# A CAR,

# SOME CASH,

# AND A PLACE

# TO CRASH

# A CAR, SOME CASH, AND A PLACE TO CRASH

## The Only Post-College Survival Guide You'll Ever Need

### REBECCA M. KNIGHT

RODALE

© 2003 by Rebecca M. Knight
Back cover photograph © by Cal Mackenzie

Printed in the United States of America
Rodale Inc. makes every effort to use acid-free ∞, recycled paper ♻.

Book design by Joanna Williams
Front cover photograph by Mitch Mandel

Library of Congress Cataloging-in-Publication Data
Knight, Rebecca M.
    A car, some cash, and a place to crash : the only post-college survival guide you'll ever need / Rebecca M. Knight.
        p.      cm.
    Includes index.
    ISBN 1–57954–626–9 paperback
    1. Young adults—Life skills guides.   2. College graduates—Life skills guides.   I. Title.
    HQ799.5 .K57 2003
    646.7'0084'2—dc21                                        2002153790

Distributed to the book trade by St. Martin's Press
2   4   6   8   10   9   7   5   3        paperback

Visit us on the Web at www.rodalestore.com, or call us toll-free at (800) 848-4735.

RODALE

WE INSPIRE AND ENABLE PEOPLE TO IMPROVE
THEIR LIVES AND THE WORLD AROUND THEM

For my mother and my father

# acknowledgments

I incurred many debts in writing this book.

Foremost, I wish to thank my formidable agent, Wendy Sherman. This book would not have been possible without her.

At Rodale, I thank Stephanie Tade and my editor, Chris Potash, whose keen eye and good ideas made this a much better book.

I am deeply grateful for the help of many recent college graduates who shared their experiences with me, especially Rachel Edmonds, Rich Forristall, Makaela Steinberg, Robert Rupe, and Jessica Strauss.

I am also thankful to: Caroline Amport, Jamie Asin, Andrew Bairstow, Roger Bairstow, John Birnsteel, Kim Boglarski, Jennifer Boutin, Kara Burch, Regina Burns, Graeme Campell, Peter Campion, Marcus Chung, Monica Civali, Erika Collins, Christopher Cotnoir, Ian Crystal, Alexandra Dalavagas, Bryan Dehmler-Buckley, Michael Doyle, Cybele Dreskin, Annette Dumont, Tina Eide, Aaron Lee Fineman, Darcie Leah Gagne, Kate Gilpin, Jeff Gregor, Kathryn Haviland, Patrick Heller, Nick Hoffa, Abby Ingber Leipsner, Courtney J. Jacobs, Lindsey Kampmeinert, Vicki Kan, Brad Keller, John Kelly, Douglas Kiker, Sarah Knight, Joseph Kuo, Catie Lazarus, Erika Lea, Susan Lineberger, Abigail Loyd, Sean Masterson, Pete Mackenzie, Garrett Miller, Danielle Mysliwiec,

Christina O'Connor, Meredith Orren, Shenandoah Pearce-Andersen, Becky Phillips, Jason Quesada, Dave Raabe, Nik Ramshand, Angela J. Rapp, Emily J. Saglimbeni, Emily Selden, Lauren Sella, Nawar Shora, Sarah Stray, Leslie Thornton, Matthew Tucker, Barbara Van Orden, Margaret Van Orden, Julie Westney, and Lisa Winegar.

I am grateful to Rose Jacobs, Susana MacLean, and Mariko Sanchanta, who were the first readers of my manuscript. Their suggestions were invaluable.

At the *Financial Times*, I am blessed with supportive and encouraging colleagues: Lionel Barber, Alison Beard, Joshua Chaffin, Mary Chung, Chrystia Freeland, Tally Goldstein, Alexandra Harney, Stephanie Kirchgaessner, James Montgomery, Robert Orr, Abigail Rayner, and Amy Yee.

I am indebted to my stepfather, Cal Mackenzie, for his encouragement and guidance.

Finally, I thank David Bairstow for his patience, humor, and unwavering support.

# contents

# preface

I STOOD IN THE TERMINAL at Ronald Reagan National
Airport on a bustling summer evening in 1998. Mr. Business Suit
trotted by purposefully. A gaggle of teenage girls giggled around
me, smacking pink chewing gum. Announcements blared from the
PA system. I had graduated from college a week before, and I had
flown to Washington, D.C., for three job interviews. I was dressed
in my black Job Interview Suit, a graduation gift. My unruly hair
was tied neatly back—someone once told me I looked older this
way. I was wearing my sensible heels.

One of my prospective employers had arranged to meet
me at the airport, but that wasn't for another hour. I had to
make a decision. What should I do about the gnawing in my
stomach, which had begun on the airplane and was growing
worse by the minute? I'd made a pact with myself that I would
not eat or drink anything while wearing my Job Interview Suit;
it was, after all, my only Job Interview Suit. I'm not a particularly neat eater, and I knew that anything I put near my mouth
would have a magnetic attraction to my suit. Don't risk it, I said
to myself.

But I was starving.

Then it came to me: Use a straw. Even a child doesn't dribble
on herself when drinking from a straw. Yes, a cool beverage,

sipped with a straw, would freshen me up and leave me with a clean suit for my interview in an hour.

Then, out of the corner of my eye, I spotted a row of greasy moon-shaped pizzas warming under fluorescent heat lamps. I was so hungry that even airport food smelled good. Perfect, I thought. I'll tuck a paper napkin into my collar as a bib. No, I'll do better than that. I'll remove my jacket, place it on the back of my chair, sip my beverage with a straw, and eat my pizza *carefully* with a knife and fork.

I got in line, purchased my edibles, and grabbed several napkins and a set of plastic utensils. Then I scanned the food court for a free seat. There was none. Every chair was taken.

I will stand and eat, I decided. Stand and eat, the way I see so many resourceful grown-ups around me doing. I ambled to the corner to be as inconspicuous as possible. Holding the beverage and napkins in my dominant right hand and the pizza on a sagging paper plate in my left, the utensils were useless at this point. I took a small bite. Then a sip. Then a dab. Another bite. Another sip. I was developing quite a rhythm. It was precarious, yes, but certainly workable.

Just then my cell phone started ringing. (Actually, to be honest, it wasn't my cell phone at all. My mother had lent me hers in case of an emergency.) I placed the beverage on the pizza plate—in retrospect, my critical error—and began to shuffle through my bag, which was slung over my shoulder. I answered the phone; it was my mom calling to wish me luck and to find out if my flight had arrived on time, whether there was turbulence, whether I'd booked a hotel room for the night, whether I'd called yet to confirm my other interviews, and whether or not I'd eaten.

Yes, everything's fine, I started to say. Then, all of a sudden, it wasn't. In my haste, in my carelessness, in my jostling, I inadvertently hugged the pizza slice to my chest. Sauce, cheese, and Diet Coke now dappled my once-sparkling Job Interview Suit.

I hung up on Mom, rushed to the restroom, and frantically applied cold water and green-colored hand soap, cursing all the while. I contorted myself under the electric hand drier in a desperate attempt to evaporate the mess. It was no use. I had a large dark circle on the left side of my chest. I looked as if I were lactating.

My prospective employers, bless them, politely said nothing about my appearance. At least not to me.

I tell this story because it is emblematic of my entire first year out of college. One day I was a beer-drinking, sandal-wearing, needs-a-haircut college kid; the next I was expected to be a full-fledged working stiff and contribute to society—or at least contribute to Social Security. Every day after graduation, it seemed, I was put on the spot to do something I'd never done before. I spent a lot of time metaphorically getting pizza on my suit.

I've lived everything in this book. In my first year out of school I got my first paycheck with a comma in it. I was berated by my boss over a misplaced fax. I graduated from downing after-hours rum and Cokes to sipping working-girl vodka tonics at happy hour. I began to read the newspaper every day. I saw the inside of the Washington, D.C., Department of Motor Vehicles six different times. I considered and reconsidered grad school. I considered and reconsidered giving up office life to become a white-water rafting guide. I quit my job and got a new one. I successfully filed my own taxes. My roommate did not speak to me for three days after a disagreement over white bread. (I'm against it.) I bought a car. I arrived at Georgetown Medical Center's emergency room at 1:00 A.M. and was scolded by the nurse when I revealed I had no proper health insurance. I started a retirement fund. I asked for a Cuisinart for Christmas. And I accidentally crashed my company's e-mail system after a friend forwarded cumbersome and inappropriate messages. Very embarrassing.

The point is, this is not the perfect person's guide to the Real World. Nor is it a love letter to your parents' way of doing things. Simply put, this is a book that I wish I had when I graduated from college: a preview of pitfalls and pile-ups, a paean to preparation and prevention.

Not very long ago, very recently in fact, I ran the gauntlet that you're now entering. I did some things right, some things wrong. Through it all, I've discovered that there are some things in life that you need to be told. I'm going to tell you a few. I hope it helps.

# introduction:
# NOW WHAT?

THIS BOOK IS ABOUT making your way successfully in what's often called the Real World. Every phase in our lives, every world, is real of course. The freedom we felt in college certainly seemed real after high school. But we'll use the term Real World here to refer to what lies beyond college. It's a term of convenience, not one meant to demean anything that came before.

Frankly, what came before was . . . a great time. For most of us our college years are relatively fun and carefree, despite the early classes, impossible reading assignments, and 10-page papers due in the morning. It was a great big party, and all of our friends were there.

But now the party's over. Once you take that final walk across the stage or turf to accept your hard-earned diploma, suddenly it is time to take ownership of your own life. For the first time since kindergarten, the last day of school is not the start of a long, languorous summer holiday but rather the beginning of your stint as a grown-up in the Real World.

The stakes are high, and it is natural for the newly minted college graduate to feel a tinge of uncertainty. Now what? Where do I go from here? From the age of five (if not younger), all we've ever known was institutions, and friendly ones at that. We moved seamlessly from elementary school to junior high to high school and then on to college, with spring breaks and summer vacations built into the annual schedule. It's what was expected of us, and we willingly obliged. Now, though, there is no welcoming institution waiting to greet us.

College may have taught us many things, but not about surviving in the Real World. There are important questions to ask yourself, and so many big decisions to make: Where do I want to live? What kind of job should I go for? How important is a career to me? What kind of social life do I want? Do I need a lot of money or will a little suffice? As one recent graduate put it, "At first the novelty of being on my own was so exciting. I thought, I can do this by myself, I can do that by myself. But then it hit me: I *have* to do this by myself. I realized that all the decisions about my future were mine; nobody would make them for me."

There are no gimmicks in this book—no secret keys to being debt-free by age twenty-five, having the perfect sex life, or even finding a good parking space. In the Real World, such successes are won mostly with discipline and commitment. At the same time, there's no need to do things the hard way. I want you to get your footing as soon as possible straight out of school. I've been there and done that, and I want to ease your way and cheer you on as you ask for a promotion, carve out a social life, and start your 401(k).

My method for introducing you to Real World sensibilities is meant to be as painless as possible. I've ordered the chapters to reflect a common post-college path: First, you look for a job. Then, or at the same time, a place to live. Maybe you buy a car. Of course you apply yourself to your job to make enough money to keep your apartment and car, all the while strategizing on how to build a career. In your spare time you make new friends and explore the world around you while trying to stay healthy enough to keep working.

Of course, real life doesn't always proceed in such an orderly fashion. For instance, you might decide that moving to a new city first would make it easier to land a job there. Or you might reason that it makes no sense to buy a car if you're moving to a place with good public transportation. Don't feel that you need to read straight through from beginning to end. Skip around. Read what interests or informs you and save the rest for later. Maybe you plan to attend graduate school right away or travel around Europe for a few months or join the Peace Corps. Hold on to this book anyway. The problem you haven't experienced yet is just that. It's coming soon. Count on it. And then the solid information in the appropriate chapter will help.

What kind of information? Throughout the book you'll read about the real-life adventures of more than a hundred recent graduates. (Names and personal details have been changed or omitted altogether to protect the guilty, including me.) These peers of yours majored in everything from art history to economics to zoology. Some graduated from state schools, some went to Ivies; some attended big-time universities, others small liberal arts colleges. After graduation, they moved all over the country, from tiny towns to large cities. They got jobs and became teachers, consultants, journalists, bankers. They all made the usually bumpy transition to the Real World—sometimes stumbling, sometimes bumbling, but triumphing often enough. Their stories are called out with oversized quote marks. Also included is practical advice and commentary from relevant experts and accomplished professionals.

I asked a whole lot of questions to a whole lot of people who know a whole lot about the issues faced by new grads, and here is what they said. Their advice is not reproachful or scolding. Rather, it's meant to gently nudge you in certain directions that will make post-college—or post-high school, for that matter—survival all the easier.

Bob Hope used to tell graduates at the many commencements where he spoke, "It's a jungle out there. Don't go." It may still be a jungle. In fact, the jungle may have gotten bigger and scarier since Bob Hope's time and there may be more snakes, wolves, and skunks out there in the Real World than ever before. It's daunting for all of us, but it's not so bad a place if you know what you're doing. You'll see. It's fun to live on your own, make your own money, have your first job.

So, with high hopes for your impending success, let me be one of the first to enthusiastically welcome you to the Real World.

Now have at it.

# A CAR,
# SOME CASH,
# AND A PLACE
# TO CRASH

# chapter one

# first step:
# GET A JOB

THE DAY OF MY BIG JOB INTERVIEW arrived and I was nervous, but I tried to play it cool. I showed up a little early at the offices of the large New England daily newspaper. The woman behind the desk with big hair told me to wait in one of the mismatched chairs in the corner of the reception area. I sat there, going over all the questions for which I was magnificently prepared: What are your career goals? Why do you want to work here? What skills do you possess that would make you valuable to us? After what seemed like several days, finally I was called in.

I offered a hearty take-me-serious-please handshake to my interviewer, a bearded, crotchety editor. There was some small talk, and some shuffling of papers. Then it was clear that the interview was about to start. He looked at me squarely and asked, "What's on your nightstand?"

What? My mind started to race. "I don't even *have* a nightstand." Then: "What business of it was his? How dare he?"

No right answers there.

Not wanting to be difficult, I slowly, rather timidly began to recount the contents of what a twenty-two-year-old woman might theoretically have on her nightstand. "A lamp, hand lotion, a clock radio, a box of Kleenex . . ."

Fortunately, the perplexed editor stopped me right there and asked me outright: "No, no. I want to know what you're currently reading. What is the book on your nightstand?"

Ugh.

Many of us leave college in the throes of a job search potentially even more agonizing than the college application process. It's an unfamiliar enterprise. Even if you were at the top of your class in high school and getting into college was a breeze, landing your first job may not be so easy.

Typically, the search is time-consuming, tedious, and tiresome. But it's also manageable. College graduates who approach the task rationally and strategically eventually find jobs. And, if you're organized, have a well-written cover letter, can present yourself confidently during the interview, and know how to negotiate with an employer once you have an offer, you'll find a *good* job. You really will.

This chapter will help clear up some of the mystery surrounding your looming job search and provide some Real World tips to get you organized for success. First, though, you'll have to do what you might have managed to put off during your entire college career: decide what you want to do with your life.

## What Do You Want to Be When You Grow Up?

*To find out what one is fitted to do and secure an opportunity to do it is the key to happiness.*
*—John Dewey*

Many of my classmates already had jobs by the time graduation rolled around. These charmed students were wined and dined by corporate recruiters and big banks. The cookies, hard candies, and fancy pens they received as part of the wooing effort were flattering to those with offers, who for the most part had selected practical majors like finance or computer science. For me, with a major in American government, their gifts served as glaring reminders that I didn't yet have a job. This feeling of being left behind is a common fear among new grads.

> *I had no idea what I wanted to do. I worked hard in college, but my days were about the little things: Which class do I have now? Will I get my English 201 paper done on time? I never bothered to think about the future in any meaningful way. Graduation loomed and I realized that I never thought I would be old enough to be out in the real world. It was terrifying.*

Difficult though it may be, try not to get caught up in the I-gotta-find-a-job! panic that hits many seniors. Take your search seriously, but remember that your first job out of school is not the pinnacle of your career, nor is it an indicator of your worth as a person. You're still young, after all.

On the other hand, you may feel that you're selling out by joining the ranks of corporate America in a nine-to-five office job, abandoning your dreams of becoming a writer, a dancer, an artist. You may fear that wearing a suit each day, marking you as just another worker bee, will somehow kill your imagination. Well, the Real World truth is—and deep down you know it—that working will probably involve some compromise on your part. Working a job is one of the most practical things adults do. You gotta eat, after all. But don't let that creeping negativity squelch your ambition or your enthusiasm for the work world. Your job can be a venue for your creativity. Writing, thinking, expressing yourself—these skills will all come into play in your professional life. Ideally, your job should strike some kind of balance between what you'd most like to be doing with your life and what someone else is willing to pay you to do.

## Why Work?

We apply for a job for all sorts of reasons: to make money, of course; to gain fame; to do social good; to hang out with like-minded people; to keep busy. Or maybe it's to follow in Dad's footsteps or because it's what Mom always hoped we'd do.

> *I felt tremendous pressure from family to find a so-called good job after graduation. My parents spent a lot of money on my education, and I didn't want to let them down. I had in my head a 'perfect job' scenario that I thought my parents would approve of. In the end, that distracted me from thinking about what I really wanted to do.*

While some new graduates have an idea of what they want to do, others are content to experiment in different jobs and fields. Despite disapproving glances that may come from your parents, this is a perfectly normal introduction to work.

> *I knew that I could always waitress again if I had to, but I had promised myself that I was done with the food service industry after graduation. I wanted to do something challenging that put my major—English—to*

*work. I was just looking for something to get me started in the working world that would offer me professional experience and polish. I wasn't interested in any given career track, and I didn't feel an overwhelming pressure to find a job that I would keep for the rest of my life, despite the fact that my parents did that without ever questioning it.*

There's a wide world of jobs out there, all offering their own perks and different brands of job satisfaction, so it's up to you to narrow the field. The truth is, you know yourself better than any fill-in-the-dot personality test or bureaucratic human resource department. You may not know exactly what you want to do, but you know what you're good at and you know what you like and what you loathe. Work from there, and seek out jobs that you think match your abilities and interests. If you don't, you may find it hard to get up in the morning—*every* morning.

## Decisions, Decisions

Your first step toward getting a job, then, is about knowing yourself well enough so that you land where you want to, or at least somewhere you won't be miserable. Do some hard thinking about what sort of career might interest you. Consider options and make decisions. Do you like writing? Do you like working with numbers? What are your interests—business, music, policy, food, photography? Reflect on experiences you've already had that might make it easier for you to decide on a job path. Maybe you've done internships or job shadowing during college to help you sort through these choices.

## Maybe You're Not Ready
## for a Real Job

It's common for recent grads to take some time off after college, or at least to opt for something different from a standard job right away. They take advantage of this rare period of freedom to experiment and explore.

"I took some months off after college and traveled throughout Europe and then spent a year teaching in Thailand," says Andy Bennett, a University of New Hampshire grad. "I needed some time to decompress from the college experience. In retrospect, I'm so glad I did it that way. I realize now that I have a lifetime to work. You don't have many other chances to take this time because responsibilities like jobs, kids, mortgages get in the way."

If you are considering taking some time off after graduation, make sure you have thought it through. Prolonging the job search because you're scared that you're on the brink of Too Much Responsibility isn't smart; you're likely to spend as much time and energy avoiding responsibility as you would just diving in. What

Think about what constitutes your ideal work environment. Do you want to work with a lot of people, or do you prefer to be autonomous? Do you thrive in high-pressure situations, or is flexibility most important? Will you be happy with a desk job, or are you interested in work-related travel?

Consider your broader life goals and values, such as quality of life and financial security, for example. Are you willing to invest body and soul in a high-paying corporate career? "A lot of people say that money doesn't really matter. And for some, it's probably true. But others might have a social life that requires are your *real* motives for taking a year off? An odyssey of self-discovery? An eagerness to see the world? Extra time to prepare for graduate school?

Will taking a year off hurt you when you begin your job search in earnest? It depends. Yes, probably, if you spend the year surfing and working at a clam shack. Unimpressed employers will read: Lacks ambition.

But a year off will not necessarily hurt you, if for instance you spend time building homes for Habitat for Humanity in Ecuador or volunteering on a political campaign.

If you're taking time off for one last summer vacation, try to fit in at least some activities that could be considered worthwhile from the perspective of an employer. Pursue some serious interests, do volunteer work, mentor a child, write articles or take photographs for your local newspaper as a freelancer, learn a foreign language, or pick up some new skill. Basically, use the time wisely.

some cash, and it's important to think about that in the kinds of companies you're targeting," suggests Amy Lindgren, president of Prototype Career Services.

Narrow down the types of jobs you think you might enjoy doing and then target the companies, groups, schools, or organizations that hire people like you to do that work. Continue narrowing your search by geography if you think you'd like to live in a particular city or state.

If you're still having a difficult time figuring out what you'd like to be doing, take heart. Work-related revelations come at strange times, and you never know when you might have an epiphany.

> *One day I was on the train and I ran into another alumna of my college; she was on her way home from work and she was holding a giant poster of female genitalia! She was an educator for Planned Parenthood, an organization I had always loved and supported. She helped me get a few interviews there, and she even put in a good word with her boss. And I landed a job there.*

If the natural progression from your joint degree in Women's Studies and French to the working world still eludes you, there are many other sources of career information. Seek advice from your campus career services department or a professor or advisor. Or perhaps speak to a career counselor. Visit your local library for self-help books and other employment resources.

## You, on Paper

Inexperience is the name of the game for most college graduates when it comes to work history. As a full-time student it's not easy to rack up the kind of job qualifications employers look for. Or is it? The trick of résumé writing is transforming experiences—however common or inconsequential they seemed at the time—into attributes, and identifying the practical skills and knowledge you gained. That summer you spent as a camp counselor: leadership skills. Your after-school job at a tourist-trap seafood restaurant: customer service. The time you helped your friends get similar jobs at the same joint: recruitment and training. Your semester abroad in London: international experience. Your intramural basketball league: teamwork.

> *I confirmed that I had actually gained a lot of skills in school that were worth something in the real world. Who knew that my experiences as a work-study library assistant, president of the rugby club, and organizer of the student art gallery would translate into a job as a full-time circulation manager at an art library? But they did.*

"Think about all the skills you learned from your past jobs, volunteer experiences, and coursework," says Regina Pontow, owner of ProvenResumes.com, an online site offering résumé tips and strategies. She recommends avoiding clichés and glossy phrases such as "quick learner," "multitask-oriented," or "keen eye for detail" when writing your résumé. "These are meaningless unless you include a statement that shows how you have possessed that quality in the past," she says. The best way to convey your energy and enthusiasm in a résumé or cover letter is to use action verbs such as *directed, supervised, led,* and *wrote.* These give the impression that you are capable of doing things and eager to take on new tasks. Avoid overusing the personal pronoun *I*, but do explain how you'll be a good fit at the company.

It's important to understand that to get the job done, résumés and cover letters should aim to serve not as a tribute to you, but rather as a short treatise on what an asset you'll be to the prospective employer. It's one-sided: Employers want to know what you can do for them, not what they can do for you.

## Top Five Personal Characteristics Employers Seek in New Hires

1. Communication skills (oral and written)

2. Honesty and integrity

3. Teamwork skills

4. Interpersonal skills

5. Strong work ethic

SOURCE: Job Outlook '02, National Association of Colleges and Employers (NACE)

## Résumé Basics

Shakespeare said that brevity is the soul of wit. Dorothy Parker said it's the soul of lingerie. Employers say it is the key to an effective résumé.

Crafting your résumé involves a few essential rules: Use simple words, keep sentences short, be clear in describing your previous experience, and do not exceed one page.

Everybody knows that your résumé should include personal contact information like your name, address, phone number, and e-mail address as well as the specifics of your educational background and work experience, however limited that may be. You might also list volunteer work, sports you played in college, extracurricular activities and hobbies, foreign languages you know, and civic organizations you belong to, in the hope that these prove you're a well-rounded and interesting candidate.

Brief doesn't mean blunt, though. Nicholas Lore, author of *The Pathfinder: How to Choose or Change Your Career for a Lifetime of Satisfaction and Success*, says that a résumé should not read like a history of your past. "It's an advertisement. Write it for whomever you're giving it to. It's something you customize. Your objective should state exactly what you're looking for: the job that's being offered. Puff everything up as much as you can. Think about what would make someone an extraordinary candi-

## Don't Mess It Up: Avoid Stupid Mistakes

Errors in your résumé or cover letter can have a ghastly impact on your chances of being considered for a position, according to the Society of Human Resource Management. In fact, 76 percent of human resource professionals say that typos or grammatical mistakes cause them to remove applicants from the pool.

Always double- and triple-check the spellings of names and the correctness of titles. Avoid the common mistake of addressing letters of inquiry to the wrong person or company. Have someone else proofread the final draft. Ask friends or people in the business you wish to enter what they think of your résumé and cover letter and get feedback for ways to make it shine.

date. What will make you stand out?" But while you're puffing and spinning, keep in mind that everything you claim on your résumé is subject to verification, so *never lie*.

"The goal is to get attention—with the design, format, structure, headings," says Regina Pontow, the professional résumé writer. "Where does your eye go first? Does it tell you what you want the employer to know about you? Your résumé should support the image you're trying to convey. Avoid a skeletal résumé that doesn't offer enough information. Employers want a little more meat."

And while you want to be distinctive, it's considered unwise to stand out because you've got the weirdest-looking résumé— written in crayon, or perhaps printed on fluorescent paper. A wacky format will distract from your attributes. Offbeat cover letters, corny poems about your college experience, or excited punctuation and diction—"Working for you would be a dream come true!!!!"—are also taboo.

There are times when something outrageous works, but you have to be really clever. Says Lore, "In advertising, design, and publishing—the more creative and liberal fields—there is more leeway to be creative. But in law and accounting, employers don't like anything more than the facts. Anything else is just not appropriate. Attract them. Don't turn them off."

## The Cover Letter

In most cases, the ideal cover letter contains three or four pithy paragraphs that link your knowledge of the field you wish to enter, your desire to work for the company or organization you're applying to, and a description of your skills that qualify you for a job there.

As with résumés, the cover letter format may be conventional, but the content should not be lackluster. Your letter should never be more than one page, but that one page should intrigue the reader with your competence, skills, and smarts.

Write clear sentences that give an overview of your qualifications. Keep related items together so the employer doesn't jump from one concept to another. You may mention some of your personal traits or special skills, but keep them relevant to the job for which you're applying.

> *I wanted my cover letter to show that I was well rounded and responsible, but my job history was limited to the usual summer work: waiter, house painter, and landscaper. I wanted to prove that I had potential since I had no real work experience. With my résumé, I attached a cover sheet to explain the importance of*

*these activities and why I thought they provided me with skills that would be of value to different potential employers.*

Sucking up is part of it, too. Employers like to see that you've taken enough interest in the company to find out about it and that you've thought about how you will fit in. Include information in your cover letter that proves you're familiar with the company's work.

Never underestimate the power of name-dropping. If you know someone who already works at the company or who once worked there, ask her if she left under favorable circumstances and if she would put in a good word for you. Then mention her name in the cover letter.

Request an interview with the company or mention that you'll be in touch soon about the status of your application. A week or two is fine. If you're going to be in the area, say that you would appreciate visiting the office and meeting your prospective employer.

Finally, learn a lesson from the showgirls on the glittery strip in Las Vegas: Don't give it all away. "Résumés and cover letters, like great music and art, have mystery," says Nicholas Lore. "Don't tell them everything; make the employer want to hear more. Make them want to pick up the phone and call you."

## Help Wanted: The Search

*A lot of fellows nowadays have a B.A., M.D., or Ph.D.*
*Unfortunately, they don't have a J-O-B.*
—Fats Domino

Some new graduates succumb to the easy inertia of post-college life. They fill their mornings with menial tasks and errands to the pharmacy and post office. Then they while away the afternoon on their parents' La-Z-Boy watching talk shows or ESPN. There's a popular term to describe these folks: unemployed.

Discipline and organization are the paths to progress in job hunting. *You* are in command of your job search, or at least you should be. Establish a routine, keep a regular schedule, give yourself something definite to do—perhaps a quota of phone calls—each day.

> *I was looking for jobs all over the country and so I had a lot to keep track of. I kept all of my information in one three-ring binder. I clipped ads from the paper and printed out stuff from the Internet that I was interested in and taped them into my binder. It also helped me keep track of when I had sent my résumé, when I had called. My sister fueled my job search, always keeping my spirits up but also pestering me to make calls and initiate contacts.*

Diversify your job-search methods, and be creative. "Job seekers must go after companies, not just open positions," says Vivian Belen, a professional résumé writer and career coach. "Work on the assumption that companies are always interested in good people and that you're not bothering them. Because once a job is advertised, there is immense competition."

If you're eager to work for a particular company, apply through different channels, suggests Don Asher, author of *From College to Career: Entry-Level Resumes for Any Major from Accounting to Zoology*. But make sure you address your packet to an actual person, rather than the nebulous human resources

## Getting Organized: Supply Yourself

For me, the best part about going back to school was buying the supplies. I loved the perfect stacks of plastic-wrapped lined paper, the brightly colored folders, the pens with fresh ink. Luckily, supplying yourself for work in the Real World only gets better.

First, dedicate a space in your room or apartment for your mission. Think of it as your command post and also your bunker when you return from your reconnaissance runs.

Second, put in some basic supplies; this is war, after all, and you need to be properly armed. Buy a notebook, or dedicate a file folder on your computer, to keep track of your job search. Other necessary hardware includes a reliable computer printer, toner cartridges, and quality cotton-fiber business stationary and envelopes. Also invest in a set of professional-looking note cards so that you can send thank-you letters after interviews. There are useful tools for the gadget-obsessed, too: PDAs, electronic organizers, and BlackBerry devices. An answering machine or voice mail is essential.

Third, you need to *use* the supplies. Make note of all the people you speak with, along with their contact information. Keep copies of letters you send, copies of tailored résumés, and notes from phone conversations or interviews that might be helpful in the future.

department. The appropriate name is usually easy to find by either calling the company's main telephone number, or through recruiting pamphlets, the company's Web site, or newspapers.

"Think: I am an octopus, this is the clam. I will get inside," Asher says. "You must keep your letter from being sent to the human resources department. That's like having your résumé flushed down the toilet."

Your goal, then, is getting out there and connecting with the people who actually do the hiring. Today, there are many ways to go about this: classified ads, the Internet, networking, informational interviews, job fairs, and temping.

## The Old Standby: Classified Ads

Sandwiched somewhere among the comics, Dear Abby, and the daily crossword puzzle, you'll find the help-wanted ads, the time-honored tool of most job hunters. They're a good starting place to find out what's out there and who's hiring. They can also educate you about the kinds of work that people do in their jobs.

The advantage of job listings is that they change every day. The problem is that every other job seeker in your greater metropolitan area has access to these same classifieds too, and in a tight job market, employers are usually deluged by résumés from a single ad. Don't be deterred.

And don't pass over ads that call for specific skills or a certain number of years of experience that you might not have. Never rule yourself out. Furthermore, don't be put off by strange ultimatums such as "Only apply if you're committed to excellence." Never turn yourself down for a job.

## The New Standby: Internet

While the Internet can be a job hunter's gold mine, it is also dangerously linked to terminal procrastination—it's easy to get distracted checking your Hotmail account or battling it out on eBay for a signed Barry Bonds baseball bat. You have to keep your eye on the prize and mine efficiently and smartly, learning through experience how to excavate the vast and intimidating databases and job lists.

# Job Hunting: Helpful Web Sites

**www.ctrc.com**
A 12-Step Plan for Writing a New and Improved Résumé

**www.monster.com**
Job postings, résumé writing services, a career center

**www.collegerecruiter.com**
Job postings, résumé bank, articles, Ask the Experts

**www.hotjobs.com**
Résumé posting, job search engine, facts on salaries and benefits, and industry news

**www.collegegrad.com**
Preparation, résumés, cover letters, employer research, job postings, interviewing techniques

**www.joblink-usa.com**
Preparing for your interview

There are thousands of e-mail lists, message boards, and online discussion groups dedicated to job hunting that you can access from any public library or from the comfort of your home computer. Web sites designed expressly for recent graduates offer career advice, job listings, sample résumés, and networking opportunities, while other specialized sites focus on particular niches and industries. With time and plenty of surfing, it will become easier to know which sites are most pertinent to your job search and which are worthless. Quickly review the names of the companies listed at a site to see if they interest you before you bother to register. Avoid sites with few job listings or ones that have not been updated recently.

Many companies list available openings on their own Web sites as well, so visit the sites of companies in which you're especially interested and find out what jobs are available there. Look for links such as "Working for Us" or "Employment Opportunities." Ken Ramberg of Monster.com also advises visiting the Web sites of local trade associations and specialized online magazines that target industries you're interested in. "Don't assume that every job is posted," he says. "And if you happen to see a posting where the job isn't right but the company looks interesting, you have to be aggressive. You have to make cold calls; you have to send letters and e-mails; you need to follow up."

## Networking: It's All about Who You Know (Sometimes)

Networking is the touchy-feely part of job searching. Some people —usually extroverted, life-of-the-party types—excel at it, while the more reticent among us bemoan it. If you are shy, now is the time to get over it. Networking can uncover job openings before they are advertised, get your résumé moved to the top of the pile, or land you a winning reference; not only that, it's something you need to do throughout your professional career.

Tell everyone you know you're looking for a job and identify every individual who may be able to help you, including bosses from internships and summer jobs, other people looking for jobs, family and friends, and neighbors.

*I had just graduated from college and my parents threw a summer barbecue to celebrate. They invited everyone they could think of. All the guests were naturally very curious about what I planned to do with my*

*life, but unfortunately, I didn't have a job yet. I knew I
wanted to work in publishing and it turned out that
just about everyone there knew someone in publishing
in one form or another. I made several great contacts
and eventually got a job—working for my neighbor's
friend's cousin.*

The nascent networker should also take advantage of fellow
college alumni. The career services office at your alma mater
probably has an online alumni network that categorizes graduates by industry, career, and geographic location.

Call the organization or do research on the Web to establish
contacts in places that you particularly wish to work. People who
have the kind of job you are looking for are your best source for
information and should be sought out by any means necessary.
You might have good luck with those who have been working for
only a few years and have perspective on how to crack into the
profession yet still identify with a recent graduate.

*I work in public relations and it's become my
way of life. I always keep in contact with people—or
at least keep their name and business card. I have
copies of all my résumés and cover letters and contact
names from jobs I didn't get. I send holiday cards to
friends I haven't seen in a while. And I have an on-
going list of all the people I know. My many contacts
have helped me get my foot in the door at a lot of different jobs. You just never know when you might need
someone.*

Keep in mind that people enjoy being asked for help and are often flattered to be asked for advice. You may think you're imposing, but many veterans find that there is nothing so satisfying as helping a young person get started in life.

## Informational Interviews

Informational interviews are excellent ways to make contacts in your field of interest and at the same time to help you decipher exactly what position you might want to apply for. One-on-one meetings enable you to get the facts about an industry and perhaps a particular career path from someone who has firsthand knowledge. Plus, for jumpy job candidates, they provide a nonthreatening forum in which to practice answering and asking questions.

Using your network, find people who do the kinds of work you're interested in and then contact them by phone, e-mail, or letter. You should be subtle but direct in your communication. Tell them you're interested in learning about what they do. (Flattery never hurts.) Propose an interview by offering to take them to lunch or buy them a cup of coffee. Informational interviews are casual and relaxed, but do some research before you arrive so that you can make the most of your sit-down. You don't want to come off as wasting someone's time. Think specifically about what kind of information you wish to glean. Ask questions like: What do you see as the potential for growth in this field? What can I do to find employment in this field? What's a typical workday like? Never ask for a job point blank; instead, ask for suggestions on whom to contact or ways to get relevant experience.

## Communications: Be Professional

Back in college, it was considered clever and kooky to have tunes from the *Reservoir Dogs* soundtrack on your answering machine. But now that you're on the verge of becoming a taxpaying member of society, immature and unprofessional greetings risk alienating would-be bosses by saying, "I am not all that serious." Upon hearing these messages, many recruiters simply hang up and never call again.

The same warning applies to electronic communication. Don't use a flaky-sounding e-mail address like Moonbeam or Hot-momma. Don't write in colored fonts, and avoid garish multimedia displays. Don't use an informal, casual tone in your e-mail letters, or a lowercase style reminiscent of e. e. cummings: "i would like to be considered for the position at company x." These undermine your credibility.

You're in the business of selling yourself now, and how you communicate affects the sale.

*I met with the radio news director for an informational interview at a local public radio station, which was also the home of the public television station in my city. We had a really good talk, and after half an hour he said, not unkindly, 'It seems you're really more into television than you are radio.' He then said he happened to know that one of the TV news programs was looking for someone to serve as a production assistant. I dropped off my résumé that afternoon and got a call back that day. I was interviewed the following day, and started my job there within a week.*

A certain amount of luck is important in any job search. Luck is tempered by persistence, though. Employers like it when you show continued interest in a professional way. It clarifies their decision that you are worth considering as a candidate when a job does become available.

## Job Fairs

Job fairs are meat markets for professionals. For employers they're an opportunity to interview the largest number of prospects in the shortest amount of time. For job seekers they offer a noisy and chaotic venue for shameless self-promotion with potentially hundreds of hiring companies.

"Employers love to see recent college graduates walk up and down the aisles," says job-search strategist Amy Lindgren. "Recent grads are the most flexible and malleable. They have a lower income need; they are more willing to travel. People are usually very enthusiastic about their first jobs and willing to learn new things. These are the stereotypes and assumptions that work in your favor."

Job fairs resemble giant mazes, so it's important to have a structured approach. Get there early and be prepared to spend the day. Look for a floor-plan handout at the entrance to see what companies are located where. Then formulate your plan of action: Know specifically with whom you want to speak and in what order. Make appointments if necessary. When you finally meet with the prospective employer, introduce yourself with a smile, hand him your résumé, and explain how your skills and personality match the needs of the company.

There will be hundreds of job seekers at the job fair with the same goal as you. It may seem counterintuitive to help people you're competing with, but be generous with your resources and leads. Many of the fairgoers will have interviewed at companies you might like to work for. Some may be looking to leave a job that you might be interested in. One of these people might know of the perfect job for you. Remember: The system rewards networking.

## Temping

Some people, desperate to find a job, find the temptations of temping too good to pass up. Temporary employment agencies fill a range of jobs, from secretarial to middle management, although some focus on particular industries or skills. If your job search is taking longer than you expected, consider becoming a temporary employee at a company where you are interested in working full-time. Usually these jobs are filled through temp agencies, but it's worth a call to your dream company's human resources department to see if there is work available.

The potential benefit of temping is that people will get to know you and be willing to help you land a permanent position at the company. Also, while most assignments are administrative, temping allows you to experience a variety of work environments, assess different types of jobs, and determine which types of employers mesh with your personality. You gain another line for your résumé, you're making money, and, if nothing more, temping can be a way to learn where you don't want to work, and sometimes that's just as valuable.

A temporary employee who does a good job is usually the first choice when a full-time job becomes available. This incentive, unfortunately, lulls many temps into a lackadaisical job search.

*I was a temp at an online market research firm and after nine months of slogging away, the company finally hired me as a full-time employee. At the time, I was just looking for a job because my parents said I needed to move on with my life. I ended up helping out the customer service department. Not really what I wanted to do, but I figured at least I'd learn something new. But the work was too easy and it got boring really fast.*

Temping is unlikely to be your wildest professional dream come true—you frankly have a better shot at getting discovered on *American Idol*. Most employment agencies work only with certain companies, so it's best not to rely solely on them to find a permanent job. Many agencies have strict policies regarding where you work, how long you work there, and when you can accept a permanent job there. Plus you're taking away precious time from the job search at hand; it's not easy to duck out for three hours in the middle of the day for a job interview.

Temping can be tempting. Beware.

## Interviewing: Talking Shop to Employers

In November of my senior year of high school, my English class was mired in those dreadful college application essays: In five hundred words or less, "Describe a life-changing experience," "Explain who you admire most," and of course, "Why do you want to attend our university anyway?"

My teacher, who often took a paternal view toward us students, dedicated a class period to talking about these essays. The first thing he said was: "You want to be serious but not too serious. Be eager but not too eager. Be funny but not too funny." We collectively groaned.

But he was right. Successfully conveying such a persona is the goal in job interviewing, too. You want to come across as a serious person. One who thinks serious thoughts, one who takes herself seriously. Seriousness of purpose sells. Be genuine. Be earnest. But be careful. You want to have some distance from yourself and not take yourself too seriously, for then you might come across as the touchy employee who can't take criticism.

You want to be eager, excited about the prospect of taking the job, and passionate about the work or industry. But not overeager, certainly not bubbling-out-of-your-chair eager, for that might imply immaturity or a lightweight intellect.

Don't be deceived by a casual atmosphere. And don't make rookie mistakes.

*The person who conducted my very first interview wore khaki shorts, a nasty T-shirt with visible food stains, and no shoes. I thought, 'This is going to be a cakewalk.' He put his feet up on the desk, chatted with me about my college classes, my semester abroad, but never really got around to anything real. Or so I thought. I realized in retrospect that he was asking me thoughtful questions, but I wasn't picking up on it.*

Finally, you do want to be funny—or at least good-natured and affable. Humor makes you seem easy to work with, likeable, and flexible. Opt for a clever comment or a simple witty remark rather than a slapstick routine or a joke. As a rule, though, use

## Dress to Impress

> *Never wear anything that panics the cat.*
> *—P.J. O'Rourke*

Now that so many offices and work environments have gone Brooks Brothers business casual, there is debate about whether suits are an absolute must.

Assume they are. A job interview is no place to dress down. Give the prospective employer the fewest possible reasons to vote against you. Dress like a grown-up—an employed grown-up. Your physical appearance should convey confidence and professionalism. Interviewers want to know you take the interview and the job seriously. Look neat, clean, and well groomed. If you do not have a suit, men should still wear coats and ties and women should wear skirts.

If you are applying for jobs in creative fields like graphic design or publishing, it is generally acceptable to dress the part, but don't go overboard. Julia Kasen, an Ivy League graduate who was trying to crack into the hip, trendy magazine scene in New York City, donned a purple suede mini-skirt for her interviews. She also left her tongue stud in, claiming she wouldn't want to work for a company that didn't allow its employees freedom of dress and expression. Julia eventually landed a job—but not without a few awkward interviews where she answered questions such as, "Have you ever chipped a tooth on that thing?"

In general, job interviews are not the venue for exposing your inner Cher and not the place to demand sophomoric entitlements. A ban on tongue studs does not a prison make. It's always better to be overdressed than under. When in doubt, go conservative.

humor only if you're comfortable with it. If it's natural, it works; if not, it's awkward. Do at least smile and look pleasant rather than down and uneasy.

## Sell Yourself

Almost everyone has botched at least one important job interview. The best you can do is to stay in control and be ready for anything. And make eye contact with interviewers. Lots of eye contact.

Prepare a minute-long statement about who you are, why you want to work for the company, and why the company should hire you. Do not enthuse about your hobbies and personal interests unless they relate to the job somehow.

> *I have had a number of awful interviews. I remember one in particular where the interviewer said, 'I see you are interested in medieval history.' I was nervous so I said, 'Yes, because blah blah blah.' I went on and on and on. I realize in retrospect that she didn't care about that, she was just being polite. It was meant to be an icebreaker, not a chance for me to chat about my major.*

Concentrate on how you can benefit the organization. Emphasize the skills and interests most beneficial to your success in the field: your quick analytical mind, which led you to apply for a job at a law firm, or your love of numbers that inspired you to pursue a career in accounting. Ask follow-up questions so that you don't get off track, something like, "Is that what you had in mind? Did I answer your question?"

## Typical Job Interview Questions

Some interviewers will pepper their interrogations with trick or just plain silly questions. "Which book would you bring with you to a desert island," for example. If you confess that you loved the sequel to *Bridget Jones's Diary*, will the employer think you're a ditzy and impractical girl more obsessed with nail polish than work? If you admit you mostly read sports magazines, will the employer see you as uneducated? Are you falsely presenting yourself?

Fretting too much about off-the-wall questions is pointless. It's best to respond by simply giving the least-damaging answer, experts say. Play it conservative. Pick a book that is neutral, a classic—and certainly one you've read.

For the most part, though, employers use a basic stock of questions. Expect to answer these:

What are your qualifications for this job?

What are your strengths and weaknesses?

What are your greatest accomplishments?

What did you like best/least about your other jobs?

Describe a time when you worked effectively under pressure.

Sometimes inexperience can work to your advantage, too. If the job you're applying for explicitly requires a recent college graduate, play up your youthful exuberance.

*I was interviewing at a lot of companies where I would have surely been the youngest employee. I'm glad that I was a bit naïve and raw when I went out on*

Why did you choose your course of study?

What school activities have you participated in?

What are your career goals?

Why do you want to work for us?

How would your friends (colleague, professor, supervisor) describe you?

How do you handle instructions and criticism?

When asked a question, pause before you respond—take time to collect your thoughts. Plan your answer and know exactly what you want to say. Be overwhelmingly positive and don't be afraid to brag a little.

If you are asked a negative question—identify your biggest weaknesses, for example—answer honestly, but don't select a weakness that is vital to the job and could remove you from the running. Mention what you've done to overcome the weakness, and always end on an optimistic note.

SOURCE: QuintessentialCareers.com

*my first interviews because I think most interviewers appreciated my honesty and my enthusiasm. I don't think being too slick is always the best approach. Just be yourself and be candid with your responses.*

Be prepared. Browse the company's Web site and read any company brochures you can get your hands on, talk to people already doing the job, review information about the organization, and know who is interviewing you. Start reading the newspaper to look for some topical current event related to your field that you can mention in the interview, some new innovation that will affect your job, or somebody in the news from the prospective company. This will not only endear you to your interviewer, it will enrich your own understanding of your chosen profession.

## Tell a Story

There are behavioral interview questions that usually start out with "Tell me about a time when . . ." The interviewer is looking to your past behavior as an indicator of future behavior and how you might react in a similar situation on the job. These are golden opportunities.

"Details make you credible," says job guru Vivian Belen. "Have at least three stories prepared that illustrate your points. How you organized a parking lot. Or how you made coworkers feel comfortable. Stories are more meaningful than generalizations."

> *With most mainstream jobs, the best bet is to be a little rehearsed, and so I practiced with friends. Know about what you want to do and have a story that intertwines with your résumé.*

Be careful, though, because employers will be looking for inconsistencies. If you have a questionable academic record, with study skills reminiscent of Holden Caulfield, be prepared to talk about it. Be candid but also have an idea about what you learned from your youthful transgressions.

> *I really didn't do all that well at school—let's just say my college threatened that I wasn't going to make it back for sophomore year. I went to my biggest interview, with a big Wall Street bank, with a black eye that was swelled shut from a rugby match. The interviewer asked me if I felt that my grades reflected my work ethic. Here I was with this pitiful 2.6 that I was actually proud of salvaging after my disastrous freshman year. What could I have said to get out of that one? I wasn't asked back for a second interview.*

"Employers are willing to believe that you will be different," says job expert Amy Lindgren. "You should not apologize, but you will need to explain." Do not divulge that pledge week at your fraternity marred the entire second semester of your sophomore year, or that a really tough breakup with your high school sweetheart made it impossible to study junior year. These excuses sound adolescent. Rather, take the opportunity to show that you've learned something from your mistakes by saying something like, "I was trying to choose a major and experimenting with different courses and fields. I don't think I handled it very well."

## The Request for References

After an interview, most employers will ask for references if they are interested in hiring you. This is standard procedure, so be prepared and don't blow the job because of a faulty testimonial.

References are people who have worked with you, know you well, and will vouch for your dependability. Ensure that all your references will say upbeat and encouraging things about you by asking beforehand: "Would you be willing to give me a good recommendation?" Never use anyone's name as a reference unless you've asked the person first. The question is, who to ask?

A former teacher or professor is a good choice. Make sure you select someone who knows you beyond the classroom, though, and has a sense of your intelligence and ambition. A faculty advisor to a club or activity, such as the school paper, is ideal.

A work reference from a summer job or internship is another sound possibility. The reference should come from someone who can describe your ability and character as an employee. Peers qualify, although a manager or supervisor is preferred. It's probably not such a good idea to ask relatives for a reference unless you have a family member already employed by the company or in a similar industry.

A forewarning is a necessary courtesy, too. As soon as you give the names of your references to your prospective employer, let them know that they should expect a call. And follow up with a formal thank-you note—even if you don't come away with a job offer.

## Closing the Interview

At the end of the interview, if the prospective employer asks you if you have any questions about the job or the company, take this opportunity to sparkle. Demonstrate that you're an engaging person who listens and has done his homework. You should have already thought of some questions, such as, What qualities are you looking for in your new hires? What are the organization's plans for future growth? Does management encourage promotion from within the organization?

Never ask questions such as, What will my hours be like? Will I have to work weekends? These always translate into: How hard do you expect me to work? Also, never broach the subject of salary in the first meeting.

Vivian Belen, the career expert, suggests asking, What reservations do you have about my background? Where do I stand compared with other candidates? "This is a horse race," she says. "As a job seeker, it's your responsibility to be proactive because you deserve to know where you stand."

Adds Wendy Enelow, president of Career Masters Institute, a professional networking organization, "As you see the interview wind down, take the initiative to share with them what you feel are your strengths. Give yourself a competitive distinction. Everyone is going to say they're a self-starter or that they're motivated. Have an example of what makes you different."

Even if the interview has gone especially well, it's still important to maintain professional decorum. Don't revert back to collegiate informalities.

*My first interview was a series of short meetings with five or six of people in the company. A woman who had a similar position to the one I was applying for was responsible for greeting me at the beginning, escorting me from one mini-interview to the next, and bidding me farewell at the end of the day. When it was*

*time for me to leave, she walked me to the elevators*
*and reached out to shake my hand. Still in college and*
*accustomed to being informal and friendly with anyone*
*my age, I proceeded to lean over and hug her. You*
*know, one of those 'Oh, I haven't seen you since lunch,*
*are you ready to go to the frat party?' college kind*
*of hugs. I was so embarrassed; but I learned my les-*
*son. I've never hugged an interviewer since, and I am*
*always poised and ready to shake hands in profes-*
*sional situations.*

## Don't Forget to Say Thank You

When the interview is over, send a thank-you note, a lost art in today's world of instant communication. Send a real note—paper, envelope, stamp, the real McCoy. Thank the interviewer for her time and remind her of your continued interest in the job. "Play up the themes you highlighted in your interview—thank-you notes are marketing tools," says Enelow.

After the interview, expect a downright painful waiting period. Nearly every prospective employer promises to inform you of your standing at the time of the interview. And there's a special corner reserved in heaven for those who follow through. Remember that when the interviewer says "next Tuesday," it might be a week or two after that. This phase is excruciating, agonizing—all because the decision is out of your hands.

The advent of e-mail has made things easier on your psyche. It's appropriate to send a follow-up e-mail to your prospective

## Singin' the Rejection Blues

If you are turned down for a position, even if it was your dream job, try to be understanding and don't get angry or defensive with the recruiter or bearer of bad news. It is acceptable, however, to ask why you weren't chosen for the position: What would have made me a better candidate for this job?

"It's important to find out why you weren't selected," says Candace Davies, a career coach. "Challenge the employer, ask why. Sometimes they will be honest with you and tell you that you don't have the skills or the experience needed for the job. Don't take it personally. People get rejected all the time."

Instead, ask how long your résumé will be kept on file, ask if the interviewer knows of any other openings in your line of work, and send a thank-you letter for the company's consideration, recommends Davies.

employer—after the requisite thank-you note, of course. Be persistent, not pesky.

# Finally, the Offer

The longer your search takes, the more desperate you'll become, but never accept a job on the spot. Take a day or two to ponder the offer: job specifics, title, vacation time, location, money, and benefits. They won't rescind the offer. It's better—more mature— to make a rational rather than an emotional decision.

> *A lot of my friends got sucked into boring jobs*
> *they didn't really want because they were terrified*
> *they wouldn't be able to get another job. They didn't*
> *think about whether they'd be happy going there day*
> *after day.*

The elation that somebody actually wants to pay you for services beyond scooping ice cream or mowing lawns wears off quickly. A job signifies a paycheck, but will it give you a chance to experience new things? Does it seem likely you'll be able to move up in the organization? And does this job correspond with your long-term career plans?

Be sure you have a clear appreciation of your job responsibilities and what's expected of you in a typical workweek. Job descriptions can be misleading, and nailing down your day-to-day duties before you start will help you make a more informed decision. Are you sure you still want the job if you're required to sort mail each day or work seventy-hour weeks? In the long run, will you feel satisfied toiling away in a tiny cubicle just to earn a fat paycheck?

Consider whether you fit in with the corporate culture and office personality. You may wish to talk to someone else in the organization to get some insight into what it's like to work there. You should also consider the chemistry and rapport with your manager-to-be; gauge whether you are comfortable with her administrative style and whether she has the potential of acting as a mentor to you.

There are practical matters, too. If the company is neither well financed nor capably managed, it's foolish to accept an offer. Be wary of small start-ups that exaggerate the benefits or potential for growth; vague proclamations like, "There's no limit to what you can earn in your first year" should give you pause.

## Negotiating

You and your employer share a common goal: ensuring that you like your job and will be good at it. If your prospective employer offers you a salary less than you'd imagined, maybe less than you think you can live on, there is often room for negotiation. You should negotiate if you feel the offer is inadequate because the impetus is on you to ensure that you receive a fair employment package. Be respectful; know when to stop asking. Don't be too pushy; don't make unreasonable demands. And negotiate only if you're seriously considering the offer.

If you have other job offers, suggest that without revealing detailed information. Employers thrive on the hard-to-get dating and mating game. You're more attractive if you're sought by other employers; being in demand enhances your marketability.

Joel Garfinkle, founder of Dream Job Coaching, concedes that recent graduates are not in an enviable bargaining position. "It's going to be tough, and as a recent graduate, you're not going to have much to back you up since you don't have any work experience. But do your homework. And have facts that show you were an above-average student and you're an above-average candidate and that is why you deserve more money."

Highlight the breadth of your education and your proven strengths. Play up your software skills, your demanding course load—anything to keep attention away from your inherent lack of experience. Throughout the negotiations, be sure to convey your enthusiasm for the job. And keep the faith: Even if you are entering a high-skill, high-demand field, you may have more leverage than you think, and employers may be willing to meet your expectations.

## The Money

You may be so ecstatic about the job offer that you feel too timid to ask for more money for fear of sounding greedy. But the fact is your potential employer expects you to ask for more money. The employer's first offer is rarely the only one, with the exception of union jobs like teaching and journalism. Most corporate jobs are set up for negotiation. There is usually a little bit more money tucked away, or at least room for negotiating a quicker review so that you can get a raise within six months of starting if you're good. Always assume the possibility of negotiations.

> *It's in your employer's best interest to pay you as little as possible. But if they want you, they're usually willing to pay more than their first offer. I asked for just a little more than I was offered in my first job. It wasn't a strategic move, I just wasn't sure I could live in a big city on what they were offering. Of course, I got so up-tight and nervous that the offer would be rescinded that I called back that afternoon and reiterated that I really wanted the job. Luckily, my counteroffer had already gotten approval. Afterward, I felt like it was so easy, I should have asked for even more.*

Always let the employer make the opening salary offer. If you get asked something like, "What were you expecting to make?" or "What would we have to offer to hire you?" throw the question back at them. Ask, for example, "What is the range for this position?"

Some possible answers to the salary conundrum: "According to my research, this salary is below market rate," or "I really had in mind a little more than that based on my conversations with other people in the field."

If the employer is hesitant to give you more money right away, you might suggest a progressive raise of a certain percentage over a given amount of time. In any case, your salary should be reviewed on a regular basis. In fact, your potential for salary growth is more important than your starting salary. You have more bargaining leverage before you accept an offer, so don't be afraid to ask for something. Get advice from other people in the company on how hard you can push in particular places.

## Benefits and Perks

Beyond salary considerations, think seriously about the employment package a prospective company offers: incentive pay, stock options, job responsibilities, life and health benefits, moving expenses and relocation costs, travel support, work schedule, vacation time, earlier evaluation for promotion, continuing education, and computers for use at home. Identify what's important to you and what's important to your prospective employer. There are usually discrepancies between the two. Use those differences to create trade-offs that benefit both parties.

The era of the instant dot-com zillionaire is over, so think

## Know What You're Worth

Salary. Benefits. Retirement savings. Stock options. Maybe a signing bonus. Your head swims. Too much information. Is it a good offer? How would you know?

Do your homework. Don't go into a negotiation without an idea of what you're worth in the marketplace—in other words, what other companies are paying employees at your level. Luckily, there are resources online that can help. These sites will tell you what someone with your job, living in your city on average makes for a living.

The sites are for everyone, so they may not be the most accurate salary calculators, but it's a starting point to know when you might be getting a sour deal.

**www.salary.com**

**http://salary.monster.com**

**www.homefair.com**

**http://careers.yahoo.com**

**www.monstermoving.com**

twice before accepting a lower salary in exchange for a ton of stock options, or the opportunity to purchase company stock, typically at a below-market rate. If the company is a start-up or about to go public, you have to determine how much faith you have in the business and how much you're willing to lose. On the other hand, if the company is doing well or is already established and it's publicly traded, stock options can be a good bargaining point.

Ask if the company offers perks that help you do your job better. Sometimes a corporate credit card, cell phone, laptop, or free parking can be worth more than the increase in salary you could negotiate. Ask if the company allows employees to work from home one day per week or one day per month; for example, it might make sense to be at home away from noisy office distractions, or maybe you have a long commute and it makes sense to spend those hours at home working.

Ask if you will get on-the-job training or reimbursement for courses that relate to your job. Many organizations have in-house training programs, provisions for outside training, or an educational assistance program. Explore the organization's policy regarding seminars and workshops. If there's *anything* else that's important for you to know while considering an offer, now is the time to ask.

## Accepting and Declining

Once an offer has been made, you should accept or reject it within a day or so. Otherwise, your inability to commit will reflect poorly on your decision making and, perhaps more dangerously, it will broadcast your lack of interest to the new employer.

If you have one offer but are awaiting another that might be more attractive, you can ask for a little more time without specifying why you're asking. You may or may not get it, but time to consider is negotiable like everything else.

Finally, when you accept, get everything in writing.

## Good Reads

In addition to the books mentioned in this chapter, you might find these helpful:

*The Complete Resume & Job Search Book for College Students,* by Bob Adams and Laura Morin (Adams Media Corporation, 1999).

*The Complete Job-Search Handbook: Everything You Need to Know to Get the Job You Really Want,* by Howard E. Figler (Owl Books, 1999).

*Cover Letters That Knock 'Em Dead,* by Martin John Yate (Adams Media Corporation, 2000).

*The Complete Q & A Job Interview Book,* by Jeffrey G. Allen (John Wiley & Sons, 2000).

*Job Hunting for Dummies,* by Max Messmer (John Wiley & Sons, 1999).

*My first job was teaching second grade at a public elementary school. I asked questions over the phone and in person and was told what I wanted to hear: Sure, you will receive benefits after three months. Yes, your teaching load will be small in your first year. No, you won't be required to perform nonteaching duties like cafeteria duty. It turned out not to be true, but I had no recourse.*

The written offer, or employment agreement letter, should sum up the conditions of the job with the position title, starting date, salary, and other pertinent information, and should specify those points that made you want to accept the position. Oral guarantees are meaningless when questions concerning compensation, perks, or benefits arise six months into the job.

If you decide not to accept the job offer, call the person you were negotiating with and follow it up with a letter. Be polite and graceful. You're too young to burn bridges.

2

# moving on, MOVING IN

IT'S NOT LIKE COLLEGE ANYMORE. For better or for worse, there is no housing lottery in the Real World. True, dorm rooms were cell-like chambers with cinder-block walls painted inviting colors like hospital-robe green, but back then things were so easy. Now, your parents aren't subsidizing your life anymore, and you have to find a place of your own.

Of course, chances are you'll love living on your own. Despite the challenges and costs, it's exhilarating and liberating—not to mention an eventuality.

I remember what it was like looking for my first apartment. "This should not be complicated," I thought. "I just need a place to keep my stuff and sleep, just a modest corner of the world, plain and simple." Each morning I rose, excited and hopeful, and sifted through the classified ads of every single newspaper in my new city. I logged on to the Internet and clicked my way through Apartments.com. I ventured out to grocery stores and community bulletin boards cluttered with fringed handbills proclaiming ROOMMATE NEEDED.

## Cracking the Code: Real Estate Speak

appl(s): Appliance(s)

bkr: Broker

CAC, C/A: Central air

cptg: Carpeting

drmn: Doorman

EIK: Eat-in kitchen

laun: Laundry

MLS: Multiple listings service

plumb: Plumbing

WBFP: Wood-burning fireplace

I quickly realized there is a secret language of real estate, and I didn't speak it. What on earth is an EIK? Riv vu? No utils? But I slowly caught on to this jargon of apartment-speak: doorman building versus walk-up, condo versus co-op. I got the hang of the nuances of layout: two-bedroom versus one-bedroom convertible, railroad, and studio. And the economics of it all—no-fee apartments, rent-stabilized buildings, prime neighborhoods, and up-and-coming ones—started to make sense. But not before some real-world experience.

One particular morning, an apartment advertised as "spacious" and "bright" with "Lg closets" and a "Brk fr plc" caught my eye. I made an appointment. A broker with shiny tie and toothy grin greeted me and presented the residence in question. It was a dingy and cramped basement apartment, the lg closet was nonexistent, and the fr plc hadn't worked for years. No thanks, I said.

Days passed. A week went by. Friends knew what it was like to be looking. They offered sympathy. They commiserated.

Finally I found a place I could live with, one with shiny hardwood floors and a black and white tiled bathroom. Still, it wasn't exactly my dream house. I had wanted an apartment with lots of natural light; this one was at ground floor. I had hoped for close proximity to a park; this one was a twenty-minute walk. I had fantasized about a dishwasher; my broker laughed at me. The point is, even when I finally found what I was looking for, it turned out to be not exactly what I was looking for. I made some compromises and tough decisions, and you will, too.

Moving into your first apartment is a venerable tradition, a rite of passage. Not surprisingly, the means of finding a decent place to live have become more high-tech over the years, and yet the tricks have changed very little. Today as always, planning is essential.

- Have a notion about what you can afford in terms of rent and utilities.
- Know what you're getting into when you meet with a landlord or a real-estate broker.
- Understand the specifics of your lease and housing contract. Grasp what it means to be a good tenant and a respectful neighbor.
- Realize that you and your roommates are business partners, sharing monetary responsibility, and treat your relationship as such.
- Learn how to furnish your apartment reasonably and how to leave your apartment with your security deposit, your integrity, and your sanity intact.

If you're patient and persistent, you will find a perfectly livable place in your price range. After all, look around. Cities in America are crawling with young people who found apartments, live with roommates, have neighbors, and pay electricity bills. Some day soon, you will, too. So while the hunt for your first place is never exactly *fun* given all the challenges, the payoff is great.

### Or You Could Live at Home

If your first place after college strangely resembles the place you lived *before* college, maybe it is. Your pictures are all over the walls. Pets are allowed here—your dog sleeps at the foot of your bed. Your two roommates are called Mom and Dad.

Living at home after college for a short while can be a financial necessity for many young people. "My first place was my bedroom back at my mom's house," says Dan Donovan, a graduate of the University of Chicago. "My doting mother loved to have me living there. Looking back, I am glad I did it because it made her happy for a short time and I was able to get back on my feet financially after spending way too much cash during the last year of college."

If you do live at home, you will most likely feel a loss of the freedom you relished in college. At school, you chose when you went to sleep, what you ate, how you dressed, and how you structured your day. It's therefore important to establish ground rules at the outset. You are, after all, still living in your parents' house and should abide by their conventions.

## Finding a Place

Landing an apartment can be a snap, or it can take several weeks or even months, depending on your city's market and how much money you have to spend. "I recommend allowing forty-five to sixty days," advises Andrew Heiberger, the president of Citihabitats, a real estate brokerage in New York City.

Two months is a long time, so you may need to secure some temporary housing while you look. There are many economical possibilities: your buddy's couch, your great aunt's davenport,

In order to work things out with your parents and siblings, you will need to clarify your expectations—and theirs. Do your parents insist you get a job right away? How much freedom do you have coming and going? How much leeway is there in borrowing the family car? Is staying out all night even an option? When, if ever, do you need to "report in?" Are you allowed to have boyfriends or girlfriends stay overnight, or do your parents subscribe to the Not Under My Roof! mentality? Getting all this clear can prevent a lot of anger and arguments.

It also doesn't hurt, living in the Real World, to act more like an adult. Help out around the house. Pay your share of the phone bill. Take your little brother to Little League practice. Ask how you can contribute.

For some, living at home is cushy. Good food and clean laundry are trade-offs for rigid schedules and nosy parents. For others, launching their adult lives from the same room where they used to play with Barbies or Tonka trucks is difficult, if not impossible. For these graduates, it's time to cut the umbilical cord.

your mother's best friend's guest room. There are also youth hostels and YMCAs that rent by the day or week.

Looking for an apartment requires a lot of effort, so it's important to prepare yourself for the potential pitfalls and to keep your energy up.

*Searching for a place to live after college became my full-time job. On the weekends I would prepare my plan of attack. I would jot down the times of open*

## Movin' On Up: Helpful Web Sites

**www.apartments.com**
Apartments.com has listings for every state, along with information on moving companies, credit reports, and furniture rentals.

**www.craigslist.org**
Craig's List covers major U.S. cities and has ads for apartments,
sublets, roommates, and used furniture.

**www.homestore.com**
Homestore.com allows you to search for available apartments by
ZIP code, and has a rent calculator to help you figure out how
much you can afford.

*houses for apartments or group houses that looked in-
teresting and would make appointments with property
managers to view units at larger apartment com-
plexes. Going to open houses never worked out, because forty or more people would show up every time,
and it was difficult to distinguish myself from the
crowd.*

Check out the city's newspapers online, and have a look at
local apartment-locating services. There are helpful and free Internet sites that offer apartment listings in almost every price
range and showcase roommate advertisements for housing all
over the country. These sites often show pictures or floor plans
and give dimensions of the apartments they feature.

Word-of-mouth is often an effective way to find a place. Ask friends and coworkers if they know of anyone leaving an apartment any time soon. In other words, make sure all your friends and acquaintances know you're looking for a place. And sometimes, when you're really lucky, an apartment search can have a happy ending.

> *We saw this small sign on the outside of a Brooklyn diner one morning that said, 'Apartments: Call Sam.' So we did. He had this great two-bedroom, no-fee apartment for rent with a backyard and storage space, reasonably priced. We signed the lease on the spot.*

## Location, Location, Location

The golden rule of real estate matters even to twenty-two-year-olds. Is the apartment close to your work? Is it close to your bank? Are there stores nearby where you'd actually shop, restaurants where you'd actually eat, bars where you might fit in? Is there parking? Or is there public transportation in the vicinity? And most importantly, is the neighborhood safe?

> *I wasn't making enough money to live in the nicest neighborhood. And I wasn't familiar enough with the city to know which areas were considered unsafe. So I moved to a popular neighborhood in Cambridge, which had a bit of seedy element to it. Gritty chic, I called it. Unfortunately, my apartment was broken into a few times. I should have talked to more people in the city to get a better feel for the different types of neighborhoods and chosen my living situation with a little more care*

*than I did. My advice would be to forgo extra space and amenities for a safe neighborhood, or at least look for apartments that are on the second floor or above and do not have easy access from the back.*

Then again, concerns such as the safety and "coolness" of a popular neighborhood are subjective. You have to know yourself *and* the territory. Do your homework: buy guidebooks, get your hands on city maps, talk to people who live in your city of choice and people who have lived there in the past. Scout out prospective neighborhoods at all times of the day—after dark, late Friday night, and in the wee hours of the morning—to see how comfortable you feel. Also, check rush-hour traffic noise.

*I walked around and got a sense of the different neighborhoods. I scanned the papers and went online to figure out what places cost. When I finally found a place that interested me, I paid close attention to where the nearest grocery store was, and whether there was fun stuff to do at night. I wanted a place with a neighborhoody feel, with kids playing outside and little coffee shops around the corner. It took me a month to find it, but it was worth it.*

And it may sound like a no-brainer, but be sure that you lay eyes on the place before you move in, even if your friends promise you that they'll take care of everything. Your new roommates, after all, may have a very different sense of how much money is too much, or what an acceptable apartment looks like.

> *My friends insisted that I go take the summer off like I had planned and they would find a place no problem. When I showed up with boxes in tow and saw my room, I almost tore up the lease on the spot. I had to walk through the shower to get there and the only thing that fit in it was a child-sized mattress. I should never have left it up to them.*

## Rent: How Much Is Too Much?

Two big questions face anyone starting an apartment search: What can I afford, and What should I expect for my money? "The first thing you should consider is price," advises Andrew Heiberger of Citihabitats. "You don't want to strap yourself and be rent-poor, though inevitably you will be a little when you're first starting out."

Demand for housing is great in most big U.S. cities and so a lot of apartments are exorbitantly priced. Once you find an apartment, you'll have to pay first and last month's rent, a security deposit—usually equal to one month's rent—and maybe a broker's fee, often one month's rent or more. If your income isn't high enough, or if your credit history is poor or nonexistent, you'll have to line up guarantors—typically parents, who are held responsible if, say, you or your roommate hit the road.

> *We signed our contracts, and my mom had to co-sign. I hadn't been working long enough to show good credit, which was a major pain. I had avoided the college credit card scene and I was now regretting it. I didn't want to have my parents backing me anymore.*

The rule of thumb is that one week's salary should be equal to or greater than one month's rent—including all associated housing costs like telephone, electricity, and cable. (Ask potential landlords for a heating estimate or an approximation of all utility costs so you can figure out the total package.) Be honest and realistic about money. Carl Cherchi, owner of National Roommates, an online matching service, says, "Most people tend to be a bit overconfident about what they can afford."

*I knew I had to satisfy some basic needs. I needed available parking. I needed to be near some sort of public transportation. I wanted to live with other people—preferably women—and I wanted to be paying around $500. I ended up making some sacrifices and I ended up paying a little more than I wanted. If you want to live in the city, you have to suffer the costs.*

Be practical and think about what you require versus what you desire. Do you need your own bedroom? Must you have a dishwasher? Do you need a parking space? Will basic cable suffice or do you risk pop culture starvation without weekly installments of *The Sopranos*?

*I moved into a small one-bedroom apartment with a friend from high school. Rather than split the bedroom, we chose to divide up the common space. This was a bad idea. In my opinion, after college, everyone needs at least four walls and a door for the bedroom. I chose not to have that due to financial constraints and it was the wrong decision. A hanging sheet in the middle of a room doesn't qualify.*

Sometimes rent is negotiable. If there are a lot of vacancies, then it's a buyer's market and a perfect time to negotiate. But when few apartments are available, landlords hold the power. Bring along advertisements for comparable apartments in the area as negotiating leverage to contest the landlord's offering price. And be creative—there may be other ways to hold down the dollar cost of renting.

> *My friend lived in a building rent-free in exchange for managing the complex of about thirty units. He wanted some buddies down in that part of town so he gave me a great deal on a very nice one-bedroom apartment. In exchange, I'd take over management responsibilities when he had to go out of town. It was a great setup.*

There are other points to negotiate. If you don't mind a little manual labor, offer to paint the apartment or refinish the floors or perform some other maintenance or refurbishing task in exchange for a reduction in rent. If you have extra time but are low on funds, offer your services as a babysitter or a housecleaner to a landlord in need. Or, if you're considering living in a place for several years, try to work out a longer lease term of two or three years. The rent may still be more than what you're looking to pay that first year, but you can save money over the long term by avoiding the annual rent increase.

## Dealing with Landlords

Understand that because of your age and lack of experience, you're already at a disadvantage. "In the eyes of landlords, young people—or anyone who has had a job for less than two years—

are considered undesirable tenants. They're immature and their careers are unstable. Plus, young people tend to be disrespectful to property and late with their rent checks," says Heiberger, the real estate broker.

And in a tight housing market, landlords don't have to rent to potential liabilities. "I want someone who is secure and stable," says Paul Hammer, a landlord in Houston, Texas. "To be honest, I don't like renting to kids. They're more likely to move, and then I have to go to the trouble of finding another tenant."

Apartments will invariably seem small and expensive. Try to manage your expectations. In fact, after looking for a day or two you'll naturally begin to decipher which classified advertisements have embellished a bit. You soon learn that "charming" means small and that "sun-filled" means that there's a window or two. No matter how B-I-G the apartment sounds, compare the amount of rent being asked with the location. It may be too good to be true.

> *The rooms were the size of postage stamps. One place we looked at had one decent-sized bedroom, two bedrooms that were closet sized and one that was so small it had a loft bed with a closet under it and barely enough room to stand in. Plus, there were no windows.*

Try to visualize any apartment the way it might look with you living in it. Don't write off apartments simply because the walls have wood paneling and the linoleum in the kitchen is a deep shade of brown. Have a vision: A dark and dingy apartment could turn out okay with a fresh paint job and some brightly colored throw rugs. (Of course, you'll have to ask the landlord before you go ahead with any renovating.)

Navigating the details of getting the apartment can be a hassle, too.

*It was a whirlwind two days of paper-pushing, signing, faxing, letter-obtaining, and guarantor-obtaining. The funny thing is, I am not actually on our lease, because I wasn't employed when my roommates and I were looking to rent, and they thought I would be a liability. Technically, I don't live here. Let's hope that never becomes a problem.*

Before committing to the apartment, try to get a handle on potential landlord or building supervisor relations. If your apartment is particularly old or decrepit, ask other tenants about how long it takes to get things fixed, or if they have had any problems in the building. Here is the chance to find out about them, too. Do they have yippy dogs or small children? Does their music blare?

*My first place had two porches, a gas stove, good-sized bedrooms, and on-street parking. The only problem was the frat house next door. My roommates and I were all so over the college thing by that point. The late-night parties and beer cans on the lawn had really lost their appeal.*

It's important to chat with your landlord to find out if she keeps the place in good working order. "Make an effort to deter-

## Credit Report? What's That?

Landlords use credit reports to determine whether or not you're a financial risk as a tenant. Based on a model derived from analysis of the credit histories of thousands of people with a financial profile similar to yours, it helps a landlord predict how likely you are to make rent payments on time. Credit rating agencies get information from retailers, banks, collection agencies, and public records. Not surprisingly, a good credit history will help you secure an apartment and a bad one will make it harder.

There are five factors that contribute to the "credit score" that makes up your credit report:

1. *Approximately 35 percent of your score is based on your payment history.* The first thing any landlord will want to know is whether you have paid past bills such as credit card statements on time. While late payments do not necessarily ruin your score, a good track record on most of your credit accounts will increase your credit score. An overall good credit picture can outweigh one or two instances of late credit card payments.

2. *About 30 percent of your score is based on your debt.* Having credit accounts and owing money on them does not mean you are a high-risk borrower with a low score. Owing a significant sum on many accounts, however, can indicate that a person is overextended, or maxed out, and is thus more likely to make some payments late or not at all. Another consideration is how much you still owe of the original balance on installment loan accounts like col-

mine if the landlord is financially responsible and honorable," says Paul Bernstein, a lawyer for tenant's rights in Chicago. Find out how the building is maintained; make as many inquiries as you can before you actually become a tenant."

Landlords also size you up. Dress nicely when meeting your

lege loans. Paying down installment loans is a good sign that you are able and willing to manage and repay debt.

3. *About 15 percent of your score is based on the length of your credit history.* In general, a longer credit history will increase your score. However, even people with short credit histories may get high scores depending on how the rest of the credit report looks. The score considers both the age of your oldest account and an average age of all your accounts.

4. *About 10 percent of your score is based on whether you are taking on more credit.* Today people tend to have more credit than ever before. But opening several credit accounts in a short period of time represents greater risk—especially for people who do not have a long-established credit history.

5. *About 10 percent of your score is based on the variety in your credit accounts.* This part of the score is a complex formula that takes into account both the types of accounts and the total number of credit accounts you have under your name. Credit account types include credit cards, retail accounts, installment loans, finance company accounts, and mortgage loans. This part of the credit score is more important if you do not have a lot of other credit information on your file—the norm with most young adults.

SOURCE: Consumer Credit Score Online (www.credit-score-online.com)

landlord for the first time. It would be a shame to lose an apartment over a pair of tattered jeans. Have some letters of reference in hand, and carry proof of employment on company letterhead and a pay stub so your landlord can be assured you're gainfully employed and able to make rent payments on time. "I always check references and I read between the lines," says Gioia Ambrette, a landlord in New York City. "When I call their employer, I ask if they show up to work on time; if so, then they'll probably pay their rent on time. I try to get an indication of a person's patterns of behavior."

Most landlords simply want to make sure you'll pay your rent and care little about your personal life and habits. In fact, the federal Civil Rights Act and Fair Housing Act prohibits landlords from discriminating on the basis of race, ethnic background, national origin, religion, and sex. If you suspect you're being discriminated against, find out about the laws in your city and state.

> *When my girlfriend, who is black, and I were trying to find an apartment, we ran into several racist landlords. One had the gall to take my girlfriend aside and say, 'Are you sure you want to share a one bedroom with that?' in a stage whisper. We just decided that if they don't want us, we don't want them.*

## Adventures with Brokers

If you're strapped for time or simply find that dealing directly with a dozen different landlords takes too much of your energy, then it may be necessary—or at least wise—to seek professional help when looking for an apartment. A broker or a real estate agent serves as an intermediary between you and the landlords or management companies. The broker's business is to maintain a database with privileged apartment listings and at least in theory can more easily match you with an apartment in your price range.

For this service, they take a fee of between 10 and 15 percent of the annual rent.

"Brokers can show you a greater variety of what's available in the competitive market," says Andrew Heiberger of Citihabitats. "Brokers help you wade through the process and steer you toward buildings where you are more likely to get approved."

> *It was mid-August, which was really the worst time to be looking for an apartment and everyone thought that I was nuts for looking that late. So I did the broker thing. After seeing fifteen apartments in a few days, I came across one that was awesome. Because it was called a walk-through studio—it had a bedroom that just lacked a door—I got a deal on it. It was only a seven-minute walk to work. It was pretty big and in a great neighborhood. I give my broker full credit for finding this place.*

But understand that brokers are not your friends. They regard you as a moneymaking opportunity, no matter how much they seem to really care. Do not tell your broker how much money you have or that you are desperate for an apartment. Do not let your broker convince you to take a more expensive apartment; he'll want to do this, of course, to earn a higher commission. Ask to see apartments at least $100 below your actual top monthly range.

> *Not to be too dramatic or anything, but my broker was so wretched that she destroyed my faith in humanity. She spent two weeks showing me apartments that had none of the qualifications I wanted, telling me all*

## Subletting

Subletting, an agreement made by a renter to rent all or a portion of the rental property to another person, is a viable option, especially if you're in the market for a furnished apartment.

But subletting is not a casual alternative to renting. Indeed, you must treat it with the same amount of seriousness. Discuss in advance as many obligations and potential problems as you can. For instance, if you sublet on a month-to-month basis and you decide to leave, you may vacate upon a thirty-day written notice. However, if you sublet for a fixed term and decide to check out early, depending on the terms of your agreement, you may be responsible for the rent even after you have vacated.

Have a written and signed agreement with the resident that explicitly states what your rent includes—gas, water, electricity. Be clear on the length of time you're renting, and that the sublet has the approval of the landlord. And remember: You are relying on the other renter's ability to pay the tab; if they get evicted, you're out, too.

*the while that I was never going to get an apartment in my price range. Then, when I finally found a place I wanted and went through the process of credit checks and lease signings and taking whole days off work to do so, she told me that the apartment wouldn't be ready for another two months. The whole thing fell through.*

And don't rely solely on your broker to select your place for you. Brokers rarely volunteer details about the unsavory aspects of a neighborhood, such as rising burglary rates or curse-worthy rush-hour traffic. Adopt a critical attitude toward all of the apartments you see, always keeping your own standards firmly in mind.

## The Big Bad Lease

It's not exactly a palace, but you finally find a place you want and you're ready to snatch it up. Before you sign the lease, do a thorough walk-through. Make a record of how the place looked prior to your arrival. With a pen and pad, note all the dents and holes in the wall, stains in the carpet, tears in the linoleum, scuffs or stains in the hardwood floors. Otherwise, you could be held accountable for them later. You might even bring a friend along, take photographs, or, even better, videotape your walk-through with the date stamped on the video.

Evaluate the appliances and amenities: the stove, the sinks, the shower, the toilet, air-conditioning and heating units, washer and dryer, smoke and radon detectors, fire extinguishers, mailboxes, outdoor lighting, locks, and emergency exits. If any of these do not function properly, no matter how slightly, it's wise to write a formal letter noting all problems and ask that they be corrected before your arrival. And, as with all formal correspondence, *make and save copies.*

"Remember, the lease was created by the landlord and it was designed to protect the landlord," says attorney Paul Bernstein. "If you have certain concerns about the apartment—say the carpeting in bedroom number one is frayed, or the front room needs a fresh coat of paint—an honest landlord should have no reservations about making amendments to the lease. But make sure it's signed by both parties."

To ensure that the landlord complies, work out a timetable

## Look Before You Lease

Your lease likely will be jam-packed with unfamiliar terminology. It's tempting to sign on the dotted line and disregard all those confusing words. Don't do it.

Instead, take the time to look over the lease to make sure you understand the terms you are agreeing to. Here are some basic definitions to help.

*Lessor:* The landlord.

*Lessee:* The person renting the premises, also known as the tenant, also known as you.

*Possession:* Lawful occupation and use of the apartment, subject to protections of "quiet enjoyment."

*Security Deposit:* Consider it a down payment. This sum, typically one month's rent, is money that should be refunded to you when you move out, if you abide by the terms of your lease and leave the apartment in the same condition as you found it, excepting normal wear and tear.

*Indemnify and Hold Harmless:* To free from any responsibility or liability.

that states when chores will be completed. "If you don't want to be disappointed, be as technical and as detailed as you can."

The lease is a legal, binding agreement between you and your landlord; it will define every aspect of your relationship. Never rush into signing a lease. Read it thoroughly so that you understand your rights, and what's expected of you as well. "Often times there will be a set of rules attached to the lease with mundane items like you forfeiting money if you play music too loud or don't empty the trash in the correct way," advises Ben

*Liability:* Responsibility, loss.

*Arrears:* Overdue rent.

*Default:* Forfeiting or losing by omission; failing to perform a legal obligation.

*Eviction:* Forcing a tenant to leave his apartment. A landlord has the right to evict without stating any reason when the lease expires so long as he gives proper notice. He can evict during the lease period only when the tenant breaches one or more of his basic obligations.

*Notice to Quit:* Warning from the landlord to tenant ordering tenant off the property, usually after thirty days from the first day of the next rental period.

*Tenant at Sufferance:* A tenant who has remained in a unit after a lease agreement has expired or was terminated.

*Acceleration Clause or Escalation Clause:* Allows the landlord to charge additional rent for certain expenses that have increased over a stated period of time or above a predetermined unit cost.

Grant, an attorney in Portland, Maine. "Look carefully at those rules to determine whether there might be a problem."

Get an explanation of things you don't understand. Don't worry about your questions appearing naïve—you *are* naïve. Never sign a lease with which you are uncomfortable. In fact, you might want to include clauses of your own—say, a release from the lease if your company transfers you out of town. If you do ask for a change, add it to the lease; writing it in by hand is okay. Do not settle for an oral agreement.

## Home Sweet Home

After you sign the lease, the only remaining business is to set a move-in date. Before you move in, have the utilities and cable service turned on, call the phone company to arrange for service, and file a change-of-address form with the post office.

Then the day comes when finally you're on your own. Expect some mixed feelings. It may not be exactly what you had anticipated.

> *It was hard to get used to living on my own. When I'd get home, I'd immediately turn on the television or throw in a CD just to have some background noise. In college there was always someone to talk to. But in the real world I was really lonely.*

On the other hand, it could be exactly what you expected and you'll relish your newfound freedom. For many of us, living on our own—out of our parents' home, away from dormitory life—is liberating. Revel in it.

> *My first apartment was cool. It was a little small, but it was fine just for me. I loved the fact that I could go home and escape from everyone. I didn't have to ask anyone else to do this or that. I had free rein to walk around in my boxers, eat what I wanted, watch what I wanted on TV, and listen to whatever music I wanted. It was great! I had a place that was mine.*

## No Place Is Perfect

Your landlord is obligated to keep the building and grounds in a good and safe condition, but be prepared to deal with the kind of annoyances and inconveniences that are inevitable in any home: creaky floorboards, drafty windows, doors that don't latch properly, ovens that heat either too fast or too slow. The problems you should address before you move in include a malfunctioning showerhead, a radiator that oozes brown syrup, and obvious rodent issues, for instance. Usually the landlord must maintain all electrical, plumbing, and heating systems as well.

Find out whom to call—the building's superintendent or the landlord himself—when problem situations do occur.

> *I was sleeping and heard something above me. I thought it was mice in the ceiling—hardly a settling thought, so I got up. When I turned on the light, what do I see flying around my bedroom but a bat. I ran out of my apartment and was standing in the hallway at 3:00 A.M. in my PJs while the bat was having his fun in my apartment. Finally, attracted to the light, he flew out into the hall and I flew in and locked the door. A few days later, I got a message from my landlord stating rather sinisterly, 'You won't have to worry about the bat anymore, he's been taken care of.'*

Be respectful and polite when requesting to have anything fixed. "Try to create a good relationship with your landlord," advises Grant. "People are responsive to people they like, rather than those they perceive to be complaining. Ultimately, they own the property and when it comes time to renew the lease, they will look less favorably on you."

Try to be patient about non-emergency repairs—a few days are reasonable—and call judiciously. It can be difficult to reach your landlord or building supervisor, especially in times of need. Landlords are, after all, running a business. You'll have your share of talking to answering machines and sending faxes and e-mails. If your oven light won't turn on properly, that might not be a priority. When the bathroom above yours is leaking into your bedroom, however, that certainly qualifies as an emergency. Even then, expect some apathy.

> *Our landlord is pretty relaxed. This can be both an asset and a detriment. When we needed him to steam clean the carpets because the dogs had stained them, it was a plus. When we needed him to come fix the stopped-up sink or repair a window, it was a bit of a setback.*

If your landlord is constantly indifferent to your problems, there are ways to get her attention. "You can call the code enforcement officer—there is one in every town—and get him to come and inspect your place," suggests attorney Ben Grant. "If he finds that your problem violates the housing code, then he will issue a complaint to your landlord." Alternatively, under "repair and deduct" statutes, you can withhold rent if you deem the problem large enough. Every state has organizations that serve to protect tenant rights, although there is not necessarily a consistently named office. A quick Internet search for "tenant rights" along with your state name will yield state, regional, and local resources.

Get permission for do-it-yourself repairs no matter how handy you think you are with a power drill. "If an ember jumped out of the fireplace and burned a hole in the carpet, and the tenant took it upon himself to fix it, and then messed it up entirely, that is a big and costly problem for me," says landlord Paul Hammer. "Realistically, how many people are really competent enough to deal with such things?"

"There is an unspoken structure between myself and my tenants," says Hammer. "On one level, they fear me—I am a faceless institution who does not care about their day-to-day problems because I need the rent by the first of the month. On another level, they need to feel comfortable enough with me to let me know when there is a problem—even when they caused it—right away."

## Protecting Your Place

Consider purchasing renter's insurance. It's a policy that covers loss of personal property from fire, weather, or theft, and pays living expenses if you are forced to live elsewhere while your apartment is being fixed. Policies are relatively inexpensive, typically about $150 per year depending on where you live.

"Most of the time, young people think that they don't have that many belongings," said a spokesperson from MetLife Auto and Home. "But if they really thought about it—the CD burner, the computer, the DVD player—it really adds up. We recommend a policy worth about $10,000." Sometimes renter's insurance is not optional. "I insist that my tenants have insurance, and I need to see proof," says landlord Gioia Ambrette. "I am not responsible for the contents of their apartment if it gets broken into."

Liability coverage is usually included in the renter's insurance. "If someone gets hurt on your property, or if they're injured
by you—say if they trip over your umbrella in the aisle of a
restaurant—then you can get sued. Liability insurance typically
covers up to $100,000 of medical problems," says a spokesperson
from Metropolitan Life Insurance.

Ask coworkers or friends to recommend an agent with
whom they've had a good experience. If that yields no leads,
check the Internet or the Yellow Pages for the local office of a reputable company. You often can save money if you apply for coverage through the company that insures your car.

Make sure to buy the amount of coverage you need for your
possessions and remember that you want the replacement cost of
your belongings covered, not just their "actual cost"—what you
paid for your killer stereo system years ago when things were
cheaper.

On the other hand, if your belongings aren't all that precious—you still have your parents' television set from the year
they got married and an IBM circa 1989—you might think twice
before investing in renter's insurance. After you've been out on
your own for a while and accumulate more things, you can always reconsider.

## Your Neighbors

Pat, the geriatric woman who lived next door to us in my first
post-college place, was gaunt with white braided hair. She was
chatty and nosey and eager to know about what "the young
folks," as she called us, were up to. If one of us, say, had parked
just a little too close to the fire hydrant on our block, she would
leave a rambling note on the windshield of our car warning us
about the tenacity of Washington's meter maids. If the weather

forecast called for a storm, she would drop by to advise that we bring our lawn chairs and grill indoors. It was mostly harmless and we mostly tolerated her. We could never tell if she actually liked us or if she considered us a nuisance.

When my roommates and I decided to throw a party one Halloween, we thought it best to tell Pat. It was a preemptive move that would lessen the possibility of Pat calling the police if we made too much noise. We promised not to get rowdy and instructed that if any sound bothered her, she should let us know immediately. She nodded primly and pursed her lips.

Later that afternoon, Pat showed up at our door. She said she had a little surprise for us. It was a giant sign emblazoned with fluorescent letters that read: The Party's Here. We knew then that she was on our side.

Get to know your neighbors, even if they're not Chandler and Joey—or even Pat. Introduce yourself in the hallway or in the lobby. Leave a note on their door, identifying who you are. You never know when you might need that neighbor to water your plants or collect your mail when you're away.

And be considerate. Most lease agreements provide for residents to have "quiet enjoyment" of their apartments. Remember that you share most of your walls with neighbors and that you're not in college anymore. Your neighbors may not share your appreciation for Lauryn Hill, and loud music, especially late in the evening, is no longer the norm. Restrict extra-noisy activities— tap dancing, vacuuming, practicing your cello—to normal waking hours: 9:00 A.M. to 9:00 P.M.

If your neighbors complain, there are ways to minimize your noise output. Place foam pads under small appliances to minimize their vibrations. Put up curtains; the fabric in window drapes will absorb sound. Replace metal garbage cans with ones that are plastic. Put down carpeting or large area rugs on your floors. Document these changes so that if you are confronted about sounds emanating from your apartment again, you can prove that you have made earnest attempts at reducing the noise level.

Perhaps you're the one being victimized by a neighbor who insists on vacuuming at 6:00 A.M., or someone who blasts AC/DC at midnight.

> *Occasionally, my upstairs neighbor complained about the loud music, but I would just turn the music down and apologize. I hate confrontations. But then he moved out and a young female occupant moved in upstairs. The only problem I had with her was that my bedroom was right under hers and she had a lot of, ahem, fun. So every other night I would hear the bed springing and her moaning. So sometimes I didn't get a lot of sleep. I guess she didn't either.*

Speak with your neighbor and ask for understanding and cooperation. But if the problem persists, send a copy of the local noise ordinance to the offending noisemaker. Finally, contact your landlord, outlining the problem and letting the landlord know the steps you've taken to address the issue. Your landlord has a legal obligation to provide you with a habitable dwelling.

## The Best of Roommates, the Worst of Roommates

Roommates: Can't live with 'em, can't afford to live without 'em. Chances are you will have a roommate or four during your first few years out of college. After all, by pooling income with some other folks you can swing a much bigger, nicer abode. Besides, living with roommates can be fun, like an extension of college life.

*I have three roommates and I love them. I love having people around. I find it lonely in the evening when no one is home. It's fun throwing parties, cooking dinner, watching movies, staying up late talking. We divide up the chores when they need to be done. We each do our own food shopping and everything works out fine.*

That's the bright side. But not everyone feels the same way. Some graduates have had more than their fill of the communal aspects of college life. Loner types or those anxious to set up their own bachelor or bachelorette pads may decide that two's a crowd. For them, living with others can result in uncomfortably contentious relationships.

*I hate having roommates. Having roommates is just hard, no matter how flexible and agreeable you are. I'm much happier now that I live on my own; I don't worry about who's going to be moody when I get home from work or who's going to be in the bathroom when I get home from the gym.*

The most important attribute in a potential roommate, beyond his or her ability to share rent, is compatibility. While you're not looking for a new best friend, you are looking for someone to share communal space. "You want to have a comfort level and compatibility with your potential roommate," advises Carl Cherchi, owner of National Roommates. "Go with your first impression. You should have things in common, be of similar age. It's not an exact science though, and you have to enter the relationship in the spirit of cooperation."

Many people upon graduation move to a new city or town and live with friends from college. But if you're not lucky enough to have a best friend moving to your city, ask around to friends of friends, put up a flier, look online, or pore through the classifieds of the local newspaper.

Reputable roommate matching services are sprouting on the Internet as well. To avoid being scammed by a service, obtain sample listings of roommate seekers in your price range before signing on and paying a fee.

*I went online and read people's advertisements seeking roommates. It was a lot like the personals. Then I went around and interviewed with all these potential roommates. This one group of women wrote that they had a friendly cat named Margaret, there were three cute boys living downstairs, they liked snowboarding, and they loved country music. It was a perfect match—except for the country music. But it grew on me.*

Interview potential roommates carefully and openly to get an idea of their tastes and habits. Be honest about your own habits. Do you stay up late and sleep late? Or are you an early riser? Are you a domestic goddess? Or do dust bunnies tend to congregate in the corner of your bedroom? Do you listen

## Let's Move In Together

You're in love. Your relationship is perfect. You couldn't imagine a finer roommate than your darling dearest. But should you live together?

It's not an easy decision. Make sure that you and your significant other have the same expectations of how your relationship will be affected: Do you plan to get married? Do you view living together as a trial that will help you decide? Or is marriage not in the foreseeable future? Talk about potential issues of living together and define how you'll handle finances and property. It may be true love, but it's business, too. These conversations will protect you later if you decide to go your separate ways.

Weigh the pros and cons and be realistic. Cohabitating will not magically change your relationship. The obnoxious traits in your beau will become the obnoxious traits of your roommate. Your nagging girlfriend morphs into your nagging roommate.

to loud rap music? Or are you an opera buff? Do you play a musical instrument? Do you smoke? Do your friends come by at all hours?

Most important, however, is the sheer economics of it all. Is your potential roommate reliable? Does he or she have a job, or at least rich parents willing to pay the tab? When your roommate can't pay the rent, you are held responsible for paying it in full. "When folks get together and say they want to live together, no one stops to think about the what-ifs," says attorney Paul Bernstein. "Even the best of relationships deteriorate, and roommates are jointly liable."

## Money Matters

No matter how strange it sounds, you and your roommate—friend or stranger—have a business relationship. Don't enter it blindly. And think twice when your buddy from college who was always borrowing beer money begs to live with you; a six-pack of Natty Light easily translates to an unpaid phone bill or overdue rent check in the real world.

Consider drawing up a roommate agreement to clarify responsibilities and set some financial guidelines such as how bills will be paid and how newspaper and magazine subscriptions will be split. If your sole use of the *TV Guide* is the challenging crossword puzzle, do you still have to pay for it?

*Costs are always an issue when you have roommates. Someone always thinks they are getting screwed because somebody ate their last cookie or someone always finishes the milk and never buys more. And those are just the little things. My roommate who has the biggest bank account pays the monthly bills, like electricity, cable, water, and we pay him back. That's the worst part so far—organizing everyone all at once to mark out their phone calls and pay up!*

Your agreement might also cover other forward-looking matters such as what would happen should one of you want to move out. How much notice is needed? How are deposits going to be handled? Discuss how overnight guests will be treated. Is it okay to have friends crashing on your couch for a long weekend? (If you live in a desirable city, you will no doubt have out-oftowners asking you to play hotel.) Are you okay with your room-mate's boyfriend or girlfriend hanging out and sleeping over for days or weeks at a stretch—for free? These kinds of issues, if ignored, can put significant stress on your relationship with your roommate.

> *There were episodes with my roommates. My boyfriend, Alex, got a job in my city and ended up staying with me—in my room, neatly and respect-fully—for two weeks. After he was gone, my three other roommates told me that he should pay rent for the time he was there. I disagreed, but to allevi-ate tension I gave them each some money. It was an ugly situation that bruised a few of my closest friendships.*

Compromise is golden. At the outset, figure out how much you're each going to pay for rent if there are discrepancies in the sizes of the bedrooms. While it's easy to claim that the big bed-room with the enormous closet should be more expensive than the tiny room off the kitchen, the hard question is: How much more? When you decide this, however, bear in mind that such agreements don't have any impact on the landlord, and that each tenant is independently obligated to pay the rent.

> *My roommate and I had our first argument over how to split the rent. The space was fair-sized, but cozy for two people. We had a wall company come in and build an extra wall for us, to cut a bedroom out*

*from the living room. This meant no light in the living room and people had to traipse through my bedroom to get to the terrace. My roommate felt we should split the rent evenly because we each had a bedroom. I didn't really think it was fair because I lived in the faux bedroom, which was smaller than hers. Plus her closets were in her room whereas mine were in the kitchen. So, I felt dividing the space up by square footage was the fairest option. It came out that her square footage was about $150 more than mine. She didn't feel it was fair. So we compromised at her paying $125 more.*

Money can cause another divide within the house, particularly if one of you does petition drives for Greenpeace and the other is an investment banker at J.P. Morgan. One of you shops at Price Club, the other at the fancy organic grocery store downtown; one of you guzzles Bud, the other insists on microbrew; one of you dines on gourmet risotto, the other Chef Boyardee. You get the picture. Discuss how you'll divvy up food and other expenses. Will basic goods like coffee, milk, and OJ be split evenly?

*Groceries were split evenly for a while. But as my roommate fell more and more into debt, my soap became his soap. My soda became his soda, then it became his friend's soda. After a few frustrating arguments we finally talked like civilized people, and I told him that I wasn't going to live with him after the lease was up. It was rough. It was also sad, because he was a good friend.*

## Chores and Behavioral Issues

One of my first roommates was the daughter of a women's shoe magnate. Hence this woman had a ton of shoes: lipstick-red velvet platforms, sophisticated navy heels, brown leather mules, baby blue designer sneakers. Since my roommate—we affectionately called her Imelda—had so many shoes, she would often wear more than one pair during the day. Who could blame her? Every afternoon she would arrive home from work and toss her shoes in the corner of our dining room. By the end of the week there would often be a mound of nine or ten pairs lumped in the corner. It drove the rest of us crazy.

We finally devised a plan. When we noticed the shoe congregation forming, we immediately gathered the pairs and dumped them on her bed. She was a good sport about it and quickly took the hint.

When you live with other people, it becomes necessary to divide up the responsibilities for cleaning, shopping, taking out the trash, getting the bills paid on time. Whether you're more Oscar or Felix, your roommates' opposite proclivities are bound to drive you batty. For the neatniks, it's an especially hard cross to bear.

*My roommate had difficulty identifying a vacuum. Chores seemed to fall on whomever got grossed out by the kitchen sink first. And it was always me. My roommate doesn't seem to notice when the bathtub gets clogged with hair or when the dust bunnies get nuclear under the couch.*

Try to deal with messiness and grime before they become issues. If you are intensely clean and neat—you wouldn't miss a "Hints from Heloise" column and you made your bed in college

## Oh, Give Me a Home

Okay. So it's a little small. The floors aren't so shiny and the walls are a morbid shade of maroon. Here are some inexpensive ways to make your apartment more attractive and livable.

*Paint:* A fresh coat of paint can easily—and cheaply—change the look and feel of your apartment. Also, color schemes create illusions of space. If your apartment is especially boxy, the key is to create a focal point; paint one wall a different color from the others. If your apartment receives hardly any natural light, paint with pale colors. Just be sure to get permission from your landlord first. Some landlords deduct from your security deposit to paint it white again when you leave.

*Slipcovers:* If the couch you inherited from Mom and Dad has the relic appeal of an episode of the *Brady Bunch*, washable throws and slipcovers are the perfect camouflage. They not only hide those ugly, busy patterns, they also protect your sofas and chairs if you eat in the living area. Many furniture and linen stores sell ready-made slipcovers.

even when your parents weren't visiting for the weekend—understand that many of your peers will never meet your high standards. It is also doubtful that they will respond well to constructive criticism. You will, in this case, end up taking on more chores and cleaning responsibility.

Consider hiring a weekly or biweekly cleaning service. "We recommend that roommates split the cost of a cleaning service. No one wants to be nagged by their roommate," says Carl Cherchi of National Roommates.

Work with your roommates to keep your collective mess

*Furnishings:* Milk crates don't cut it anymore. If your first apartment has a small or nonexistent dining room, consider a temporary ready-to-assemble breakfast bar with stools or collapsible wooden chairs. These RTA items are sturdy and storable, and not as expensive as traditional pre-assembled furniture.

*Plants:* Whether your pleasure is Aglaonema or Zebrina, live plants do wonders to brighten your apartment. And luckily, many houseplants thrive in little to moderate daylight. Thrift stores sell a variety of containers, but a galvanized pail is an inexpensive alternative as well.

*Accessories:* Those needling items like bath mats, wastebaskets, napkins—not to mention the necessary accessories like towels, shower curtains, and silverware—add up. Discount department stores such as T.J. Maxx and Marshalls have great deals on brand-name items and usually have a plenty in stock.

under control. Sometimes that requires straight, often uncomfortable, talk. But it's usually better to confront problems than to let them fester. And sometimes the offending roommate doesn't even realize that behavior that was acceptable in the family home or in college doesn't cut it in your shared place.

## Time to Say Goodbye

Some roommates are blessed with a natural affinity. Chores are never an issue, money is not a problem, and interior decorating tastes are shared.

*I live with a good college friend. We don't divvy up chores. You do what you want in your bedroom, just keep other areas picked up. We take turns, though not officially, when it comes to vacuuming and mopping. Our groceries we share—we eat the same things and usually go to the store together. It just comes down to respect and knowing the individual. If she buys something I know she particularly likes and I eat it, I tell her about it and then replace it. It's pretty simple.*

On the other hand, sometimes you and your roommate just plain don't get along. Not every roommate problem is about who owes grocery money or who forgot to empty the trash. Sometimes two—or three or four—people just don't belong together, and for the sake of all parties involved, something must be done.

*I lived with my sister's good friend and I hated it. She used to watch those stupid WB and Fox hour-long shows and had girly parties for the Oscars and Grammy awards. She and all her friends had pools about who would win and would scream and squeal whenever the winners were announced. I wanted to jump out of my seventh-story window.*

What should you do if things get really bad? The discussion should simply be about who has to leave. The answer is simple, too: Whomever can't stand living there any longer. If the lack of love goes both ways, then you might ask a trusted mutual acquaintance to mediate. This can be especially helpful when there are financial issues involved. Remember, this was a business relationship when you entered it; try to keep it in that category when ending it as well.

## Furnishing Your Pad

Although minimalism has a certain modern cachet, you ultimately will need to get some furniture. And while you may page through the glossy Crate and Barrel catalogs dreamily, it's hard to fathom shelling out $319 for that darling Auburn Kitchen Cart when you're living on a new grad's measly salary.

When you're just starting out, furniture should not break your bank. Luckily there are ways to decorate and furnish your place within a reasonable budget—especially now that your trusted futon is not so comfortable anymore and you're tired of looking at that poster of *The Scream* you hung up with fun-tac in your dorm room sophomore year.

> *Our house is the house that keeps on giving. In many ways it was furnished when we moved in. My roommate's brother lived there before us and we inherited a lot of things from him. We got some items from tag sales. And the house has been furnished bit by bit and continues to evolve. Nothing matches, and not much is off-limits for the dogs.*

Foraging for furniture will occupy a good deal of your time during the first few months in your new place. You will spend hours of your life waiting for the couch to be delivered, wandering the halls of discount furniture stores, and comparing screwdrivers at Home Depot. Even after those few months, you might find you have yet to hang pictures.

Start with Mom and Dad, or older siblings. Hand-me-down furniture is cheap and easy and usually available. Perhaps your parents have had an epiphany: your old room—still filled with your high school yearbooks and lacrosse sticks—might make a cozy home office or a great place to store the Nordic Track. If they plan to convert your room, they just might be ready to shed some furniture. Take advantage.

Be patient. Realize that furnishing your place to your satisfaction will take time. Shop in increments to avoid carpet malaise—when your eyes glaze over and you no longer detect the difference between sea foam green and spring forest sage. Make sure the furniture is sturdy, using it the same way you would if it were in your living room.

> *When I first got my own place, my parents took me to a shopping mall and we looked at loads of beds, tables, couches, chairs, pots and pans. I just wanted to get a good idea of how much these things cost. A lot, basically. So I didn't buy my first chair till Christmas, but at least I was sitting on my own floor.*

Do some research before you shop. Draw up a map of your apartment with the basic dimensions so that you can determine whether that bookcase is too big for that corner. "Get a magazine or a catalog and tear out pictures of things you like. You'll start to see a trend: 'I like traditional things,' or 'I have funky taste.'

Otherwise you might end up with something you really don't need," suggests Jill Davis, interior designer.

It's important to have a plan because little things add up fast. Prioritize your furniture purchases based on the immediate needs of your lifestyle, and remember that you don't have to buy everything at once. Eclectic furnishings are the norm—although some would say the bane—of first apartments.

Many young people just starting out find that IKEA, the Swedish superstore packed with sturdy, vividly colored couches, tables, chairs, bookshelves and bureaus, is their savior. IKEA offers decent furniture at lower-than-average prices, and their stores are accessible to many of the largest metropolitan areas in the United States. While IKEA is hardly designer furniture, the pieces are not frumpy.

> *We furnished our apartment through a combination of hand-me-downs from my parents, IKEA, and flea markets. Most of the furniture is serviceable, but I'm not crazy about it. I'm looking forward to the time when I can invest in some nicer, more permanent things. Of course, for holidays and birthdays, my parents buy different items—pots and pans, bedspreads, sheets, just different stuff.*

But if IKEA stretches you too thin or you have a strong aversion to primary colors, there are other options. Yard sales and dusty antique stores are not just for your great-aunt anymore. If you go this route, bring cash because dickering is the game and you'll have better bargaining power with a wad of dough. Don't

## Good Reads

*Steiner's Complete How-To-Move Handbook,* by Shari Steiner and Clyde L. Steiner (Independent Information Publications, 1999).

*The World's Easiest Pocket Guide to Renting Your First Apartment,* by Larry Burkett (Northfield, 2002).

*Rules for Roommates: The Ultimate Guide for Reclaiming Your Space and Your Sanity,* by Mary Lou Podlasiak (iUniverse.com, 2000).

*How to Decorate and Furnish Your Apartment on a Budget,* by Lourdes Dumke and Denise Sturnad (Prima Publishing, 2001).

be afraid to ask questions. Ask the garage sale holder why she is selling the item—obviously a blender that doesn't work anymore is not even worth the $2.50 asking price. "Check to see if the chair is wobbly or sturdy, whether it's scratched or stained, or if one leg is shorter than the rest," advises Jill Davis.

Charity-affiliated stores like Goodwill and the Salvation Army also provide solid, cheap secondhand furniture. Attend estate sales and auctions, too; many of the goods are still in excellent condition.

Once you have a steady paycheck, you might not be able to resist purchasing one or two pricey pieces of furniture. Still, be smart. "Spend the bulk of your money on a great upholstered piece like a durable and well-made sofa bed, or you might invest in a table and four chairs," recommends Jill Davis. "I wouldn't put all my money toward a coffee table because that's something you can pick up rather cheaply at a flea market."

# Moving Out with Your Security Deposit

After a while, you'll begin to regard your apartment's quirks and irregularities as charming: the creaky floorboard that sounds the "Ode to Joy" when stepped on in just the right way, the knob in your kitchen drawer that will forever be loose, or the window that was painted shut in the late 1960s.

Someday, though, after you've put in a couple of years, the time will come to move again or to relocate to a new city altogether. You'll wonder: How do I get out of my lease with my money and integrity? The process of ending your lease is easy— that is, if you do things right.

Be sure to give the landlord thirty to sixty days notice that you are leaving. She needs this time to advertise the place to new tenants. "The lease usually says to leave the apartment in the state that you found it," says landlord Gioia Ambrette. "Don't leave anything in the refrigerator. Don't leave a disgusting bathtub. Throw all your trash away."

Bottom line: Leave the place in good condition. Move all of your belongings out of the house. Vacuum the carpet and sweep the floor. Defrost the freezer. Make sure that light fixtures have working bulbs and that smoke detectors have good batteries—believe it or not, these items can be taken out of your security deposit.

If you leave the apartment in good condition, then your security deposit rightfully belongs to you. The landlord may keep your security deposit if you fail to pay rent or leave before the end of your lease, but otherwise your deposit should be returned to you, with interest in most cases. "The security deposit is the tenant's money," says attorney Paul Bernstein. "Every apartment is going to have ordinary wear and tear, and a lot of unscrupulous landlords will deduct it from the deposit."

Your landlord must furnish a written statement showing the specific reason for withholding any part or all of the security deposit. The landlord cannot charge the cost of repairing any damages that existed at the time you moved in against the security deposit. If you did not take the time to perform an inspection to check the damages before you moved in, however, you may find yourself arguing with the landlord over those tears in the linoleum or that scuff on the floor.

If you believe that the landlord does not have good reason for withholding any of the security deposit, inquire why the money was withheld. If your landlord cannot adequately explain the withholding, and if the amount of money involved is significant, it may be worth pursuing return of your deposit in small claims court.

Lawyers are expensive, but that may be the least of your worries. "Most of the preprinted leases have provisions that say if the landlord takes the tenant to court, then the tenant must pay for the landlord's attorney's fees. In some cases, there is a reciprocal benefit. Look at your lease to determine whether there is a landlord and tenant ordinance," says Paul Bernstein.

Further, if you are asked to leave—or put more crassly, you are evicted—"The issue is how egregious the conduct is and whether or not it's repeated," says attorney Ben Grant. "If it's multiple times, then the judge will be less sympathetic."

Finally, if you break a lease, you will probably lose your security deposit. But if you plan carefully, making sure that the landlord suffers no loss of rent and has no unplanned expenses, there is a chance that you may recover some or all of the deposit.

3

# car
# TALK

IF YOU THINK YOU WANT TO become a car owner in the lonely state of nonsubsidization, there's good news and bad news. First, the good news: Cars are fun. They help you get from a point A to point B comfortably and on your own schedule. And driving is fun: You can turn up the radio, pop open the sunroof, and shift gears until your wrist hurts. Shopping for cars can be fun, too. You can ask yourself deep philosophical questions like: Am I a Jeep kind of person? Does a hatchback mesh with my personality? You get to choose from an array of glamorous-sounding colors: midnight, sapphire, or lunar mist. You can opt for small conveniences like electric windows or steering wheel–mounted control keys to save your arm strength when changing radio stations.

Now, the bad news: All this fun has a formidable price tag. Cars are very expensive pieces of machinery—probably the most valuable possession of the average recent college grad—and ownership will lead to unexpected and untimely costs and headaches. Know that you're considering a serious long-term cash commitment when you enter a dealership, and prepare yourself for costs you never hear about in those inviting automobile ads: sales tax, service contracts, insurance, tags, and registration. Also, depending on where you live, monthly parking fees and daily bridge-and-tunnel tolls—not to mention filling up the gas tank— can add up to hundreds or thousands of dollars per year. And no matter how much you pay, you'll still get stuck in traffic. Lots and lots of traffic.

So, you first need to decide whether you really need a car at all. If you're moving to a large city, maybe you can get along without one. It's worth considering, especially while you're trying to find your financial footing. You'll be forced to become an expert on public transportation, and that's not necessarily cheap either, but you can't compare the real cost of car ownership with the cost of getting around on trains, subways, and buses. A car can be a great convenience, but is it worth the money?

For me, the answer was yes. And so, after graduation it was time to trade in my trusty—and rusty—Nissan. She had served me well throughout high school, from my abuse on a learner's permit through the licensed hellion stage. She had stuck by me through the overloaded treks to and from college and on frequent road trips to other snowy campuses all over New England. But my little sedan had had her share of accidents, and her age was showing. The crumpled front bumper, the dimple on the passenger's side door from the fire hydrant that attacked me sophomore year, the crack in the rear brake lights that appeared after I backed into my mother's car in our driveway were but a few of the visible chapters in the old gal's history.

There were other scars, too. Her horn was not as powerful as it once had been. Her gray coat didn't gleam as it once had. Her clutch had grown so sensitive that only I knew how to handle it just right.

It was time to let her go. I was a grown-up now and I needed a grown-up car, something dependable, something handsome. But I didn't want a car that was Too Adult. I was still young, and there was no need to get a station wagon or a minivan or some other dowdy, suburban soccer-mom car. I wanted something zippy, sporty, and sleek. And so my car-shopping adventure began.

As you will see, car shopping and ownership can be a confusing collection of choices. Are you truly prepared to splurge for a new car, or will a used one serve your purposes? Should you buy or should you lease? How do you negotiate a good deal? What type of insurance should you purchase, and how much do you need? And how does one maintain a car? For some knowledgeable car talk that can help you decide, read on.

## Shopping for Your Car

*Everything in life is somewhere else, and you can get there in a car.*
—E. B. White

After deciding that my old Nissan wouldn't do, I took comfort in visualizing the ideal replacement. I knew that the car of my dreams was dark green— I've long had an affinity for the color green—and had a stick shift. But, as a relatively levelheaded college grad, I also knew that such shallow parameters did not make for the most informed automobile purchase.

Luckily, you don't have to be a hardcore car enthusiast to be a savvy car buyer today. There are resources out there: car magazines, Web sites, books, customer pamphlets. Both *Consumer Reports* and *Consumers Digest* publish comprehensive annual issues about the most dependable cars, by model and year. If you're buying used, you might want to invest in a copy of the *Kelley Blue*

*Book*, which is considered the industry standard for determining the actual price for used vehicles based on the year and mileage. The *Blue Book* is available in most bookstores, or online at www.kbb.com.

The people you know are another good information source. If your best friend's cousin drives an Acura and you're in the market for one, find out what he likes and what he doesn't like about it. Spread the word that you're in the market for a car among your own circle of driving acquaintances because advice will flow in and friends looking to sell may come to you first.

Unfortunately, car shopping is about more than engine power and decor. You also have to figure out how much you can spend. It's only natural to yearn for a bigger, nicer car than you can afford, but inflated auto aspirations can lead to financial downfall. To figure out which car fits your budget, take your monthly income after taxes and deduct your fixed expenses such as rent and utilities. Then subtract your variable items like food, clothing, and entertainment. The amount left over should help determine what you can afford.

## The Right Model

Cars had always been somewhat of a mystery to me. I didn't know anything about fuel injection, and the function of a fan belt eluded me. So, before I shopped, I researched. I visited some dealers and spent hours poring through car magazines. I boned up on particular brands and models. I learned about engines and rack-and-pinion steering. I even pondered different safety features.

With my research complete, I went off in search of my dreamy dark green car. By this point I had narrowed it down a bit: My heart was set on a Volkswagen. It wasn't a frivolous decision. I decided that VWs were flashy enough to be youthful and fun, yet had high ratings in safety categories—much to my parents' relief. The real shopping had just begun, and I was already hooked.

Think about what you want in a car and what you're willing to spend to get it. Since this is probably the biggest purchase you have ever made, be patient in your search for the right car at the right price. And trust your instincts.

> *Before looking at cars, I thought about what I was going to be using it for: It needed to be able to fit a bike, a surfboard, and a big dog. Since I don't commute to work by car, gas mileage and highway performance were less of a priority. I decided on a Jeep.*

Are you no-frills? Or do you desire a sunroof and a CD player? Think about where you live. Do you need to parallel park your car often? If so, think compact car. Or will you be driving through snow a lot? Four-wheel drive, maybe? Will you be spending a lot of time in your car for work? Look for comfort and good gas mileage. Any plans to traverse Kansas? Then you may want cruise control, Dorothy.

> *I knew I wanted an SUV, and after looking at different makes and models, I thought the Ford Explorer was the best deal in my price range, mainly because it was bigger than the other cars I looked at. I bought a new car and I think it is both fun and practical. Practical in the sense that I can take a lot of stuff with me, but not practical in that it does not get the best mileage, and it is a pain to park in the city.*

Try *not* to narrow your choice down to one model. You
lose bargaining leverage. "Never fall in love with a car," says
Jack Gillis of the Consumer Federation of America and author
of *The Used Car Book.* "Once you do, you lose the psychological ability to walk away from a bad deal. Remember that the
dealer needs you more than you need him." Instead, once you've
decided on the type of car you want, say a basic compact,
explore the comparable models of competing manufacturers,
for example, the Ford Escort, the Toyota Tercel, and the Volkswagen Golf.

## The New-or-Used Conundrum

My next dilemma was: Do I get a pristine, new, sparkling dark
green VW or a more experienced—read *used*—dark green VW?
Let's face it, a new car is easy to love. You're the first person to
drive it, the interior smells deliciously factory fresh, and the engine roars magnificently.

But other than sensual pleasures, there are very few benefits
to buying new cars. New cars are more expensive to buy, to
insure, and to register. A new car depreciates almost the minute
you drive it off the lot and loses at least 20 percent of its value
after the first year you own it. Four years into ownership, your
new vehicle will have dropped at least half its value. So I made a
practical move: I went with a slightly used model and loaded up
on new-car-scented spray.

If your parents or grandparents buy you a brand-new car of
*any* make or model for graduation, then thank your lucky stars
(and them). But if you're financially on your own, think twice,
then think again about buying new.

> *I bought a brand-new car at my parents' encour-*
> *agement—my dad and I split it. When I sold it three*
> *years later, I had to split what I got from the buyer with*
> *my dad and the car had depreciated 50 percent. My*
> *eyes were most definitely opened. New cars are a waste*
> *of money.*

It is wise to consider buying a reliable almost-new car—in some circles known as *pre-owned*. Owning virtually any old car that's new to you is bound to be exciting, especially after you get it out of the shadows of the shiny, straight-from-the-factory models at the dealership.

> *I was given a used Saab for graduation that had*
> *over 80,000 miles on it. I packed my bags a couple*
> *days after graduation and rolled down the windows*
> *and sunroof of my new car, proud and free. I cruised*
> *around town in the comfort of leather seats, air condi-*
> *tioning, and cruise control. I truly felt like I had made*
> *a big step forward in my life. So what that I had a col-*
> *lege diploma? I had a vehicle in my name!*

The market has been improving for used cars, and there are plenty of reputable dealers who specialize in used cars or "program" cars. Program cars are often an especially attractive option. Typically, they're a year or two old and have been owned by a rental car company or a corporation. They often have low mileage, are still on warranty, and have been well maintained. The standard for used-car mileage is about 12,000 per year. Higher mileage severely deducts from the market value of the car. It's best to avoid very high-mileage cars altogether. The math is simple: the more miles on a vehicle, the shorter its remaining life.

Unless you are buying a certified used car from a certified used-car dealership, you should take a car to a trusted mechanic for an inspection before you buy. For about $90 the mechanic will run a computer diagnostic on the car and you'll get a detailed printout of the vehicle's condition. You can also request an itemized repair estimate and use it in your negotiations. You'll be sorry if you fail to heed this advice.

> *I searched the newspaper for anyone selling an affordable Subaru station wagon. All I wanted was a cheap car that would fit my stuff. I did no research, and I didn't take it to a shop to have it inspected, which was very, very unwise. I paid $600 for it. I thought it was a good deal until I had to buy a new oil pump and brakes three months into ownership. Six months later, the mechanic told me I was driving a death wish. I ended up selling the thing for parts, but all of the problems could have been avoided if I had only taken it to a mechanic before I bought the car in the first place.*

If you can, talk to the previous owner to discern how the car was treated. Ask the owner why he's selling the car. Sometimes there are just too many things starting to go wrong, so he'd rather sell it to you. If you're buying from a private owner, it's a good idea to run a vehicle history check to find out whether the car has ever been in a wreck. You do this by calling your state's department of transportation and checking out the Vehicle Identification Number, or VIN. The VIN, located on a metal plate at the lower corner of the windshield on the driver's side, is composed of seventeen letters and numbers and acts as a fingerprint for the car. Many states keep records of VINs and are willing to perform a free title search.

*I tried going the private owner route, but I realized after a few meetings and several phone calls it was just too hard. I initially fell in love with a Nissan that appeared to be in perfect condition. But I opened up the trunk to discover that the back bumper was held together by duct tape. When I did a check on the VIN, all that came up was one word: salvaged.*

Sean Roberts, owner of a large auto repair business, says it's essential to do your own visual inspection as well. "On the outside, examine the paint job. See if the panels are straight. Search for any corrosion. Find out whether the lights work." Then, he says, "Start up the motor and let it run for a while. Look for oil leaks under the car and pull the dipstick to check the color of oil—it should not be black or milky; ideally it will be clear. Also, smell to determine whether the oil is burnt. If the brake pedals are worn down and the tire tread is shabby, that's a bad sign."

When you buy a used car from a dealer, you might consider buying an extended warranty to cover repairs and minimize your headaches. Most used-vehicle warranties begin 30 days or 1,000 miles from the dates on the contract, so be careful about timing your first claim. Moreover, never sign an "As Is" waiver at a car dealer. You want at least a 30- to 90-day warranty.

## The Test Drive

The test drive is crucial. Budget plenty of time for test drives and try to take the car on as long a drive as possible to know if it really suits you. Take a few tests. Your goal is to find the best possible car for you.

"The things you end up hating about your car—the blind spot when you back out of the driveway, or that it doesn't have the acceleration you'd like, or that it's uncomfortable for your friends in the back seat—could have been avoided if you had taken a good long test drive of at least one hour," says car expert Jack Gillis.

If you can, head out onto the highway and tour around neighborhood streets. Throw it into reverse. Listen closely when turning and braking. On a quiet street with no traffic nearby, step neatly on the brakes. The car should stop without pulling. On a level road, take your hands off the steering wheel for a few seconds—the car should track straight. Pulling could mean either that the body has been twisted as the result of a crash or the car has an alignment problem.

Try out all the controls and displays and make sure all the lights are working. Also, be sure to get in the back seat to determine if there's enough room for your friends and your dog and your camping equipment. Whether you are buying a used car from a private owner or dealer, take them along for the test drive. That way you can quiz them in case you hear any strange noises.

## To Buy or to Lease

If you go to a dealership, you'll have to decide whether to buy or lease your car. Leasing is becoming more and more popular because of the combination of little money down and low monthly payments. Up-front costs are typically a first month's payment, a refundable security deposit, taxes, registration, and tags. Monthly payments are based on the difference between the car's initial price and its expected residual value at the end of the lease term. Leasing allows you to get a nicer or newer car than you would be able to afford if you were, in fact, paying for it.

There are two types of leases. With a closed-end lease, the leasing company is obligated to take back the vehicle at lease end. The lessee may then choose to buy the car for its value at the end of the lease, plus any other charges or fees stipulated in the lease, but there's no requirement to do so.

With an open-end lease, you are responsible for the residual value of the vehicle. At lease end, you are obliged to pay that amount to the leasing company with any other charges or fees stipulated in the lease. You have to buy the car.

*I was in a position of uncertainty after graduating, and I had no idea where I would be or what I would be doing in two or three years. Maybe I'd be in school and wouldn't want or need a car. Maybe I'd score a great job with a huge salary and want a much nicer car. So, I thought tying myself to a three-year lease on a Subaru made the most sense.*

But there are some important considerations before you decide to lease a car. Leasing is a valid option for people who drive no more than 12,000 to 15,000 miles per year. The typical lease has an annual mileage limit, and you have to pay per mile for every mile exceeding that limit. The cost of the additional miles can add up quickly.

*I had no money to put down, I didn't have a trade-in, and I could only afford low monthly payments. Leasing my Isuzu Rodeo appeared to be the best option. In the end, I don't think that I got that great a deal. It was all to make sure that I lowered the monthly price to fit my budget. I didn't take into consideration that I had to actually stick to the mileage limit. I was well over, driving 50,000 miles in three years rather than the "allowed" 36,000 miles under the lease agreement. That would have been a significant cost had I given the car back. To mitigate this cost I ended up buying the car.*

You should take very good care of a car you lease. Damage from accidents, dirt, or abuse might allow the dealer to stick you with an "excessive wear and tear" charge, and this could add up to thousands of extra dollars.

Remember, too, that leasing, like everything else about acquiring a car, is negotiable. Compare leasing options and look carefully at the specific terms. Closing fees can be extravagant, and early termination of the lease is costly. If you think you'll drive 20,000 miles a year instead of 15,000, see if you can negotiate a higher mileage limit for a slightly higher monthly payment.

*I knew that I wanted a car that was reliable, fuel efficient, and somewhat roomy so I could fit people, bags, equipment, skis, camping stuff, and, since I am a drummer, my drum set. When I visited the car dealers, I discussed financing options and did some*

*preliminary pricing so that I knew what I was get-*
*ting into. I knew approximately how much money*
*I had to spend. I knew that the kind of cars I wanted*
*were between $18K and $25K new—way out of*
*my price range to buy. I decided to lease because*
*it allowed me to get a brand-new car that would*
*have the greatest functionality and reliability. Also,*
*leasing would give me the best possible warranty*
*protection.*

In the short term, buying a car is a bit more expensive, but
there are many advantages over leasing if you can afford the difference. When your loan is paid off, you own the car and that is
a nice asset, albeit a depreciating one, for someone in their midtwenties.

*I needed a car, and I needed it fast. I took the ad-*
*vice of family and friends and I went with stability and*
*affordability. Leo, my little red Geo, was a good car*
*and lasted past the last payment for the loan, which*
*was entirely in my name, so I was happy. I bought*
*rather than leased so that I would have a solid trade-in*
*the next time around.*

## The Salesman Shuffle

We've all heard the stale clichés about used-car dealers. You
know: cheap plaid suits, inane gimmicks, supermarket cologne,
cunning winks, and blow-dried coiffures. While most of these

chestnuts are outdated—or are they?—there is one enduring truism: Car salesmen, new or used, will say almost anything to make a sale.

Dickering with a car salesman is, when done correctly, a remarkably exact science—or so said the sage men in my family. It's a rhythmic and predictable chain of actions and reactions, they counseled. You can expect lots of discussion, several absurd lies, and many exaggerated facial expressions. You'll wander through the lot, eyeing several cars, perhaps taking a test drive or two. All the while, the salesman—and they are usually male—will prattle on about mileage and safety, and might even make lofty promises about giving you a great deal later on. Secretly, you'll have selected one of the cars on the lot. But you mustn't let on that you have found your dream car, for that would spoil everything. Stay cool. Stay calm.

You and the salesman will enter his cubicle just off the showroom. It's time to talk numbers. He'll tell you the astronomical sticker price and then say—out of the goodness of his heart, of course—that he is willing to knock some money off that. He'll shuffle some papers, punch the calculator purposefully, and offer a price that is still by most standards enormous but seems to him quite reasonable. All this is accompanied by a smile meant to suggest he's the best friend you've ever had.

You'll look unimpressed. Roll your eyes, perhaps. You'll offer an amount significantly less than his "rock-bottom" price.

A look of utter shock will come over his face. He'll heave a disappointed sigh and say something like, "I just don't think we'll be able to give you that kind of price. I will have to speak to the manager about this."

You'll balk.

He'll leave the glass office, still shaking his head, incredulous at your impossible offer price. He'll return a while later saying that, just as he suspected, the manager was not willing to go so low. Miraculously, though, the manager was able to shed some more off that "rock-bottom price." You will raise your eyebrow, utter a suspicious, "Mmmm." Sit back.

And so it will go from there until you've gotten the salesman to go as low as he will go.

## Don't Be a Sticker Sucker

I had the keys in my hand and was ready to drive off into the sunset. But not so fast. We had yet to agree on a price.

I stepped into the Volkswagen showroom that was plastered with fluorescent signs: LOW, LOW PRICES, and WE DON'T TAKE NO FOR AN ANSWER. Posters of scantily clad women sprawled over hoods adorned the walls. The glass partitions of the car salesman's office were covered with regional sales awards and pictures of the dealer's summer softball team.

I was on the salesman's turf. He wore an impish grin. But he didn't know that I was ready for him; my research was about to pay off.

The sticker price is never the final price, unless you're gullible enough to let it be. That number represents what dealers would, in the their wildest fantasies, get for a particular car. You are not expected to pay that amount. But you must have a valid reason why you shouldn't be expected to pay that much.

Enter the dealership armed with prices, quotes, and invoice numbers. Volley. Use competition to your advantage and bring

## It's Not Easy Being Female

No question, women are at a disadvantage in the car market. Dealers do not think that women are as savvy as men about buying cars. But there are ways to overcome that. Be no-nonsense. Be businesslike. Do not participate in "typical girl" behavior like fawning over the purple interior or exclaiming "What a perfect place to keep my lipstick!" when you see the hidden compartment on the driver's side. When all else fails, "If you get the hint you're being patronized or you're not given the same respect, walk. That is the most powerful tool you have," says Jack Gillis, author of *The Used Car Book*.

"I bought my Golf from a questionable used car dealer. I knew he was sleazy but I was desperate for a car," says Carrie Copps, a forthright Dartmouth grad. "It turned out it was a total lemon, and by the third time it broke down I called him to complain. He told me that it sounded as though my car just needed a tune-up and that if I would have a drink with him then he would fix it for free."

As much as I hate to admit it, it might be wise to bring your brother, your boyfriend, or your dad on your car search, if only to even out the testosterone level.

along advertisements of similar cars to your liking. You might even try playing dealers off against one another with varying quotes. It's laborious and time consuming, and they will make it as tedious as possible, but it's a good way to save money.

You're matching wits with a seasoned professional who does this every day. Don't feel bad when the dealer acts indignant at your offer and accuses you of low-balling. A dealer will never go lower than he really can afford to, so don't feel guilty about haggling. And don't be intimidated by pressure. A dealer might say that the given price is good for today only. Other times, he might mention that someone else has expressed interest in the exact same car. Don't be afraid to walk away and take your business elsewhere if the price is unsatisfactory. And never pay a cash deposit on a car. If the deal turns sour, it's almost impossible to get your money back.

There are some other tricks: find out if the dealer's lot is filled with a certain model. You might be able to get it for less if he's eager to unload. You should shop at the end of the year or during winter when business is usually slower. Shop at the end of the month, when salespeople are eager to meet sales quotas. Many dealers, mindful that new cars make excellent graduation gifts, have sales in the spring and special deals for recent graduates. Also, consider purchasing a bare-bones model, without a top-of-the-line CD player or stock security system; you can always add those later, and it's often cheaper that way.

## Buyer Beware

When it's time to sign on the dotted line, be sure to read the small print carefully, and be sure that no sneakiness has occurred. You didn't want power windows or power locks or a car alarm that electronically sings "La Cucaracha." Ask for a fully itemized bill detailing all the various charges and speak up if you suspect anything fishy. You might want to shop for a car with someone who has experienced the drill before, like your parents.

Before you zoom off, make sure you have the title in hand, a signed copy of the bill of sale, and the maintenance records. Make sure you have all sets of keys, owner's manuals, repair manuals, and your car's equipment.

If you're trading in an older car, try to get more for the trade than first offered. That's a common and essential negotiating strategy. A warning: You will invariably feel robbed by the money you receive from your trade-in, especially if you have a powerful emotional attachment to the car.

> *My pistachio-pudding-green Monza was very special to me. It had nice round, bald tires, and I bought it from my friend's grandmother. It was such a unique car. Everyone could see me coming from miles away. And all my friends would talk about what a cool ride I had. It lasted a few years, and I couldn't bear to let go so I sold it to my sister for $200—basically to cover the tape deck I installed.*

Typically the dealer will offer you only the wholesale value of the car. You will almost always get more money for it by selling it yourself. Sometimes all that's required is a classified ad in your local paper and a couple of hours of your time.

If you aren't in the haggling mood, there are fixed-price cars like Saturns or low-cost dealerships that do not cut deals since their prices generally can't be beat. For inexperienced car shoppers it can be comforting to deal with salespeople who do not work on commission.

And, an increasing number of people are finding that using the Internet is more comfortable than venturing into a flashy showroom.

> *I started by going to used-car lots to see what was out there, and I also read the classifieds to see what years were available at what price. Once I narrowed it*

*down, I went to the dealership, but was discouraged by the salesperson's 'buy it now or never' attitude. It was my first car, and I didn't want to be pressured into it. During one of my searches, I ended up on an Internet site for used cars. I ultimately ended up buying my Jeep Cherokee from them. They did my financing for me and even registered it for me. It was the ideal way to buy my first car—very low-impact and zero pressure.*

## Financing Your Car

For most of us who don't own homes, a car is the biggest purchase we've ever made. The average American will own a dozen or more cars in a lifetime, making car ownership one of the biggest expenditures in our lives. Yet because cars have more personality and pizzazz than, say, a mutual fund, many of us don't take the money aspects of car ownership as seriously as we should.

The cheapest way to buy a car is to negotiate the best possible price, then pay for it in cash. But most people borrow the money to buy their cars, especially their first car.

Whatever you do, do not discuss financing until after the price of the car is settled, as these negotiations should be entirely separate. Most car dealerships offer their own financing, usually a loan from a bank with which the dealer has a relationship. This may be the most convenient way to get a loan, and salespeople will try to convince you it is. But it's not likely to be the cheapest loan—at least you should assume it's not until you've shopped around. Dealers usually get a finder's fee for arranging the loan and this adds to your cost. And car dealers, knowing

## Total Cost of a $20,000 Loan at Varied Durations and Interest Rates

| Years | 6% | 7% | 8% | 10% |
|-------|------|------|------|------|
| 3 | $21,904 | $22,232 | $22,562 | $23,232 |
| 4 | $22,546 | $22,988 | $23,436 | $24,348 |
| 5 | $23,199 | $23,761 | $24,332 | $25,496 |
| 7 | $24,542 | $25,356 | $26,185 | $27,890 |

that twentysomethings are less likely to notice outrageous interest rates, tend to prey on your inexperience and vulnerability.

Wherever you decide to finance your car, create your own spreadsheet and do your own math to determine how much the monthly payments will be at different interest rates and over different lengths of time. To seek out a bargain, compare the annual percentage rate (APR) and the length of the loan. It may be tempting to grab the lowest monthly payment, but keep in mind that the lowest amount you will pay depends on the price of the car you negotiate, the APR, and the length of the loan.

Be wary of concentrating too much on the monthly payment, because in the meantime your total interest cost will skyrocket. (See the table above.) Dealers with dollar signs in their eyes eagerly promote the seventy-two-month payment plan or the luxurious five-year lease, but it is a scam to make you believe that you are spending less money. Ideally, you should pay off your car as quickly as you can so that you can reap a better trade-in value and save money on your loan or lease. Most spreadsheet programs have a formula that allows you to see both the monthly principal and interest and the total cost of a loan. Familiarize yourself with all the elements of a loan before settling on one.

Because interest rates vary from bank to bank, be sure to shop around for loans. There are plenty of lenders eager and willing to do business with you. Call at least three banks, since some offer their account holders a "good customer" rate if you meet a minimum balance. If you or someone in your family is a member of a credit union, shop there, too. Often credit unions have highly competitive car loan rates. And don't forget the Internet, both as a place to compare bank rates and to find and negotiate a loan.

If you're coping with several big student loans, you might want to ante up the biggest down payment you can afford so you can reduce the overall amount of your debt. If, however, a car loan is your one and only debt, then you might want to skip the down payment altogether and opt for bigger monthly payments.

## Registration

Ah, the Department of Motor Vehicles. Or what some people like to call Hell on Earth. Registering your car, depending on where you live, can be a snap: a simple exchange of papers and money, or even a quick Internet transaction. But don't count on it. My first car registration experience was anything but simple or pleasant. Nightmare was more like it—but a nightmare that experience and a little knowledge might have prevented, or at least shortened.

My goal was to register my vehicle in the District of Columbia. This simple task required me to visit the DMV, with its ugly fluorescent lighting and snaking lines, no less than six times.

In retrospect, I realize I was foolish to think that registering my car should be simple in the nation's capital where, after all, bureaucracy is ingrained in the soul of the city.

On my first visit I was most anxious about whether my Maine driver's license would be transferable to Washington, or whether I would need to take a written or road test. How I dreaded parallel parking. I finally made it to the head of the line. I looked into the eyes of the bored bureaucrat and proceeded with my question. She snapped her gum and looked bothered. "Maine?" she asked. "Is that in the United States?"

And so it went.

Registering your car can be a pain and it can also be expensive, but you pay a bigger price for not registering appropriately.

> *I was given a new car for graduation. But I could not afford the $2,000 price tag of registration so I never got the appropriate license plate stickers. Parking is zoned in the city where I live and when I left the car on the street during the day, I would get a $15 ticket. If I drove to work, it cost me $11 to park. It ended up getting towed because I had allowed $395 in tickets and late fees to accumulate on the car.*

Registration fees vary depending on where you live and the make and age of your car. When you register, there will be a box for you to enter the purchase price. This is used to calculate the sales tax. Be aware that this amount can runs upwards of $1,000 for a new car. Many people are tempted to pencil in a lower price than they actually paid to lessen their tax bill. But states are not ignorant of this trick. Once the clerk enters the title number into her computer, a printout with the *Blue Book* value will appear. So be honest.

Read your registration carefully. It might require you to get an emissions test or stickers from an entirely different building. Or you might need to get a parking permit for a different section of town.

> *My apartment building has a garage attached to it, but the monthly rate was $350, so I decided to park on the street. But in order to be able to park in my neighborhood I needed a residential parking permit, which meant that I had to register my car in Massachusetts, get a Massachusetts license, and all that. At the time, I foolishly thought that this required too much effort on my part, so for six months I parked it outside the neighborhood, having to move it at least once a week for street cleaning. Of course, there was a lot more effort and stress involved in having to move the car and find a new spot—often before 8:00 A.M.—than in just going to register my car, but I was still too lazy to drag myself to the DMV. Finally, after several tickets and much fear of going to move my car only to realize that it had been towed, I decided that it was time.*

Think ahead when you go to register your car—or, better, call ahead and find out exactly what you'll need. In addition to all the paperwork about the car, you may need to prove residence in the place where you're registering. So take proof of insurance, title to the car, sales tax records, VIN, proof of employment or pay stub, and proof of residency: a printed, authorized copy of your lease or a utility bill addressed to you is usually sufficient. Bring along proof of your identity, too: Social Security card, passport, or birth certificate. If you're prepared, you should be able to get registered and duly stickered in one trip. But take a sandwich; it could be a long one.

## Car Insurance

Car insurance covers harm done to you, your car, other people, and other people's property. The total amount of coverage you need depends on the health insurance you have, the condition of your car, the value of assets you must protect in case you're held responsible for an accident, and the rules of your state. Premiums—or periodic payments for your insurance—are based on your age, where you live, the kind of car you drive, your driving record, and how much driving you do.

When you're young, car insurance is pretty expensive. Aside from eighty-year-olds and teenagers, we in our early twenties are the highest-risk drivers on the road. From an insurer's perspective, then, our through-the-roof rates are entirely appropriate. We have more accidents and more insurance claims, and we cost the companies more, so we should pay more.

There are some ways to reduce the cost of car insurance, though. The first is to shop around; premiums can vary widely from company to company. "Ask your relatives, friends, and colleagues where they have their insurance and what kind of service they receive," says Loretta Worters of the Insurance Information Institute. "Also, contact your state insurance department for information about agents and companies in your area. Many state insurance departments have cost-comparison surveys." Call firms to get quotes; insurance agents are listed in the Yellow Pages and online.

> *I shopped around and got quotes from four places. Cost was not the most important thing for me. I cared more about quality. I would rather err on the side of caution and get a lot of insurance protection, especially if I were to cause a lot of damage to another person. My insurance choice was driven by fear.*

Sometimes the best offense is a good defense: avoid cars that are likely to have higher risks for insurance claims. "The cost of insurance added to the monthly car payments can be a real financial burden," says insurance expert Loretta Worters. "In order to save money on your auto insurance, think about purchasing a car that has relatively low repair costs and is not very popular with thieves." You can find this information in any consumer magazine.

## Varieties of Insurance

There are several types of car insurance and some of them are an absolute necessity. Some dealers and lenders may encourage you to purchase credit insurance to pay off your loan if you should die or become disabled, but this is usually not a good idea. Credit insurance is not required by federal law and in many cases you may be duplicating policies.

In most states you need liability coverage, which typically constitutes more than half of your premium. Liability insurance is designed to compensate other people for your mistakes. If you crash into someone's car—or worse, someone—your liability insurance

## 10 Smart Ways to Lower Your Insurance Costs

1. Drive safely. This one is obvious. Don't peel out. Don't do doughnuts in the parking lot. Don't speed. If you have a clean record, point it out when you are pricing policies.

2. Take a defensive driving class. It may not be the most pleasurable way to spend a Saturday morning, but participation in these classes, designed to reform the speed demons of America, can lower your rates by up to ten percent.

3. Don't drive often. Some insurance companies charge smaller premiums if you drive fewer than thirty miles per week.

4. Get old. Auto insurers have lower rates for "adults." For women, the magic age is twenty-five, for men it's thirty. (What was that about girls maturing faster than boys?)

5. Don't be shy about your Dean's List distinctions. Recent college graduates are often eligible for discounts based on their good grades, until they reach twenty-five or get married. Ask your insurance company about this option.

6. Ask for a higher deductible. A deductible is the portion of a repair cost you pay out of pocket before the insurance coverage

will pay for the damages to that person's car and his medical and pain-and-suffering expenses.

But how much liability coverage do young people need? While it varies from state to state, normal coverage is about $20,000 worth of bodily injury coverage per person, $40,000 worth of bodily injury coverage per accident, and $15,000 worth of property damage coverage. If you don't own a home and have some money saved, get at least $100,000 bodily injury kicks in. The more coverage you have, the higher your premiums will be. The higher your deductible, the lower your premium.

7. If you buy a new car, get airbags, antitheft systems, antilock brakes, and your VIN etched in the windshield. All these safety precautions can reduce your premium significantly.

8. Try to bundle policies if you happen to own other types of insurance. If you still live at home, you may be able to get a discount if your car is insured under your parents' policy. Or if you're buying renter's insurance, ask about discounts on auto policies.

9. Get a heavy car or one that's cheap to repair. Insurance companies aren't stupid: If you drive an expensive car, your insurance will be expensive, too. Certain types of cars, however, are harder to damage and are stolen less often. If you can, buy a low-risk model car that has high ratings by consumer groups or a car that is quick to fix.

10. Keep your car parked in a garage if at all possible. This way the car is less likely to get broken into or be damaged by bad weather.

coverage per person, $300,000 per accident, and $100,000 coverage for property.

You have to protect your assets, says Loretta Worters, and special situations may call for more. If you happen to own a home, or have some cash stashed, you should opt for more insurance coverage. "It's best to have as much coverage as you can comfortably afford," she says. "In today's litigious society, bodily injury claims can be hundreds of thousands of dollars."

Medical payments coverage pays for your and any passengers' medical and hospital bills up to a certain dollar amount when you're injured in a car accident. Accidents in which no one can be proven guilty or negligent won't be covered by liability insurance, and liability will not cover your own injuries in accidents you've caused. If you already have decent health insurance, you probably won't need to have your own medical bills covered by your auto policy. But your passengers will still need some coverage.

Collision and comprehensive coverage are optional in every state. If you are leasing or have taken out a loan to pay for your car, however, lenders or dealers will require you to have this to protect their investment. Collision insurance pays for repairing the damage done to your car in a traffic accident, while comprehensive insurance covers damage caused by fire, flood, theft, tornado, and just about anything else.

After your car is five years old and the loan is paid off, you might want to drop collision and comprehensive insurance altogether if it's not required by your state. To determine whether it makes sense for you to continue this coverage, consider the value of the car minus the deductible. Compare that to your annual premium.

One good strategy for keeping your insurance premiums down is to protect your car from the kinds of situations that might lead to an accident or other damage. Try to avoid driving on snow and ice, and even on a picture-perfect day drive safely. Beware when parking on the street and in large parking lots. If you have any misgivings about parking in a certain spot, pass it up for one that seems farther out of harm's way. And don't leave things in your car that will be attractive to potential thieves, like cell phones, briefcases, suitcases, sports equipment, and portable CD players. Instead keep valuables in your trunk or stashed under the seats. In big cities it's a good idea to leave an empty glove compartment open to show there's nothing there worth stealing.

> *My car got broken into once when I was parked outside my apartment. Insurance covered the price of replacing the window, and when we called the police, they suggested leaving it unlocked with no valuables inside so the next time someone wanted to poke around they wouldn't have to break the window. I did that for several months, careful not to leave anything in the car, and no more windows were broken. Several times, however, I noticed an odd stench in the car—I was sure some homeless person was sleeping in it on cold and rainy days. It was nothing that a little air freshener couldn't fix.*

Be aware that insurance covers only damage to or theft of the car, not the things inside. A car stereo *would* be covered under insurance, because it's considered part of the car, but CDs would not be covered. In other words, personal items are generally not insurable except under renter's or homeowner's insurance.

> *I was visiting a friend in New York City and someone broke into the trunk of my car and stole a number of things, one of which was my new pair of rollerblades. The trunk was covered by my insurance. However, my car insurance didn't cover the contents of the trunk. I was out of luck. I bought renter's insurance shortly after that.*

And sometimes, even when you have insurance, it might make sense not to file a claim. Cars get dented. They're only made

## Real World Common Sense: The Perils of Lending Your Car to Friends

Lend out your car at your own risk. Literally. If you permit someone to drive your car and the borrower has an accident, most insurance policies will pay for the damage but there will still be long-term costs for you. Your premiums will rise as if you had been the one behind the wheel. A quick jaunt to the store that results in a fender bender could mean years of higher payments.

There are other risks, too. What starts out as an act of generosity can lead to a souring of a friendship. "My roommate's car died, so she had no way to get around unless she used mine," says Sarah Sulzberg, a University of Vermont graduate who drives a Honda Accord.

"She was only going short distances—out to the store, across town to visit her boyfriend—but she was going all the time. She never once filled my tank or chipped in for gas. But the worst was when she got a $60 ticket for leaving the car in a no-parking zone overnight. She refused to pay for it."

If you must borrow a friend's car or you want to loan your own, it's best to be explicit about the arrangement. How long? For what purposes? Who pays for what? How will an accident be handled? This may seem overly fussy compared to normal interactions among friends. But cars are large and expensive and dangerous. Loaning or borrowing one is not like sharing sweaters or CDs.

of metal, after all. In your early twenties when money is tight, it might make sense to fix things that are necessary, but let the little dimple in your rear bumper or a cracked piece of trim go untouched. Every claim you file becomes part of your future rate structure. Use your insurance coverage wisely.

## Maintaining Your Car

Perhaps the rudest awakening to solo car ownership comes on the day you realize that you alone have to take care of it. This large piece of machinery worth thousands of dollars is yours to park, clean, fix, and maintain.

> *When I was in school, my car broke down six times in eight months and my mom—God bless her—always paid for it because I was just a poor college student. Now, though, I have to pay for insurance and maintenance because I am a mature, employed, responsible adult. Of course that doesn't mean my mom has given up constantly nagging me with reminders of when to change the oil and when to get a tune-up.*

While every car is different, there are some basic guidelines for keeping your car running well. Have your emission control system inspected; keeping it in top shape can improve a vehicle's fuel efficiency by six to seven percent. If there is no emission inspection program where you live, you should have a mechanic do a visual check of your vehicle's emission control devices to make sure they are in place and properly connected.

Use a high-quality gas cap. Check belts and hoses. Check the air conditioning system for leaks. Change fuel filters and air filters regularly. Your car's air filter keeps impurities in the air from damaging internal engine components. Not only will replacing a dirty air filter improve your fuel economy, it will protect your engine.

> *I drive a gold 1989 Volvo 240 sedan named Frenchie. She's got 135,000 miles on her, and I plan to keep Frenchie for a long, long time. The one key thing that I do religiously every 3,000 miles—no more—is to change the oil. I bring it in with my own oil filter that I order off the Internet. It's the best investment you can make. I also keep her washed, wax her once a year to keep the finish protected, and have her underbody oiled at the beginning of the winter to ward off salt and sand. If something goes wrong with the car, I get it fixed right away. I don't wait until there are a million things going wrong, because then everything starts to snowball, and it gets too expensive to do all at once.*

Changing the oil regularly will increase the life of your car's engine. Change your oil as recommended by the vehicle manufacturer—usually every three months. Check oil, transmission fluid, and radiator coolant regularly. One of the easiest things you can do to improve the fuel economy of your car is be sure the tires are properly inflated. Under-inflated tires not only increase your fuel consumption, but also can affect your car's handling.

The biggest shock to many of us owning a car for the first time is just how expensive even small problems can be.

# Get Your Motor Runnin':
# Helpful Web Sites

**www.cars.com**
National Public Radio's popular show, *Car Talk*, has a Web site where you find mechanics in your area who have been recommended by NPR listeners.

**www.consumerreports.org**
Auto advice, information, and ratings.

**www.womanmotorist.com**
Cars A to Z: shopping to safety to Frequently Asked Questions.

**www.autobytel.com**
Research, purchase, maintain, or sell your car.

*I was prepared for most of the costs of having a car—rotating the tires, new brakes, replacing the muffler. But the $120 tune-up always gets me. You can't even tell the difference afterward, and you don't even really know what your money went to.*

Tune-ups, even in this computerized age, are still important. About every 30,000 miles, you should take your car to a garage and have the service technicians check its engine functions by hooking it up to a diagnostic analyzer.

## The Mechanics of Mechanics

It's not easy finding one, but a trustworthy grease monkey who will be straight with you is worth his weight in gold. Talk to your friends and coworkers in your city about where they've had their cars fixed, particularly if they own the same brand or model you have, and whether they were pleased with the results. Look at the mechanic's history and ratings, too. Chaiyant Sanchanta, who owns an auto-repair shop in northern Virginia, advises car owners to look for a shop that has a AAA rating, "because they have a pretty tough standard. You should also call the county's Better Business Bureau to see if that shop has had any complaints registered."

*A few months after I got my car, it suddenly started shaking when the car was idle. I took it to a repair shop that I found through the Yellow Pages. I tried to act confident and very knowledgeable, but I think they may have seen through me. Anyway, it turned out that they found a lot of things wrong with the car—even though it was only a few years old—and, foolishly, I agreed to all of the repairs. The total bill was quite high and pretty much wiped out the meager amount I had been able to save from working only a few months. Needless to say, I changed repair shops.*

Mechanics are famous for taking their customers for a ride, so to speak. Sean Roberts, my trusted auto mechanic, says young people often divulge too quickly their ignorance about cars. To protect yourself, "Never say: 'Would you please look at my car, I know nothing about them.' Instead, say something like, 'My father usually works on my car, but he is not around today. Would you mind having a look at it, then my parents can come down here and talk to you about it?' That way, the mechanic knows there is some adult supervision and they are less likely to take advantage," he advises.

## Good Reads

*Simple Car Care and Repair,* edited by Mark Thomson (Reader's Digest Association, 1997).

*Car Smarts: An Easy-to-Use Guide to Understanding Your Car and Communicating with Your Mechanic,* by Mary Jackson (Avalon Travel Publishing, 1998).

*The Lady Mechanic's Total Car Care for the Clueless: An Easy-to-Use Guide for the Mechanically Challenged,* by Ren Volpe (St. Martin's Press, 1998).

Communication is also important. Spend time with your mechanic and explain exactly what the problem is. "If your car is making a certain noise, then try to mimic the noise. Take your mechanic on a drive with you so that he can hear what is going on too," says Sanchanta.

It can't hurt to invest in a book that teaches you the basics of car repair so that you and the mechanic will at least speak the same language and you can take some comfort in knowing what to do if something does go wrong.

The awful truth is that no matter how honest a mechanic you find, getting your car fixed is an expensive endeavor. All those rubber hoses and pieces of metal are costly. If you receive an estimate on car repairs that sounds ludicrous, however, you're not helpless. "If the price exceeds $500, then get a second opinion," says Sanchanta.

Roberts adds, "Never say, 'Oh, that's all?' Because the next time you bring it in, the bill will go way up."

# Accidents Happen

Auto accidents, no matter how insignificant, can be traumatic. As a driver, you're used to being in control. You direct where the car goes and how fast it goes. An accident, whether it was your fault, the fault of another driver, the fault of weather, or the fault of an animal, defies that control and will shake you up.

Although accidents are distressing and scary, it is important to have enough composure to deal with the minor ones as best you can. Get the names, addresses, and phone numbers of all drivers involved in the accident. Also, get each driver's insurance policy number and the company's name, telephone number, and policy number. If there were witnesses, be sure to get their names, addresses, and phone numbers.

Jason Schmickle, a personal injury lawyer in Minnesota, advises people to always call the police. "No matter how small you think the accident is, you are entitled to property damages. Otherwise, the whole thing is botched and it turns into a he said/she said ordeal because there is no record." Cooperate fully with the police in preparing the accident report; after all, it's imperative to have all the information for your own insurance records.

Be honest about what happened—but, says Schmickle, "It's probably a good idea not to make any admissions. See if the other driver is hurt, but do not discuss the details of the accident. Wait for the police."

If it was a substantial accident—more than a fender bender, more than the cost of your deductible—report it immediately to your insurance company, whether or not it was your fault. "When you call in a claim," says a spokesperson for MetLife Auto and Home, "be sure you have all the pertinent information, like your license plate number, name and address of the other driver, the exact location of the accident—including street names—and weather conditions. Deal with your own insurance company. If queried by the other driver's agent, refer them to your company's representative. Everything you say can be used against you."

*After my accident, the other driver came rushing up to me saying she was so sorry and making sure that I was okay. When I called her insurance company the following morning and told the agent that the accident had been her fault, the agent said, 'That's funny, she said it was your fault.'*

If the accident is not your fault, you have the right to file a claim against the driver who caused the accident. This claim could entitle you to payment of your medical bills and the damage done to your car. In most cases, your rates will not increase. "Almost any personal injury lawyer will give you a free consultation. If you're injured or just confused with all the forms you have to fill out and you have no idea what you're signing, call a lawyer. They will help you figure out what your rights are and sort through the preliminary questions. Avoid the lawyers who are always on TV or whose billboards are the biggest," says attorney Schmickle.

See a physician if you are having any pain. Cuts and scrapes will heal with time, but sometimes internal bruising and whiplash will not subside without some treatment. "Many times, young people will feel sore or notice swelling and decide that they are going to tough this one out. But you need to go to a doctor if you are in pain," says Schmickle.

## What to Do after an Accident: A Checklist

Copy this list and put it in the glove compartment of your car—
after you have added any phone numbers you might need in the
aftermath of an accident.

1. If possible, get your car off the road and out of harm's way.

2. Review your own physical condition. Get out of the car and
walk around. Seek medical help if you think you have any injuries
that may need to be examined.

3. Ask any other drivers involved in the accident if they need medical or other emergency assistance.

4. Call the police to report the accident.

5. Exchange names, phone numbers, driver's license numbers, license plate numbers, and insurance information with other drivers
involved in the accident. Do not discuss who is at fault. Anything
you say in such conversations may haunt you later.

6. Observe the accident scene closely and take notes on the condition of the cars involved and their angles relative to each other.

After a crash, you may have some hard choices to make about
the future of your car. Even if an auto body repair shop says it can
return it to its previous condition, that may not be the wisest idea.
Automobiles are complex systems, and a shiny appearance may
belie lots of problems that can't be seen but affect operation.

*After my accident, my heart wept at the sight of
my car, scrunched and bleeding radiator fluid all over
the street. It took all summer and $5,000 to repair the
car; the car looked shiny and new again. There were, of*

Make notes on weather conditions. Call a friend who might be able to bring a camera to the accident scene. Try to get pictures before the cars are moved from the accident scene.

7. Ask the police officer who arrives to visually observe and note the condition of other people involved in the accident. If you suspect other drivers of being under the influence of alcohol, call this to the attention of the officer and ask that a sobriety test be administered.

8. Talk with the police about the removal of your car from the accident scene. If you are close to home, call your own mechanic or auto body specialist for advice on whether you should drive your car or to get it towed if necessary.

9. As soon as possible after the accident, report it to your insurance company. Do this even if you do not think you are at fault or will need to file a claim.

SOURCE: Edmunds (www.edmunds.com)

*course, some residual problems: the air conditioning has never worked since, the alignment is slightly off, the oil always leaks.*

Yes, many of us grow very attached to our vehicles, especially our first set of wheels. But after a frame-jarring crash, or when a rash of things starts going wrong one after another and the car has a substantial number of miles or years behind it, it's best to be realistic about cutting your losses. After all, you don't *really* plan on driving that clunker forever, do you?

# chapter four

# climbing
# THE LADDER

I WAS EAGER AND BRIGHT-EYED when I arrived at my first day of work. I had great expectations. My game plan: I would dazzle my superiors with my quickness and aptitude. I would be conscientious, organized, amenable to suggestion and instruction. My superiors would love me and I would love them. I would be hardworking but not an office drone, always light and breezy. "Ah, she is invaluable," they would remark. "Whatever did we do without her?"

My long-term plan was to be an exemplary worker *and* coworker, impressing not only management but my colleagues as well. I would indulge in idle watercooler chitchat so my coworkers would know that I cared about them beyond the workplace but not so much that I wasted precious company time. I would befriend the office outcast and be thought kind and generous.

I dreamed I would have a brilliant start to my career. I would be learning all the time, continually challenged with greater responsibility as I received promotion after promotion. I would be in my element. I would be deemed a star. I would be a Person Who Loves Her Job.

It didn't exactly turn out that way. My first day was just under way, my enthusiasm still undimmed, when I was introduced to what were described to me as the four F's: faxing, filing, photocopying, and fixing coffee. My glorious plan began to evaporate, and I'd barely started.

In all fairness, I had been warned. First jobs are generally pretty terrible, or so said the parental crowd who swarmed around me at graduation. They spewed wisdom so conventional I paid it no heed: You're the low man on the totem pole. You have to pay your dues. You'll have your fair share of grunt work. They chuckled knowingly. Now I was standing in my fluorescent-lit office—correction, I was *kneeling* in search of coffee filters—and I wanted to cry.

Long before that first day was over, I found myself counting the hours until six o'clock. I was introduced to my officemates, but no one really spoke to me the rest of the day. I had only foggy notions of what I was expected to do and knew even less how to do it. And my new boss, who had seemed so nice and encouraging when he interviewed me, looked my way only once, and that was to scowl when I took too long to photocopy some papers for him. When I got home that night I fell into a heap on my sofa, exhausted and dismayed.

A first job is sometimes torturous, sometimes wonderful, but always unforgettable. Whether you grow or grovel, whether it accelerates your career plans or obliterates them, whether it's awesome or awful, your first job will be a pivotal point in your life. You'll be underutilized and overextended, praised and blamed, delighted and demeaned. But you'll learn new lessons almost every day, and some of them will profoundly shape how you eventually fit into the working world.

For most people, even those who stumble into their first job, beginning life at the office plops you into a nest of uncertainties. What kind of relationship should I expect to have with my boss? What happens if I don't get along with my coworkers? What if I make a mistake—a really big mistake? How do I get ahead? And, if the time comes to leave, how do I exit gracefully? So many questions, so many anxieties.

## Your First Job

This is it, the day you've been anticipating—with joy or dread—after sixteen years of education. All that homework. All those school lunches. The all-nighters. The unpaid internships. All that preparation and persistence with your job search. Now the big day arrives when you finally take your place in the work world.

> *Having grown up most of my life in a small town in West Virginia, I came to the big city not sure of what to expect. It was a very prestigious job and I didn't want to disappoint. I remember when I spoke with people at the office, they seemed very friendly, but the phrase that they wanted me to 'start yesterday' put some unnecessary stress on me. My first day I ended up getting to the office about half an hour before it opened, so I went to the nearest coffeehouse, got a mocha and a* Wall Street Journal, *and read*

*up on my stocks. I still remember it clearly. That is when it hit me that I was—dare I say it?—an adult. It scared me.*

Your first days and weeks on the job are likely to be by turns exciting and scary, exhilarating and overwhelming. That's natural. Even just going to work every day, day after day, will probably come as somewhat of a shock to your system, which may still be tuned to a casual collegiate schedule.

*The wonderful thing about being a student is that you really do have so much time for yourself and you're able to set your own schedule. Not the case with work. I remember riding the bus home my first week of working 8 to 6 and thinking, 'Wow, is this my life now?' I still miss the freedom to set my own schedule that only school allows.*

But what may strike you most powerfully is the complete lack of stature you're afforded as a new hire. Or, to paraphrase Rodney Dangerfield, you won't get no respect. "The role of the employee is to help make the employer productive," says Steven Rothberg, president of College Recruiter, a job-hunting Web site. "New college graduates don't always understand that they are there to improve the bottom line of their company."

## Awkward Adjustments

In most corporate offices, real nurturing is in short supply. Nobody much cares if you're happy or satisfied. You have tasks and you have deadlines. You're there to contribute to a cause or to the earnings report by doing good work.

Being new to the workforce, you are likely to feel particularly vulnerable, but chances are that sooner or later you'll get comfortable in your current position. Until then, go with the flow.

> *My first week was difficult. I didn't have a computer to work on. I didn't even have a cubicle to sit in, and this being my first job, I had no direction. It took me a while, but I settled in. But at first I was all alone in this weird place. I'd sit there in my suit and tie, all choked up, and twiddle my thumbs. It really didn't feel right.*

One of the things you'll come to realize rather quickly is that there's no grade inflation in real life. What earned us a perky B+ in college gets tossed back to us disapprovingly by our new boss, needing "a lot more work." Don't expect to be showered with the feel-good praise you received from professors and TA's and the campus counseling center.

> *In high school, I was a superstar—great grades, captain of two sports, class president. Then I got to college and I had to work a bit harder, but no sweat. When I got to the working world, I had my comeuppance. 'Everyone here is like me—only better,' I thought. 'Everyone in this office is a star.' It was a lot more competitive.*

"Some people are hired as future leadership in the company; for better or for worse, they're treated differently. Others are just bodies, another $35,000-a-year worker that you could replace off the street. But it's important to remember that a company needs both to grow," says Ed Vincent, a college recruiter for a financial services firm in New York City. "You need people who are cogs in the organization, just as you need people who are passionate about the work. People are replaceable. In college, you're coddled. It's a very nurturing environment. But the harsh reality is that a company is focused on output. You get points for results, not for effort."

## Playing by Somebody Else's Rules

"Every organization has a personality and style," says Teri Fisher of Insight Strategies Inc., author of *Demystifying the Unspoken Rules of Career Success*. "You have to set yourself up to learn about the infrastructure and the culture of your organization."

Adapting to that culture requires the skills of a good detective. Be on the lookout for hints about what is and is not acceptable in the workplace. How do other people dress? (Is the leopard-print miniskirt too much?) Communicate? (They kinda sorta talk, like, grown-ups, like, you know?) Get along? (Are office disagreements settled over a business lunch or a heated game of foosball?) Keep in touch with one another? (E-mailing is generally okay, but avoid cutesy expressions like :-) please.) Clues and cues from more experienced employees can be helpful, so keep your eyes and ears open, and navigate your way carefully.

Despite the competitive nature of business, or because of it, some organizations try to make the office a happy place to work.

Some are even creative about it. Maybe the company mandate is: "Go ahead, wear those khakis." Or perhaps you're indulged in bagels and OJ on Friday mornings, or treated to happy hour on Thursday afternoons. Maybe inviting e-mails flood your inbox, announcing company-wide birthday celebrations, promotion parties, softball games, and the like.

Whatever the character of the workplace, your first job will be different—probably radically different—from college, and that's not necessarily a bad thing.

> *Although I missed the academic lifestyle, the structure and set hours of a job were good for taking care of my procrastination. In school it was too easy to skip classes or assignments because there were no immediate ramifications. Sure, my grades suffered and my parents suffered, but you couldn't get fired from class. Once I was in the office I had to do my work in order to keep my job, and if I was going to do the work then there was no way I wasn't going to do as good a job as possible. I didn't love the work or the company, but I did like the challenge of proving myself in the working world. Even if I sometimes think about work outside of the office, I like the separation between 'work' time and 'play' time. I also like that things I now learn, the books I read or any courses that I take, are done solely because they interest me and not for a grade.*

Indeed, many recent graduates thrive in the workplace and prefer it to an academic setting. They love the competitive pace or the meaningful work they're doing. They discover that working

### Real World Realities:
### Reporting for Duty

In case you're wondering who else is joining the professional work force this year . . .

*There are more of us than ever.* Nearly 1.2 million bachelor's degrees were conferred by the nation's colleges and universities last year, and that number continues to grow.

*Women lead the way.* According to the National Center for Education Statistics (NCES), women earned 131,789 more degrees than men; women earned about 56 percent of bachelor's degrees, compared to 44 percent for men.

*Show us the money.* According to a 2000 study by NACE, students from a wide variety of disciplines are getting top dollar. Fields like computer science and information science have recently been at the top of the pay scale. Teaching and journalism compete for the bottom.

*We are vid-kids in demand.* Employers want the total package, according to the College Employment Research Institute. Emerging skills and aptitudes include an understanding of e-commerce, programming skills, computer aptitude, and ability to adapt to constant change.

*Loyalty, at least initially, is not in the game plan.* Nearly two-thirds of new college graduates say they plan to stay with their first employer for three years or fewer. And more than 10 percent of those expect to leave their first job in less than a year.

9 to 6 with no homework is preferable to endless afternoons in the library or pulling an all-nighter to churn out a term paper. Or they find that they're able to excel at their jobs more easily than they ever did at school.

*I am better at the working world, and I like the day-to-day performance aspect. The show begins at 8:00 A.M., I am on, and then it ends at 4:00 P.M. and I go home. In college I always felt academic stuff looming over me. Too much work to get done in too little time. I always had papers nagging at me and I felt I never had time to do all the reading.*

## Feeling Overqualified

If your post-college experience is typical, you'll initially be working at a job for which you may feel you are overqualified, probably doing some kind of quasi-administrative work. You'll learn some skills in this job, but even more important, you will learn a great deal about workplaces and organizations and how adults interact under a variety of conditions.

*I had all these lofty expectations that people in the working world were going to be so much smarter and more worldly than I was. I expected that I would be surrounded by the best and the brightest, an upgrade from college. Instead I saw a lot of midlevel corporate lifers who came to work every day and seemed really bored. They weren't motivated at all. I gradually accepted that not everything at work is exciting and challenging and inspiring. There's a lot of tedium in the workday.*

You should always be looking to learn some things about yourself: what aspects of the job you enjoy, which ones you could do without, and how to function effectively and interact successfully with bosses and coworkers. Above all, try to avoid any outward show of defensiveness. Treat the people in your workplace—all of them—with respect. Be kind to the people who sort the mail and empty the trash. Try to meet staff from other departments and learn about their jobs and their functions in the organization. Accept that you're at the bottom of the heap and be good-natured about it. Present a positive attitude no matter what. Don't steal office supplies no matter how badly you need envelopes or a stapler at home. Don't leave your leftover Chinese takeout in the office refrigerator for weeks on end, and keep your cubicle clean.

It can be that simple. Yes, you'll have an adjustment to make when you start a job and you may well feel awkward making it. And yes, you may get much less guidance than you feel you need. But a healthy attitude helps a lot. The best thing you can do to keep your sanity and your job is to learn tact, an acquired skill for many of us that will keep on giving over the course of your professional career.

## Your Boss and You

*By working faithfully eight hours a day, you may eventually get to be a boss and work twelve hours a day.*
—Robert Frost

The summer I turned fifteen I worked at a homey little deli named Ed's. Its pink neon sign and greasy curtains in the window made it look like the ubiquitous small-town eatery. I was hired as a stock girl; my job was to fill up the cooler, make sure there were enough napkins in the dispensers, and ensure a steady supply of ketchup. On my third day of work, no doubt due to my pluck and diligence (and perhaps the untimely resignation of the incumbent), I was tapped for a promotion: counter person. I would take orders, then ring them into the cash register. But first I had to prove myself.

The boss of the place, Wanda, was a stout woman with beady black eyes and what my mother would delicately call "problem skin." She pulled me aside on her lunch break and, over a taco salad, explained to me the rigors of my new position.

"Let's say someone walks in here and wants to order something," she began, with tiny bits of hamburger flying from her mouth. "What do you do?"

"Well," I answered rather matter-of-factly, "I would say, 'Hello, can I take your order?'"

Wanda nodded. "Good," she said. "I would like a roast beef sandwich."

"Okay," said I, seeing where she was headed. I took out a napkin and pretended to write her order.

"What kind of bread do I want?" Wanda asked.

"Oh, right. Of course, 'What kind of bread would you like?'" I asked sweetly.

"What kind of bread do you have?"

I squinted, then whispered, "What kind of bread *do* we have?"

Wanda rolled her eyes. "White, wheat, rye, pumpernickel, or a roll."

I repeated the bread selection to her satisfaction. "Rye," she answered.

"Great. I will get that out to you." I thought it was over.

"Don't I get a side order?" Wanda was exasperated; I was hopeless.

"Sure, what would you like," I stammered and scanned the booths for clues on people's plates. "We have chips . . . coleslaw . . . pasta salad . . ."

"Chips are fine."

"Good. Thanks for ordering." I said. "We're done, right?"

"Nope. I want a soda, too," she said. "Then my whole family has to order." She looked over her shoulder and nodded at her imaginary family. And I took their orders, too. All thirteen of them.

Wanda was my first boss, and she was a piece of work. But I learned from her. Bosses come in all shapes and sizes. Some are everyday folks. Some are bumblers and fools. Some are strong and determined. Some are wishy-washy and indecisive. Some will respect and nurture you; others will try to mow you down during their daily power trips. And, like your parents, you can't choose them.

How do you get along with your boss, then? Let's start with first impressions. They're very important and they may shape your relationship with your boss for a long time. Nella Barkley, author of *Take Charge of Your Career*, offers this advice for your first weeks on the job: "Figure out how your boss likes to receive his or her information. Is it written or orally? In an e-mail? Is it first thing in the morning, or is it at the end of the day? Lay low in the first few weeks while you figure that out," she says, "then put together your questions briefly and succinctly. But before you even ask, check with coworkers, check manuals, textbooks, or even a resource library. Bosses are extremely appreciative of people who solve problems on their own. And be sure to let them know you're doing it."

> *I got in the habit of arriving before my boss in the morning and leaving a little later than him in the evening. I wanted to prove I was a team player. I had to sell myself all the time, because no one else was going to do it for me. I had to keep my name and face on my boss's radar screen. After meetings, I would send a 'Here are my thoughts'–type e-mail to my boss so he knew that I was always thinking.*

Good bosses coach you and support you but don't stifle you. They allow open communication and encourage you to take on more responsibility once they have given you enough guidance and support to succeed. According to Barkley, a good boss is someone who "recognizes your personality and skills and gives you opportunities to use them with appropriate autonomy."

Enough about good bosses. If you're lucky enough to have one, you'll find it a breeze to get along, and you'll probably enjoy your job and grow in it. But good bosses are usually the exception rather than the rule for graduates in their first jobs. Much more often, the boss poses a set of problems—in part because so many of us are encountering this sort of authority for the first time. And failure to solve those problems can make your work environment intolerable. Here are prototypes of problem bosses you might encounter, and some tips on how to cope with them.

## The Boss Who Thinks You're His Personal Servant

"A common complaint is that my boss—and some people are notorious for this type of thing—gives me secretarial work, and I am treated like an administrative assistant. I came in here and I thought I was going to be challenged and that I was going to learn, but my boss sees me as an opportunity to take all the mundane work off her plate and I am not learning anything," says Ed Vincent, the recruiter.

> *Every morning my neurotic boss would send me out to Starbucks to pick up his coffee—one sugar, no milk—and a lightly toasted raisin bagel with butter. During the day, I spent my time collating, stapling, filing, and faxing. I was the highest-paid photocopier in the world. One day he asked me to pick up a book for him at Borders. He was about to go to Greece on vacation and he needed a travel guide. Was I going to say no?*

Being saddled with grunt work does not necessarily reflect a lack of employee competence or initiative. It's often just that the newest hire—you—gets bogged down in the mundane, day-to-day minutiae. Try not to be offended, that is simply the nature of many first jobs.

## The Not-So-Smart Boss

Egomaniacs, take heart. You just might be smarter and more talented than your boss. But the trick is not to let on that you know that. Sometimes that's not simple.

> *I worked at an Asian think tank in Washington during my first year out of college. I had lived in China for several years and spoke Mandarin fluently. My boss, Becky, claimed to be a China specialist and bragged*

*about her superior language skills, yet no one had ever heard her speak Chinese. One morning we were planning a conference call to Beijing. As it turned out, we were unable to hire a translator for the session, and Becky started to get visibly nervous. I said casually, 'Let's just do it in Chinese, we both speak Chinese, right?' But Becky was adamant that we do the call in English. I realized then what was going on. She didn't speak Chinese at all.*

You might have read more, have gone to a better college, or even have a better understanding of the job at hand than your boss, but keep it to yourself. Smart-alecks need not apply, and nobody likes a know-it-all.

## The Twenty-Something Boss

Recent college graduates may run into supervisors who are only a couple of years older, say in their midtwenties. Having a young boss is typical in youthful organizations, particularly nonprofits, where it is normal to move up quite quickly.

*My boss was only a few years older than me but she wasn't patronizing or condescending. And she was always accessible to me. Whenever I came into her office—no matter how busy she was—she would swing around in her chair and devote all her attention to me.*

Having a boss who's a contemporary can be a benefit or a liability. She has recently been where you are and might be willing to listen to your suggestions and implement your ideas; you might even strike up a friendship. On the other hand, your unseasoned boss might lack the necessary experience to manage people effectively.

> *My boss was only twenty-four. It was a little weird having this guy who was my big brother's age telling me what to do all the time, especially since most of it was administrative work. I guess it was an ego thing.*

## The Boss with Multiple Personalities

Bosses with mood swings—some days friendly and supportive, other times icy and uncommunicative—can be frustrating. You never know what's coming.

> *He was the classic control freak–bipolar personality. One minute you were his buddy, the next he was yelling at you or giving you the cold stare. We used to refer to this as getting tossed the grenade. Out of nowhere you get an e-mail or phone call indicating you were in deep trouble for something. I remember one time actually just hanging up on him because I was tired of dealing with his crap.*

It can be exasperating to deal with a Sybil-like boss. They're impossible to read. Most irritating of all, however, is that they are in the position of authority and you, as their subordinate, have little recourse.

> *My boss would sashay in from her spa lunches and talk about the latest sale at Ann Taylor and prompt me to admire her recent Kate Spade bag purchase. She'd tell me about her boyfriend troubles. Then, without any notice, she'd switch gears and start critiquing a presentation I'd given that morning. It was hard to navigate. It was fine for her—she had the upper hand—but I was on the bottom and I didn't always know when to make the switch. I had to train myself not to cry at work.*

## The Condescending Boss

Like Mr. Rogers, the familiar cardigan-clad public television neighbor, some bosses have an uncanny knack for speaking slowly, cocking their heads to the side, and nodding like a hypnotist on autopilot. "Do you think you can handle this?" they might ask, pointing at the intimidating flashing buttons on the fax machine. They notice a small error in your work and with a hand placed gently on your shoulder and a disappointed smile they'll say, patronizingly, "This is not the way we do things here."

> *My boss had the same name as me, so rather than refer to me as Pete, he decided to call me Petey Boy. It was my first job and I was young—and young looking—so I'm not sure everyone thought of me as a fellow employee. Sometimes it seemed that people thought of me as the intern. 'Petey Boy' certainly didn't help reverse this image.*

## The Boss Who's Never Satisfied

My first boss out of college was a pear-shaped man with thinning silvery hair. If you saw him on the street you might think he was a softie grandfatherly type—one who wears zip-up sweaters and leather slippers and sucks on hard candy. No such luck. He was grouchy and gruff and cranky. He bellowed through our seventh-floor suite if he was dissatisfied with anything—"sloppy" photo-copying of some very important document, a "stupid" use of grammar he'd noticed in a paper, a roast beef sandwich that was too soggy, or even the dripping humidity of a normal Washington summer.

Most people in the office either avoided him, clashed with him openly, or warily endured his constant grousing on the side-lines. We took solace in his equal-opportunity temper tantrums; there was comfort in numbers. But to me, the youngest person in the office, he was downright terrifying. He could make me shrivel up with just a few sharp words.

> *My boss was constantly on my back about when the next report was coming out or why the database was down. If it was not done immediately, she would humiliate me in front of the office.*

It's no fun being a punching bag for your boss, especially when there's an audience.

## The Boss Who Crosses the Line

We graduate from college with hardly any knowledge of the working world, only to discover that the people we work for are sometimes immature, overgrown frat boys, demeaning witches, or manipulative schemers.

> *My boss had a tendency to take a long 'lunch' on Friday and come back drunk. It never affected me directly; he was a good drunk. But there were times that I was put in a position to make excuses about where he was. He certainly never asked me to do this, but I liked him and didn't want to see him get in trouble. I had no problem making excuses, but there is definitely some respect lost when your boss comes back with the giggles. I didn't care that he went out drinking, but he made it seem like he was getting away with something. It didn't mesh with the professionalism I had expected to find in the working world.*

These bosses have so little respect for the company and their work that they are willing to make utter fools of themselves. The problem is magnified, however, when they are willing to make a fool of you, too. Being humiliated at work is probably not something you signed on for.

> *I worked as an administrative assistant at a hotel chain's headquarters in Chicago. It was the kind of place where men wore conservative J.C. Penney–type business suits and the women were required to wear stockings. My boss was a hot-shot diva named Ruby. Ruby wasn't your average executive there. She blasted L.L. Cool J in her office, chain-smoked Pall Mall*

*cigarettes, and had a propensity to slam doors, files, and folders. Ruby was married and having an affair with another married man. She would send explicit pornographic e-mails and Internet downloads to a printer that happened to be situated on my desk. I was initially scared to talk, but I mentioned my problems with her to one of my coworkers who informed me that she had gone through four assistants in only six months.*

## OK, Boss, Let's Make This Work

Face it, your boss may never be the president of your personal fan club. But no matter how nightmarish or demoralizing bosses may be, there's no avoiding them. You have to work with the boss. One way to avoid problems is to get a clear understanding of what your duties will be before you accept a job. Once you're in the job, if you find it to be very different from the one described to you during the hiring process, you're not necessarily stuck. Some tasks are inappropriate, like running personal errands, and some tasks are intolerable, like standing all day, every day, at a photocopy machine. If you find you're asked to do that kind of work, seek out a one-on-one conversation with your boss and indicate that you don't think your talents are being well used and that you didn't realize the job you accepted would include the components you now find so inappropriate or demeaning.

"Many young people have an ideal vision of how they're going to add value, how they'll be appreciated, but it bears no relation to how it actually works," says Ellen Bayer of the American Management Association. "Do not confront your boss; do not challenge your boss. Say, 'I am concerned that I am not understanding what is expected of me.'"

Try to be positive. Suggest alternative tasks for which you feel better suited. Ask the boss to suggest ways in which your talents might be put to better use in your organization. Give the boss an opportunity to see things as you see them and to work with you in making corrections.

There's certainly no reason to accept all the responsibility for a sour or uneven relationship with your boss, but it may help you to move forward if you understand that it's a process of mutual understanding and mutual adjustment. Sometimes you're part of the problem. "You need to rationalize the situation and come up with a pragmatic approach. Why aren't you getting along? Are they not listening to you? Are you listening to them?" says Matt Riley, director of human resources at a dot-com.

Howard Figler, author of *The Complete Job Search Handbook*, advises, "Solicit feedback from coworkers and friends. Ask them 'What are my flaws?' to help uncover any blind spots." Then when you talk to your boss about your working relationship, you'll approach the conversation realistically and be able to offer some suggestions for making the workplace more comfortable for both of you.

## Make Your Boss Look Good

If you are *really* smarter than your boss, then you should understand why it's a good move to use your resourcefulness to help her shine. Be wily. Be clever. Be generous. "You have to figure out ways to make your boss look good," says Figler. "She has got to feel good about herself. Don't show her how dumb she is. Don't butt heads with her. Don't make it a contest between you and your boss. Let your boss take credit for your work, but let her know privately that we did this together."

Request feedback and communicate regularly with your boss, but understand that some are simply unwilling to offer any compliments. Perhaps they fear fawning over employees; perhaps they are reluctant to show their sweet side; perhaps they are joyless, finicky curmudgeons. But there are many ways to get a pat on the back every once in a while. During a review, or even during a personal meeting, ask your boss to delineate your strengths and weaknesses on the job. Tell your boss that you would appreciate his input and insight. Ask how you can improve your skills, but couch your request by asking for a critique in a specific area so you get constructive feedback.

While a few bosses may genuinely enjoy taking young people under their wing, many others lack the wherewithal, the time, or the interest. Luckily, you don't need your boss for that. These days, *mentoring* is a buzzword. A mentor shows you the ropes of your business, and teaches as well as trains, encourages, and supports. Often she does it so well you might not realize it's happening. A mentor, says Helen Harkness, author of *The Career Chase: Taking Creative Control in a Chaotic Age*, is someone who helps you understand the environment and the culture you're in and how to move through it successfully. "Mentors give you information about how things work."

"Any chance you get to be on a team with a knowledgeable senior person, take it," says author Nella Barkley. "But avoid using the term *mentor*. Instead ask them if you could join them for a sandwich in the cafeteria and say you've noticed their competence or sophistication in an area. Ask if they'd mind if

## Punching the Clock: Helpful Web Sites

**www.jobweb.com**
JobWeb provides career development and job search advice to graduates.

**www.jobhuntersbible.com**
This site offers tests and career advice; created by Richard Bolles, author of *What Color Is Your Parachute?*

**www.wetfeet.com**
WetFeet helps inexperienced job hunters make smarter career decisions.

---

you approach them in the future when you need advice. Let the relationship grow naturally." Most people are receptive to enthusiasm and interest. If you are humble and honest, they will be inclined to cultivate a relationship with you. Seek such allies out, then keep in touch.

## Keep a Paper Trail

Without getting too Linda Trippy here, you need to keep good records if your boss crosses the line, sexually or otherwise. Tell a superior or contact the human resources department. Be sure to tell a neutral third party. Preserve all communication you have with the harasser, and find out the company policy and local laws regarding harassment. If possible, make an effort to resolve the problem interpersonally. But if you feel threatened, violated, or afraid of your boss—or anyone at work—you need to speak up.

"If you're being abused by your boss, you need to get out," says Helen Harkness. "But you need to understand how you set yourself up to be abused in the first place. Identify what's really happening. People who get in bad situations have a tendency to get in them again unless they get some insight and knowledge. Analyze what you did to contribute to the problem. Understand what the problem is so that you do not repeat it."

# Your Coworkers

*It isn't what they say about you, it's what they whisper.*
—*Errol Flynn*

In the early days on my first job I was struck by the remarkable accuracy of so many of the office stereotypes I'd heard about: everything from the rah-rah folks who organized the company-wide softball league to the sniping congregation at the water cooler to the overachieving go-getters who worked nights and weekends. It was as though we were all cast in some low-budget Fox drama series. Wherever you work, some of your coworkers will be good, hardworking people trying to get ahead in their careers as you are. But you may well encounter the following types, too. They seem to inhabit almost every workplace.

## The Suck-Up
She is the insufferable one who arrives early and leaves late and never lets you forget it. Slurping sounds echo through the corridor as she compliments your boss's new shoes, her haircut, her blouse. "Have you lost weight?" She smiles sweetly.

> *I worked as a kindergarten teacher at a small elementary school for my first job. My coworker Jennifer was young like me, but all she wanted to do was impress the other teachers. She even started dressing like the older teachers, with those long corduroy jumpers with white turtlenecks. She wanted to fit in so desperately. Jennifer wrote a song for the kids about a frog and a dragonfly and then put it on for the school. She made these huge sets for it and elaborate masks out of Popsicle sticks—it must have taken her forever—and it was just for an assembly. Then she bragged about how imaginative she was, how all the kids adored her. All the other young teachers simultaneously admired and loathed her.*

Suck-ups are the ones who loudly volunteer to do extra work and appear tethered to the office via cell phone, laptop, and PDA. But their worst trait by far is seizing any opportunity to make themselves look better to persons of authority—nitpicking your work and pointing out your mistakes.

## The Slacker

He's a shirker, a loafer. He's the one who waltzes in late and skidaddles early. While he delights in his lackadaisical approach to work, you will find him infuriating. He rarely chips in, yet no one ever seems to notice.

> *I had to deal with two slackers on a time-sensitive project. One of them announced on the first day that he was just not effective before 11 A.M. and that we*

*should not expect to see him in the mornings. Then when he finally arrived at the office, he would sit at his desk checking e-mail or playing a computer game. The other one had a large sense of entitlement and refused to sit in a cubicle like the rest of us. She would figure out which partner wasn't going to be there that day then take over a corner office. She talked on the phone with her feet up on the desk, and when I came in to tell her something she would roll her eyes, put her hand up to halt me, and mouth, 'Now is not a good time.' It was infuriating.*

Whether he is just *that* lazy, or not particularly interested in the project at hand, it doesn't matter. It sometimes feels like the slacker shows up solely to sabotage your career.

## The Chatterer

She is above and beyond your average conversationalist. And, as if laser guided, she manages always to think of something mundane to say just as she passes your cubicle: Did you happen to see *Will and Grace* last night? My mother is driving me batty. How about those Redskins, eh?

*My colleague had weight issues. She loved to probe what we thought of her weight, the new diets she was trying: 'I think this diet is really working, don't you agree?' I specifically recall having to listen to her recite each week what her routine was at the gym and how men there couldn't take their eyes off*

*her. The thing that baffles me is that I never once
solicited information from her. She would just come
up to my cubicle, fold her arms, and begin the torture
session.*

Some days you might enjoy these mindless interruptions,
considering them a break from the tedium of the day. But most of
the times you'll go to great—and inventive—lengths to avoid the
gabby babbler.

## The Gossip

Having mastered the art of hushed tones and downcast eyes, the
professional gossipmonger always seems to know who's in and
who's out. She knows everyone else's business but rarely seems
engaged in any work of her own. The loose-lipped one scurries
about the office, sometimes landing at your desk. "You will not
believe what he just said," she whispers, her hand cupped to her
mouth.

Some misguided managers even *encourage* gossip when they
think it serves their purposes.

*After firing a director with whom I was working
on a project, a senior executive said that while he
didn't want to make a formal announcement that this
person was 'fired,' he wanted to let it leak out that
this person was, indeed, fired because of unacceptable
behavior. It was this executive's belief that this would
educate the workers that such behavior was not tolerated in the organization.*

## Perhaps, Even, a Genuine Friend

If you're really lucky, you might end up with a coworker who becomes not only your ally in the office, but also a real friend. It is especially fortuitous if this coworker's skills complement yours, so that you not only learn a lot, but together you make an effective team.

> *I found that the best way to forge ties in a large office is to make small offers of generosity and thoughtfulness. People are so glad just to be noticed and singled out in such a big office that they are soon ready to be your confidante after only offering them crumbs of civility! But the important thing to keep in mind is to choose your friends wisely and with much deliberation. Ask yourself what you think their motives are or what they might gain in extending you friendship. You will be safer and saner for it.*

## Coping with Coworkers

Successfully navigating the workplace is never simple. You are expected to work together harmoniously with a wide variety of personalities and often with people ranging over several decades in age. Working conditions change, crunch time comes, stress levels elevate, bosses come and go. "Getting along with your coworkers is like getting along with your family. You need to get a handle on their working style," says author Helen Harkness. "It is a mesh of personalities more than a mesh of competence."

But, cautions recruiter Matt Riley, keep your own role in view and in perspective. "Stop and think: 'What am I? Am I the loud one? The shy one? The slacker? How do others view me?' If you want to be effective, you have to remember that you are one of these personalities," he says. "Work on your personality skills; be professional and level-headed. But if coworkers make it difficult or impossible for you to do your job, you should talk to your manager."

Your goal is not to win the office popularity contest. When you're first starting out, avoid making strong bonds with any one person too soon, warns expert Nella Barkley. "Don't go out to lunch with the same person every day. There will be worker bees, loners, people interested in nothing but politics, and folks who don't do much of anything. Get friendly with a lot of people. Know the lay of the land. Form alliances with the people you're most compatible with. Spread your friendships. Be elaborately cordial but arms-length with people who are political."

Try to stay out of the flow of office gossip; it can be cruel, untrue, and unproductive. Save your gossiping for off-work hours with nonwork friends. "Know that you are a professional person and that you carry a professional air," says expert Helen Harkness. "Stay out of the gossip chain. It's difficult sometimes because some of the things they're gossiping about are very interesting and you want to know all about it."

While some chatter is plain fun, and it's still considered okay to grumble about the big boss every once in a while, always remember that once your words enter the gossip train there's no telling where they'll end up. The best thing to do about your bad opinion of a boss or coworker is nothing at all. To paraphrase Calvin Coolidge, you don't get in trouble for things you don't say.

# Romance at the Office

The ratio of men to women in the workplace is approaching 50–50, and you might well find love in the cubicle next door. After all, people are working longer hours, some of them at night and on the weekend. And in high-stress situations, when the adrenaline is pumping, romantic attachment seems to come easily. Many long-term relationships begin at work.

But office romances require special care and consideration. According to a study conducted by the American Management Association, three-quarters of managers polled said that office romances were fine as long as the couple was "unmarried and discreet." One-quarter even admitted to dating an office colleague themselves.

But it's never simple. "Office romance? Bad idea," says Matt Riley. "Unless you're in Finance and she's in Purchasing, then it's a different story." But how do you make sure your office tête-à-tête does not interfere with your job—or your sweetheart's?

> *I met my girlfriend at work. And I've noticed that the logistics of office romance cut two ways. It's nice that you get to see the person all the time, but the drawback is that you're together all the time. Work is no longer your refuge. It's also good because the other person knows about your situation at work and can give you feedback and advice and counsel. You share a context. But, then again, you end up talking about work all the time. It really depends on*

*how you make it work, but it's hugely distracting. When you have an office romance, you find yourself going to work with a different purpose. I spent so much time and energy focused on her and not really on work.*

First, be sure you know company policy. More and more organizations these days have protocols and rules about office romances, especially those between supervisors and subordinates. Many try to put limits on office romances for their own protection. Coworkers dating can result in coworkers breaking up, and that can lead to an unhappy and unproductive workplace or even to lawsuits over everything from discrimination (if one is terminated or demoted) to sexual harassment. It is, for instance, professionally off-limits and emotionally dangerous to date your boss. Someone is bound to get hurt, and it's likely to be you.

*My boyfriend—who was also my boss—and I were honest with each other from the start and were up front about what will happen if things don't work out. We try to keep things really professional, although we did make out in his office the other day. No regrets, but I probably won't do it again any time soon.*

Office romances affect more than just the two lovebirds. In a busy workplace, secondhand romance can be as toxic as secondhand smoke. Young organizations in particular are notorious for their high levels of sexual tension. Most employees are recent grads and view the office as an extension of college.

## The Skinny on Company Parties

*Drink the first. Sip the second slowly. Skip the third.*
*—Knute Rockne, legendary Notre Dame football coach*

Beware the company party. They typically occur around the holidays, often at a luxury hotel, ballroom, or fancy restaurant—unless you happen to work at a nonprofit or at a company having a bad year. Then the party may be at the boss's house.

The free liquor, crowded dance floor, and plastic-looking disc jockey make this event a sure bet for spectacle, unruly behavior, and bad dancing. "Last year, a receptionist got rather friendly while dancing with one of the IT guys, and people were calling them Baby and Johnny—a reference from *Dirty Dancing*—for months afterward," says Rana Edward, a Georgetown grad.

"I wore my best suit that day to make a good impression during cocktails and maybe have the opportunity to engage in witty conversation with some of my colleagues. It turned out to be a bit different," says Sean Marks, an Auburn grad. "The company had issued two drink tickets per person. I'm not sure if this was so nobody would get out of control or the management was really cheap and wanted to limit the drink budget. Whatever the reason, I thought nothing of it since this was going to be my first office gathering, not a drink-up. My image of the party was destroyed

*My office was a hookup fest. In general, most of the romances were kept on the DL, but figuring out who was shacking up with whom was a favorite office pastime. Clues were often dropped when people came in together in the morning or were seen together on the*

within twenty minutes of arriving. Many of the women had traded in their work attire for clingy dresses showing lots of cleavage, bad makeup, and strong perfume. Many of the men were trying to figure out how to scam more drinks than they were allotted.

"Well, a lot of people must have managed to exceed their drink limit, since it started to become a sloppy night. A few hours into the party, while I was in the middle of a conversation, one of my coworkers kept coming up behind me, hiking up her dress, and slithering up and down against me until she would go so low that she couldn't get off the floor without help. Sure enough, as soon as she was helped up she would do it again."

There's nothing wrong with socializing with coworkers, even having a drink or two. But remember that you'll be back working with these people tomorrow, and the crimes committed while DAS—drunk as a skunk—can stay news for a long time in the lunchroom and at the watercooler. The woman with whom you flirted too aggressively, the supervisor you insulted, the coworker whose weight kept creeping into your karaoke lyrics won't be so forgiving when the alcoholic haze is gone and you have to face them again in the workplace. Professionalism and self-control are as important at party time as they are during work time.

*street. Most of us had fun just picking on the couples and dropping references whenever we could. But there is also a rumor around the firm that the reason that there are no doors on our storage closets . . . well, you can guess why.*

If you find yourself confronted with the evidence of someone else's office romance, the best advice is to try to ignore it. Stay out of their relationship; do not acknowledge what's going on between them; continue to treat them professionally. But if you're upset by cooing between the cubicles and the quick straightening of clothes when you enter the photocopy room, then it might be time to have a discreet conversation with at least one of the romancers. Suggest that some people in the office are distracted by their relationship. Never go to the boss to complain before trying to intervene directly with the offending parties. But if the distractions persist, perhaps it's time to discuss the problem—carefully documented, of course—with your supervisor.

## Mistakes Happen

*Experience is the name that everyone gives to their mistakes.*
*—Oscar Wilde*

We've all had embarrassing moments in life: the bungled parallel parking job on your driver's test, the first dinner with Mr. Hottie with spinach in your teeth, the day you discovered that the professor you'd just described to your friend as a huge bore was standing behind you in the elevator. Your first job, you'll find, is overflowing with opportunities for those kinds of embarrassing moments.

Mistakes are going to happen. You might have filed a report incorrectly, coded something improperly, inserted wrong data, or dropped a large paper clip into the mechanical innards of the photocopy machine. In the modern workplace, every task, every machine, every interaction can seem like a mistake in waiting.

> *I worked as a general assignment reporter at a small-town newspaper in southern Virginia. After working there nearly a year, I offered to write about a restaurateur who operated a posh eatery in Washington, D.C. It was a big deal since I was going to drive up there in the company car, meet with the owner, eat a meal, and hang out in the kitchen. But I never got that far. As I merged onto I-95, I crashed the car—a 1998 white Plymouth Neon—and did not make it to the interview. I was sobbing the entire time. Of course, I had to call the photographer, exchange numbers with the person I hit, call my editor, deal with the tow truck. Then I called my mom. I was sure I was going to get fired. But insurance took care of the damage, and the paper didn't fire me. I walked into the office Monday morning and everything was fine. People were concerned, and then everyone had a big laugh.*

Not all mistakes have such an impact, and not all offices are as good-natured. But any good boss knows you learn from your mistakes, just as any good worker knows never—or hardly ever—to make the same mistake twice.

## Own Up

There are some simple practices that can help you avoid embarrassing mistakes and cope with them quickly when they do occur. A good starting point is to become an aggressive mistake-avoider. That doesn't mean avoid risks or challenging assignments. It means do the basic things that protect your work from infection by insidious mistakes.

Double-check anything you submit to your boss or to anyone else in your workplace. Be sure the columns add up and that all the pages are present and numbered in order. Proofread your copy and, if possible, ask a coworker you trust to review your work before handing it off to your boss.

But even then, some mistakes are inevitable. When they happen, confront them immediately by telling your boss. Don't try to hide or cover up a mistake that could affect others or your organization, and certainly don't try to shift blame to someone else. Confession—a heartfelt mea culpa—is much better than having someone else discover your mistake and confront you about it.

## Solve the Problem

Try to come up with a solution to the problems caused by your mistake and, if you can, suggest it at the same time you confess the mistake. Most managers believe that how you handle mistakes is more telling than the mistake itself. Show your boss how much effort you have made to correct the problem and to prevent it from recurring. Express regret in a succinct and sincere way, in a personal conversation.

But don't wallow in your mistakes. That only draws attention to you and your wrongdoing. If you walk around the office bemoaning what a stupid fool you are, pretty soon your coworkers may begin to believe it, or at least get tired of having to reassure you that you're not. Confess to the boss—then move on. Everybody makes mistakes.

Still, it's far better to avoid a problem in the first place than to try to solve it after the fact. Because the fact is, there are real costs, for your organization and for you, when you screw up, and it's impossible to tell how they will affect you. As your parents used to say, an ounce of prevention is worth a pound of cure.

> *I had been working for six months before I made my first mistake. I completely spaced on a project that should have been occupying most of my time. My direct supervisor and manager told me how disappointed they were and how this was a terrible reflection on me and on them. They told me that they would have to do weekly check-ups to ensure that I got my work done. I started working harder and longer, getting my work done long before the deadline. I took on more difficult cases and started coming in on the weekends. I was really feeling good. But when it came time for my year-end review, under the section about getting work done on time, I was given a two—the lowest! The incident happened six months prior to that and I had really gotten my act together since then. It was incredible to me that someone just starting out would be judged on one mistake like that.*

Any mistake you make on the job may become part of your permanent image at work. When that happens, it may become difficult to move up the ladder at that particular company. If you find that you're stuck with a negative reputation that even your best efforts can't erase, you may have to think about changing jobs.

## Office Etiquette:
## How to E-mail like a Pro

In the professional world, electronic communication is a way of life. It is critical that you use sound judgment about whom you e-mail, how you e-mail, and where you surf. Postpone personal e-mail and surfing until after normal work hours. Don't forward to coworkers chain e-mails you get from your college friends. E-mailing pornography or using office computers to surf sexy Web sites is a very effective way to lose your job. You never know who's reading your e-mails or looking over your shoulder at your computer screen; lots of companies electronically monitor their employees' Web surfing and e-mailing. It's legal, and it's done.

When you do send e-mail to friends or to professional contacts, you should rein in your electronic alter ego. Are you someone who routinely indulges in homeboy slang? (Yo, yo, whad up brotha? Peace out.) Or someone who virtually shouts? (WHEN USING LOCKED CAPS, FOR INSTANCE.) Perhaps you write flowery prose loaded with symbols. (Just **wanted** to brighten your day ☺.)

Cool it. Neither your boss nor your hard-at-work coworkers will appreciate your e-mail witticisms. It may have seemed hip in college, but in the workplace it just seems childish and maybe even offensive. Always keep in mind that most of the time you're at work you're expected to be *doing* work.

# When It's Time to Say Goodbye

One day, you will leave your first job. It might be difficult. On the other hand, it might prove a great relief to walk out those frosted glass doors and know that you'll never have to go back. In today's dynamic workplace, no one expects a recent graduate to stay at a job for more than a couple of years. You need not feel guilty about leaving.

## All the Right Reasons

Some people leave because they feel there's no more to learn. Think of your first job as a continuing part of your education. Use it as an opportunity to expand your skills and broaden your understanding. But when your learning curve flattens, recognize that it may be time to move on.

> *I relocated to Jackson Hole, Wyoming, after graduation. I moved out here with the intention of actually trying to make a real life for myself and not just be a ski bum. I took a job as a guest manager at a ritzy resort. I was really excited about my first job. I thought it would be serious and a good opportunity, opening up a lot of doors. That is probably what we all think about our first job. It has been that and it hasn't been that. I did learn quite a bit the first two months. Then it just plateaued.*

For others, quitting a first job is a strategy for getting ahead, an important career move. Fifteen to twenty years ago, job-hopping was considered a negative, a sign you lacked stamina or commitment. But now it's become routine, almost expected. "Job-hopping can be a general fast-track," says human resources manager Matt Riley. "In a good job market, a rule of thumb is that you should never stay in a corporate job for more than two years until you're twenty-eight. You can make a lot more money by switching jobs."

## Desperate Measures

But for some, quitting a first job is an act of desperation. You've tried to make the job work, to make it fun, but failed. Maybe it was the boring, repetitive work. Perhaps you could never please the boss, or your coworkers were hostile. Maybe it was the long hours and the low pay.

If you're thinking of leaving, question your motives and try to understand the basis of your discontent. Why am I unhappy here? Is it the industry? Is it the job? Would I function more effectively and be more satisfied in a different kind of setting—a smaller company, for instance, or one with a younger workforce? What did I like about this job, and where can I find work that allows me to do more of that? If you don't answer honestly, you may well find your next job no more satisfying than your first.

If there's a chance you would stay, be sure to provide the employer an opportunity to retain you. Perhaps the company can keep you by offering a pay raise, a broader scope of responsibilities, a title change, or a job elsewhere in the company. Be explicit about what you would need in order to stay. Better yet, be positive. Don't complain about your current job, tell your boss you've learned *so much* that you'd like to move on to the next phase of your career and learn even more.

"After two years with the company you're so much more valuable to us, because we have invested time, money, and effort to train you," says Ed Vincent.

Resignation may be a sound response if the problems run deeper than money or work responsibilities. After all, it's far easier to make a move when you're twenty-three, childless, and mortgage-free. It's still hard, but it's worth it.

> *I realized that I was unhappy for nine hours a day, five days a week. Things weren't going to change and improve unless I changed them. I needed to seek something else. So I quit my job. It was liberating. The hardest part was telling my parents.*

Generally you'll know when your job has lost its allure and your creative needs are not being met. "If you're not stimulated, you have got to get out," Howard Figler says. "You need to move toward something maximally motivating. If you scale yourself down too much, then you might be making decisions like that for the rest of your life. Idealism is very important; it's at the heartbeat of a good career."

## Next . . .

So we've ended up where we started: searching for a job. If the sociologists are correct in their predictions about the character of workers in the twenty-first century, you'll probably do this many times in your life. But it will get easier as you go along. You're a veteran now—of work and of job searches. You know yourself better, too.

Your job—any job—should be a learning experience. You'll hopefully learn about the kind of environment in which you thrive and the kind in which you suffocate. You'll meet people who are generous and helpful—and some you would like to forget. You'll confirm where your strengths lie and discover ones you didn't know you had. You'll learn a lot on your first job—but nothing more important than what you want from your next one.

# Climbing . . . or Crawling

*There are many ways of going forward, but only one way of standing still.*
*—Franklin Delano Roosevelt*

From where I stand—or sit—I can barely see the top of the corporate ladder. It's the young, working person's conundrum: How do I improve my station? How do I charge ahead? How do I separate myself from the pack?

College is about thoughts and deliberation and introspection. The working world rarely cares much about those things. Your theories about multiple meanings of the green light on Daisy's dock or your groundbreaking analysis of Machiavelli's *The Prince* aren't important any more. At work, you're judged by new standards, different benchmarks.

*In some ways it's easier to be a success at work than it was in college. The things that impress people are really very simple: You're punctual, you dress professionally, you get work done on time. You end up making this impression as an amazing employee.*

You'll soon discover that there's much more to career success than raw intelligence; qualities like drive, initiative, ambition, and perseverance are what really matter. But whether you climb the ladder to success two rungs at a time, ascend at a sloth's pace, or barely make any traction at all hinges on your performance when it counts. Here are some final tips to help you on your way—hopefully, up.

Find your passion. Get ahead by exhibiting enthusiasm. Work doesn't feel like work when you're enjoying yourself.

*I was really excited by work, and I thought that I was making a difference. I started to learn Russian in my spare time and going to speeches on topics that interested me. I was working weekends and I made sure the bosses saw all the work I was doing. I was promoted after six months.*

Show that you're a diligent worker. Your supervisors will be impressed by your conscientiousness.

*After graduation, I took a job translating Arabic for the Department of Defense. During training, someone would sit over my shoulder and correct everything I did wrong. I got in the habit of writing down my errors on a little notepad next to me so that I would not make the same mistake twice. It was something really simple, but it turned me into a much more thorough worker.*

Does getting ahead necessarily mean sacrificing weekends and personal time? Chances are, your boss cares a lot less about how much time you spend in your cubicle than about your doing quality work and getting it done on time. Then again, it depends on the culture of your company.

*For me, just being at the office meant a lot. It was all face time. You needed to be seen there at 9 o'clock at night a couple of times a week. If you only worked 40 hours a week, people wondered, 'Who do you think you are?'*

If you're worried that you're not meeting expectations about the amount of time you spend in the workplace, then schedule a conversation with your manager. Be honest and up front. Ask her what she expects regarding time spent at the office.

Figure out ways to expand your job responsibilities. It's often easier for a boss to augment a job description than to give a formal promotion, so try to identify new areas in which you can make useful contributions. If you increase your productivity, you'll be in a much better position to be considered for more challenging assignments and upcoming promotions.

> *My first job was so dull that I began to fill my time by volunteering to take on other people's work. I'd pick up rogue reports and analyze the data, attend meetings where my presence was not always necessary, set up lunches with clients. One day I went to a meeting about loan quality and I started taking notes. When I got home and started reviewing what I had written down, I realized I could make a job out of what the meeting was about! I was so excited that I drafted a letter to the woman who had run the meeting and faxed it to her the next morning. Of course I mentioned, 'Oh, by the way, I'd really like to do this job.' Three weeks later, I had a new position.*

You might also investigate the possibility of a lateral move. Consider taking a different job at the same company that will provide a new experience or challenge, even though it might not necessarily be a move up in salary or prestige. A lateral move—where you acquire a new skill set and expertise—just might open up other possibilities.

Be genuinely helpful, a complementary force. Perhaps your technophobic boss thinks a backup disk is part of the human anatomy. There's an opening for you. Become her technology guru, the one who shows her computer shortcuts, sets up her Excel spreadsheets, and helps troubleshoot problems. Be omnipresent when she needs help, and be humble in delivering it.

"The sanest way to get ahead is to keep an eye out for what seem to be your boss's priorities. Then make a real effort in line with those," says Nella Barkley. "Your boss may be brilliant but disorganized. Helping to straighten out a mess may be the best way you can contribute. Volunteer for special projects, but don't stretch yourself too thin."

The bottom line is this: *Be a good employee.* Talent and its aggressive application to an organization's goals are the keys to success in any work setting. Work hard. Avoid mistakes and learn from those you do make. Know your boss's goals and commit your energies to their accomplishment. Be alert to growth opportunities and ways to expand your responsibilities. And finally, don't be surprised if the clouds begin to part, suddenly, and you find the higher rungs on the corporate ladder coming into view.

# chapter five

# money
# MATTERS

YOU'VE WAITED ALL YOUR LIFE to be making your own money. Now you are, but you're unsure how to handle it. And when you're on the brink of credit card catastrophe or are donating a large portion of your paycheck to Sallie Mae each month, worrying about money can be exhausting.

Wait a minute, aren't these years supposed to be fun and carefree? You're only young once—you're supposed to be sowing those oats. Right?

But in these early years of earning and saving and spending, it's important to make sound decisions about where your money goes. Living the high life and spending beyond your means can quickly lead to some downright frightening consequences. Already you're creating saving and spending patterns that will lead to either financial success or a lifetime of struggle.

I first learned money matters from my best childhood friend, Stephanie. At eight years old she had everything a girl could want: a canopy bed, a red boom box, a brand-new bicycle with blue streamers hanging from the handlebars, a miniature Ping-Pong table, every Barbie accoutrement imaginable, even a swimming pool in her backyard. To me it became obvious that Stephanie was rich, or at least her parents were. Even as a kid, I knew that things were bought with money and that more money equaled more things. It was, after all, the mid-1980s, and "Material Girl" was the most popular song in the country. While my upbringing was hardly Dickensian, whenever I visited Stephanie I couldn't help feeling deprived.

I've grown up a little bit, and I know intellectually that there's more to life than money. I make rational choices about how I spend my money and I know that new things aren't the key to everlasting joy. But all sanctimony aside, I *love* new things. Capitalism is the American way, and I take immense pleasure in consuming. No matter how idealistic I'd like to be, money makes a difference. It allows me to do the things I enjoy: go out to dinner, take a trip, see a show, buy a new pair of shoes.

The trouble is, money isn't always there when you need it.

This chapter is Personal Finance 101: how to save money— I assume you already know how to spend it—and how to avoid the prickly pitfalls of debt. Add to that a few lessons on how to create and maintain a disciplined budget, how to manage your credit cards and student loans, how to do your taxes, and why you should invest your hard-earned cash sooner rather than later. This is important stuff, even if you're not so good with numbers, never dared to take an economics class in college, or learned all you know about the arcane world of money and investing from an issue of *Business Week* you read on an airplane.

Luckily, there are ways to have a life on a skimpy salary

without needing to survive on Ramen Noodles and Pop Tarts. Plenty of recent grads have done it before you.

## Paycheck Realities: Why the Net Is So Gross

Earning money—real money, grown-up money, we're talking a dollar amount with a comma in it—is an exciting prospect. At last you could *afford* things, you think, and instant gratification would be yours.

Like most recent graduates, I eagerly awaited my first paycheck, dreaming of what I could buy. Nothing extravagant, of course: the latest U2 CD, the blue cashmere sweater I'd spied in the window of Banana Republic, a dinner with friends at Marcel's, the Zagat-certified French restaurant in my neighborhood.

Then the check arrived in its sleek blue envelope with my name and address in a wax-paper window. Excited, I tore it open. There must be some mistake, I panicked. This paycheck is far too small.

Nobody had warned me about the difference between the gross and the net. The gross is what I'd been told I would earn when I took the job—a number that seemed quite healthy and reasonable to me at the time. But no one will ever actually see his gross pay. When the paycheck comes, a lot of what you earned has already been removed for other purposes. What's left is your net pay: the gross minus all the deductions. The first time this happened to me I felt like I was personally supporting several levels of government.

Taxes were taken out—lots of taxes: federal and state income taxes, Social Security and Medicare, city taxes. My contribution to a 401(k), also gone. Suddenly old Uncle Sam is a wearing a maniacal grin, wagging a scolding finger, and plotting to take my money. Bye-bye, Bono. See you later, blue cashmere. Au revoir, Marcel.

Where does the money go?

Your first paycheck is a staggering lesson in the difference between gross income and after-tax income. Fair or not, the more money you make, the more money you'll pay in taxes. Be sure that you understand how much money you'll be making *after* taxes—usually about two-thirds of your quoted starting salary; otherwise you'll be spending illusory wages and living a take-home reality, all the while wondering, Why am I broke?

> *I was absolutely shocked at how much of my paycheck goes to taxes. I had some mental preparation beforehand—I had heard my parents moan about taxes —but still, my jaw dropped to the ground when I got my first paycheck and I saw just how much is taken out. Suffice it to say, I wasn't a Republican when I entered the working world, but it won't be long now.*

Most of us pay taxes throughout the year, when our employers withhold tax from our paychecks. The law requires it. Your company, using tables provided by the government, figures out how much of your salary goes to taxes and puts it into a government bank account.

Your Employee's Withholding Allowance Certificate, commonly known as the W-4, that mystifying sheet with all the 1's and 0's you fill out your first day on the job, indicates the status of your filing—single or married—and the number of allowances you're claiming. Those binary digits represent an exemption, credit, or tax benefit you plan to claim. The more allowances you claim the less tax will be withheld and the bigger your take-home paycheck will be. Keep in mind, though, you'll owe even more when the bill comes due in April.

Experts recommend that you aim to withhold 90 percent of what you think you'll owe on April 15. While a fat refund check may seem attractive in theory, it also means you've given the government a yearlong, tax-free loan, says Michael Dentamaro, a certified public accountant. "Because of the time-value of money, you could be earning interest on the amount you're withholding. But if you lack discipline and have a hard time accumulating cash, you should use the refund check as a forced vehicle for saving," he says.

Deductions are taken from your paycheck each period for federal income tax. Depending on where you work, you may be paying state and local income taxes as well. In addition, you pay Social Security and Medicare taxes. The FICA tax, from the Federal Insurance Contributions Act, is deducted from your wages to help cover the federal cost of providing care for the aging, the disabled, and their survivors. The Medicare tax covers the cost of hospital insurance for the elderly.

Most employees also pay the cost of benefits and health insurance through their paychecks. Typically, the cost of the employee's portion of the benefits is added together with the taxes to come up with the total amount of paycheck deductions. (We'll talk about this more in Chapter 6.)

If you don't understand how a number on your pay stub was computed, ask someone in your payroll department to explain it to you. Human resources departments aren't infallible, so be sure to check for errors, especially when you're newly hired or there's

## Real World Common Sense: Your Life in a Box

Getting organized is an important first step in managing your money wisely. Go to a discount department store and buy an accordion file or a plastic box with hanging folders to store your important papers: receipts, income statements or pay stubs, canceled checks, and paid bills. This is also a good place to keep a copy of your birth certificate, Social Security card, 401(k) information, passport, and other important documents.

"Paper has to be addressed," says Stephanie Winston, a time-management guru and author of *The Organized Executive*. "Stuff comes in and sits literally or figuratively at the edge of your desk and you must decide what to do with it. There are four things you can do: throw it away or delete it, refer it or pass it on, act on it personally, or file it in a paper or computer folder. But paper must move."

been some change in your status. This isn't Monopoly; an error in your favor will have to be repaid, often with interest.

# The B-Word Is Not a Dirty Word

In college it is fashionable to blithely claim that money isn't all that important. Students survive on very little of it and their lives can still be full and enjoyable—food aplenty, Internet service, cramped though toasty living quarters—if their wonderful, generous parents are paying for most of it. Like mine did. That's the beauty of college.

In the Real World, money *is* important and we need to be aware of how we're spending it and how to go about saving it. I'm talking about the dreaded B-word: budgeting.

Budgeting is something we promise ourselves we'll do but never quite get around to. Somehow spending a Sunday afternoon sitting in front of a computer spreadsheet, tallying receipts and balancing our checkbook, seems less than thrilling. We get defensive, fearing that creating a budget is confining. "Nothing will hamper my three-dollar latte addiction!" we say defiantly. "My Nine West habit is here to stay!" We love money for what it buys us. And we hate it for what it denies us. We grow fearful that budgeting will turn us into frugal curmudgeons before our time.

But just because you're limiting your indulgences does not mean that suddenly you'll crave all-you-can-eat early bird specials, or that you'll become the cheapskate everyone dreads in the Secret Santa office draw. The truth is, people who aren't in the habit of living beneath their means and saving money will never achieve financial security. Living large may be fun for a while, but it's financially shortsighted.

Good money management is about adopting a healthy attitude toward money. Part of this is creating—and sticking to—a realistic budget. Budgeting forces you to prioritize your spending according to your values and goals. This pushes you to consciously determine where your money—savings, investments, and earnings—goes. The aim of budgeting is to bring your dreams, your expectations, and your finances into harmonious agreement.

## The Numbers Game

Successful budgeting is little more than doing at home what most of us have been trained to do at work: analyze problems and solve

## Make Online Banking
## Your New Best Friend

Banking online is the best way to keep a watchful eye on your finances. For a nominal fee, you can actively manage your money from your computer and on your schedule. You can transfer funds between accounts, check balances, stop payment on checks, even schedule bill payments such as rent and cable—saving you the cost of a stamp. Online banking can eliminate late fees and returned checks for insufficient funds.

Online banking also makes savings a snap. It enables you to institute a regimen and save on autopilot by setting up transfers to your money market or mutual fund on a weekly or monthly basis. It's an easy form of discipline.

Ask at your bank or visit its Web site for more information about this helpful service.

them. Before you can figure out how to align your spending with your income, you need to know how much is coming in and how much is going out.

Get a handle on the money flow. Total your big, fixed bills, such as rent, student loans, utilities, insurance, and car payments. Then add in smaller—but still necessary—expenses, like dry cleaning, transportation, clothing, and food. Finally, tack on your weekly spending habits or variable expenses: the bagel with cream cheese you pick up before work, the issue of *Sports Illustrated* you buy at the newsstand, and other discretionary purchases such as cable, movie tickets, dinners out, Internet service, and gifts. The other side of the equation is your income—after tax, that is—and any other money you receive during the week or month.

It's tedious, but tracking your spending is the only way to double-check your checkbook and hold yourself accountable. Once you've added up all these expenses and categorized them, it should be obvious whether or not you have a problem—a deficit will be a signal—and where your spending has to give.

> *It helps to take a step back and really look at where the money goes. I remember very distinctly going to the grocery store for the first time after college when I was footing the bill and being completely amazed at how much everything cost. My buffet-style college cafeteria and enormous campus store did not exactly prepare me for the reality of the high cost of living. After the first few months of floundering, I started keeping every single receipt of almost every penny I spent. I would sit down at the end of the month and see where I spent my money and how I could cut back.*

This little exercise is not meant to make you feel guilty. You can't save every cent you earn, and in twenty-first-century America it's almost impossible to lead a perfectly Thoreauvian lifestyle. Most of these expenses are unavoidable costs of living; consider them the costs of independence.

Prioritize your spending, says Mari Adam, a certified financial planner. "Don't think of budgeting as a How Not to Spend plan. Rather it's a way to know where your money is going so that you can make choices. Those who get into trouble are the ones who overspend on every discretionary purchase: clothes, going out to dinner, travel. You can't do everything, and it's up to you to decide what to spend your money on."

## Charity Begins Now

Earning money should not swell your sense of entitlement or en-hance your selfish tendencies. Rather, these early years of earning an income are a good time to begin a habit of charitable giving.

It's simple to find a cause you wish to support by asking a few questions about your values and interests: What issues concern you? The environment? World peace? What are you passionate about? The arts? Local government? Your alma mater? What would you like to see changed in the world or your community? Construction of a new Little League field? A cure for cancer?

Work your charitable-giving goals into your financial plan. Earmarking money for your favorite causes allows you to give reg-ularly and without worry.

Molly Jansen, a University of Michigan grad, insists that giving money to charity helps her maintain a sense of fiscal conscien-tiousness. "I was raised Catholic and my parents are famously charitable, so I believe that one should donate a good portion of her income to a worthy cause. This is quite a feat early on, but I think choosing a few charities that you really believe in, and making a point of giving them $50 to $100 per year is a good idea. It imposes a minimum amount of financial responsibility and makes it seem less difficult to start giving more later in life."

*I cut out luxuries by making small sacrifices. I pare costs by always eating breakfast at home, by bringing my lunch to work, and by cooking most nights of the week. That way I can enjoy a nice dinner out a few times a month, go to a concert, save up for events and outings that are more worthy of my money and time.*

"Be forward-looking and don't beat yourself up for past blunders," says Sheryl Garrett, president of Garrett Planning Network and a certified financial planner. Garrett recommends giving yourself an allowance each month after you've paid the necessary bills like rent, utilities, and savings contributions. "Give yourself the authority and permission to spend it. Give yourself the freedom."

## Financial Dieting

Identifying your expenses as well as your income is meant to give you a broad sense of your financial picture. Seeing how much you are spending on daily non-necessities should provide some motivation to cut back. And as you get used to how much money you spend in a typical month, it will become easier to gauge where you can skimp or how to save up for a splurge.

*The hardest thing about my first year out was trying to live on very little money. It was really hard for me to cut back my spending so that it remained within the bounds of what I made. Sure, I had gobs of education, but I didn't have ten bucks in my wallet to get a small pizza. Just day-to-day living in a city is so expensive.*

Budgeting is just discipline. Start with accurate information about what you spend. Identify the expenditures that matter least to you or those you are most willing to forego and trim away. Every time there's a significant change in your life—new job, place to live, expense, or income source—re-do your basic budget. You'll find that the discipline is really not that hard or time consuming, and there's great satisfaction in feeling in control of your money.

# Saving(s) Yourself

It's difficult to resist the urge to splurge. Temptations to spend—
Red Sox tickets, a group ski condo at Tahoe, the new Sony
PlayStation—are too powerful to resist. Saving is okay, but
spending is so much more fun.

But it's crucial to have a spot in your budget for savings.
Accumulating a stash of cash will establish your financial independence. It will also give you a big sense of accomplishment. It's
what you've always heard from Dad: Pay yourself first. That
means put a small amount of each paycheck—ten or fifteen percent, or a larger sum if you can afford it—into your savings. After
a while you will no longer even notice you're spending less cash,
and that's a good time to increase your savings deposit and save
more. Save until it hurts. Make it a priority.

"You must get in the habit of saving money and have the
experience of having money and not spending it," says Jim
Kniffen, certified financial planner and owner of Trinity Capital
Management.

*I have a self-imposed savings rule about automated
teller machines, the most insidious creations known to
man. I get paid twice a month: One paycheck a month
is sent directly to savings and one paycheck a month to
checking. By depositing them that way, it forces me
to be more conscious of how much I am saving. My
biggest downfall is getting money out of the ATM and
spending it as petty cash with absolutely no concept of
what it was spent on. So I try not to withdraw as much
at one time so that I am more conscious of what is in
my wallet.*

# The Fine Art of Scrimping

*Money is better than poverty, if only*
*for financial reasons.*
*—Woody Allen*

Don't waste money because you simply can't be bothered to save. Stop talking endlessly on the telephone without regard for evening and daytime phone rates. Buy and use a low-rate phone card, even at home. If you use a cellular phone, shop around to get the best plans for calls that you actually make and receive—there's no use paying for minutes and special features you don't even use. Stop purchasing brand-name products at the grocery store when generic ones will do—after all, the status attached to a bottle of Windex or a box of California Raisins is nil. Better yet, join a wholesale club and buy your groceries in bulk at discount prices. Stop spending a few dollars at the gym each day on a sports drink the color of antifreeze. Bring your own tap water instead. Compare gas prices at different stations and then pump it yourself.

Limit your consumption of new hardcover books; opt for a library card instead, or wait until the title comes out in paperback. Stop paying useless, unnecessary fees in the name of convenience: Return your DVD rental on time and walk the extra block to your own bank's ATM. Turn the heat down or the air conditioner off when you're out of the house all day. Take your lunch to work. Stop taking cabs everywhere you go and instead use public transportation—it's much cheaper and better for the environment, too. Buy items out of season when they are on sale. And if you're strapped for cash, don't rule out creative ways to make money outside of your regular job: bartending, an occasional babysitting gig, or helping your friends' parents with their landscaping.

Financial planners recommend saving a significant percentage of your net income in addition to building up your retirement fund. The goal is to create a healthy savings habit and, more important, begin building funds to pay for the things that grown-ups—and this means you—buy: a house, a car, large household appliances. "When you're just starting out, you have very few commitments—the time before you have babies, spouses, and houses. You have to put steps in motion to save money," says Garrett. "Save ten percent of your income—a dime of every dollar. Then don't touch it. Consider it sacred."

*I have become a saving fiend. After graduation I opened my first mutual fund with the leftover money I had from some lucrative summer waitressing jobs and monetary gifts from my family. No big deal, I thought, a little just-in-case money. Then I decided to donate a hundred dollars each week to my account. To my shock, this added up to more than five thousand dollars a year! Then I reasoned that I could donate an extra two dollars per week—would I really miss two dollars?—and save a hundred dollars a year more. It was too easy.*

Keep motivating yourself by setting goals and attempting to save a certain amount. The secret to successful saving is that you must make realistic, and occasionally tough, choices.

## Three Types of Savings

It may seem daunting, but your financial goal should be to have three types of savings accounts: for-emergencies-only, short-term, and long-term. Experts suggest saving an amount equal to three months' salary for emergencies. Without this fund you are defenseless against life's little—and, unfortunately, big—setbacks, such as losing your job, getting into a costly car accident, or contracting an illness that requires an expensive hospital stay or surgery. You can never control risk and there is usually no warning for such crises, so it's wise to protect against them.

Short-term savings—investments that maintain a stable value, pay interest, and can easily be liquidated for needed cash—can pay for big expenses you'll incur over the next three to seven years. Savings accounts are popular short-term savings vehicles for recent college grads, but banks may not be the best place to keep your money. While money in a savings account is insured by the federal government up to $100,000 and account minimums are often low, the one to two percent you earn in interest is paltry. You should keep as little money as possible in conventional savings accounts.

Your short-term savings and emergency fund should be in a higher-yielding savings vehicle such as a money market account. A money market, available at banks and other big financial service companies like Merrill Lynch and Vanguard, is marginally riskier than your standard savings account but you are compensated for that risk with higher interest payments. The interest gained from these accounts is usually anywhere between one-and-a-half to four percent. These accounts, which are typically offered by brokerages, banks, and mutual fund families, enable you to get hold of your money very quickly. Often, you can write checks or use an ATM card, which makes the account liquid. But do not let extra money languish in your checking account when you could be earning interest.

Long-term savings, on the other hand, is money that you don't need right away. You can tolerate greater risk—the ups and downs of the stock market, for example—with long-term savings

## Real World Common Sense: Savings

*Saving is a very fine thing.*
*Especially when your parents have done it for you.*
*—Winston Churchill*

Unless you're a trust fund baby, a rock star, or an agile seven-footer, the best way to get rich is to save. Saving works financial wonders for several reasons:

**1. The miracle of compounding.** When you save, your wealth not only grows by steadily adding more money to what you've already saved but also by what your money earns. Let your money work for you. Your savings earns interest, and then your interest earns interest. Your money never sleeps. While you're eating dinner, your money is working; while you're partying, your money is working; while you're watching TV, you're money is working. Compounding is relentless—and wonderful.

**2. Long-term perspective reduces risk.** One of the best long-term investments is the stock of healthy companies. Every company experiences ups and downs in the value of its stock, but over the long term the trajectory for most healthy companies is upward. The

because chances are you will come out ahead over time. Long-term saving is for things like a home, retirement, and your child's college education. Those are the big-ticket items in our lives, and they require some special planning.

## Good Debt, Bad Debt

In some ways, debt is one of the great tools of modern life. Without it, we would struggle to get an education, own a car, average annual return of the Dow Jones Industrial Average over the last thirty years is more than twelve percent. If you start saving early in life and do it regularly, you get to reap the advantage of this long-term growth.

**3. Save your raise because you don't miss what you haven't had.** If you've learned to live on a budget and you get a raise or bonus, some extra money from a source other than your primary job, or an inheritance, you can save much of the unbudgeted income without a change in your lifestyle. It's easy to let spending rise to the level of your income. But if you get in the habit, it's also easy and practically painless to let saving rise to the level of unneeded income.

**4. Take away the trial of taxes.** One of the great benefits of some long-term savings is that we can do it without paying taxes. Every dollar we spend in the year we earn it gets taxed at our highest marginal tax rate. But if we put that dollar in a 401(k) or an IRA or some other tax-deferred savings plan, we don't pay taxes when we earn it and we don't pay taxes on the income it generates through compounding or investment while it's in a tax-deferred savings plan. There's no savings like tax-deferred savings.

*never* own a home, or get through life's rough spots. There are times in life when it is perfectly rational to borrow money and create a debt for ourselves. But debt is also one of life's great dangers, as there are many young people who accumulate more debt than they can possibly repay.

It's important at the outset to distinguish between good debt and bad debt. Good debt has two prominent characteristics. First, we are borrowing money for something of long-term, permanent value that we couldn't afford without going into debt. Loans for getting an education or a mortgage for owning a house are good debts. These are good investments for most of us and they're too expensive to purchase without a loan. They have long-term value in our lives.

The second characteristic of a good debt is that we've undertaken it with a rational plan for paying it off. We've carefully calculated what our financial resources will be over the life of the debt and we've determined that we will have enough funds every month to pay the principal and the interest on the debt. We entered the world of the indebted with our eyes wide open and our plans for survival hatched.

Bad debt is what we acquire when we spend more in the short term than we earn. Our monthly or annual expenditures exceed our incomes. We have to borrow money to pay our electric bills or our rent. If you find yourself in debt because you've been eating out too often, or buying clothes that are more expensive than you can afford, or otherwise living beyond your means, you're headed toward debtor's prison. Unchecked, those habits are sure to become a source of severe financial—and soon legal—pain. And for many young people, the road to bad debt is usually paved with plastic.

## Understanding Credit Cards

The unofficial initiation to the Real World often comes in your mailbox in the form of gratuitous, too-good-to-be true credit card solicitations. Expect to receive several letters each week luring you to sign up for one card after another: "You've been pre-selected to qualify for this fantastic offer!" Better yet, you receive phone calls from agents: "We're only extending this great introductory rate to our most valued customers—this means you!" they trill; "Low interest rates, no annual fees!"

Credit card companies send out millions of solicitations for cards every year and dangle lots of incentives to entice you to sign up. They offer an array of sweet, fun trinkets: free plastic goodies like Frisbees, thermoses, magnets, and pens. But really, these are low-cost bribes. For once you've signed up, that low introductory interest rate may increase to a much higher one.

There are two primary kinds of credit accounts. Revolving accounts—MasterCard and Visa, for example—allow you to pay in full each month or make a partial payment that is a percentage of your outstanding balance. Revolving credit card accounts can have very high interest rates, so it's definitely in your financial interest to pay your bill in full each month.

Charge accounts, like most credit cards, don't even give you the option of paying a portion of the balance each month. You have to pay it all. This can be a good option if you want to avoid getting in over your head with long-term debt.

Credit cards are fun and convenient. The danger of credit cards, however, is clear: They enable you to spend more than you can afford. Those sexy slivers of plastic beg you to fund extravagances and then declare innocence when the tab arrives. After all, it seems painless enough; the bill says you owe thousands, but the credit card company expects only an itsy-bitsy token payment. No biggie, you think. Ordinarily you might not have splurged on that sweater, those skis, that Caribbean vacation, but credit cards made it so easy.

*I knew that I had hit rock bottom when I was paying for my groceries with a credit card. I got out of school and quickly realized that I had no idea how to budget myself and manage my expenses. I thought*

*credit cards were my savior, but eighteen-percent in-*
*terest rates later, I see how misguided I was. I think all*
*college students should be required to take a class on*
*how credit cards can ruin your life. I wish I had.*

But we can't blame the plastic. Credit cards don't rack up debt; people rack up debt. "Credit cards make it so that you spend money you don't have to buy things you don't need to impress people you don't like," says Jim Kniffen, the financial planner.

Dependence on credit cards often begins in college. The average undergraduate owes a jaw-dropping $2,748 on credit cards, an increase of almost $1,000 in just two years, according to Sallie Mae, the nation's largest student loan agency. And today, U.S. household credit card debt is a staggering $600 billion. Americans are addicted to debt.

## Piloting the Pitfalls of Plastic

There is a good reason to have and use a credit card beyond the obvious one of convenience. At some point in life, you'll seek a loan for something that's very important to you. You'll want to have a good credit history when you do. Your credit history is an indication of how reliably you pay back money you borrow for credit purchases, car loans, home mortgages, and other debts. Your credit report will reflect whether you pay these bills on time, and whether you pay the entire amounts due.

Think of your credit report as an SAT score that indicates your financial smarts. Not only will a good credit report increase your purchasing leverage, but prospective loan officers, potential employers, and landlords may use it to judge your character and

## Real World Realities:
## Credit Card Glossary

*Annual percentage rate*—The interest rate reflecting the total yearly cost of the interest on a loan, expressed as a percentage rate. With credit cards, usually high.

*Annual fee*—A bank charge for use of a credit card imposed each year, typically ranging from $15 to $300. The fee appears on the customer's monthly statement. Many credit cards come without an annual fee—definitely the way to go.

*Grace period*—The interest-free period of time a lender allows between the transaction date and the billing date. The standard grace period is between twenty and thirty days. Those who carry a balance on their credit cards have no grace period.

*Balance transfer*—The process of moving credit card debt from one issuer to another. Many issuers offer low rates to encourage balance transfers coming in and balance transfer fees to discourage them from going out.

*Cash advance fee*—A charge levied by the bank for using credit cards to obtain cash. This fee can be stated in terms of a flat per-transaction fee or a percentage of the amount of the cash advance—in either case, an expensive prospect.

*Minimum payment*—The smallest amount a cardholder can pay to keep the account from going into default. Some card issuers will set a high minimum if they are uncertain of the cardholder's ability to pay. You should be paying off your credit card balance completely each month, but at the very least make your minimum payments on time, to avoid costly late fees.

determine whether you're trustworthy. There are several ways to maintain a solid credit history.

First, keep your account active. A zero balance doesn't demonstrate you can manage debt. It simply shows you refrain from breaking out the plastic. Use your card for small items; low-cost purchases make it easier for you to pay off a bill.

Second, pay your bill on time. Pay off as much of your balance each month as you possibly can so that you won't rack up finance charges. Credit cards make it easy to charge a "must-have" purchase, even when your cash supply is low. But when the bill arrives and you can't afford to pay the full balance, you start accumulating finance charges. Credit cards enable you spend more because the pain doesn't register immediately, as with cash.

Third, do not maintain more than one credit card. This holds true particularly if your goal is to increase your borrowing power. We've all seen the folks who pluck out their wallets and their credit cards fan out like a glorious plastic poker hand. You should have only one card that you use regularly—one without an annual fee.

If you are prone to credit problems, there are other options to consider that will enable you to build a good credit history. You might opt for a credit card issued by a local store or a gasoline company. Use this card responsibly and you'll show you're able to handle your finances. Or you could cajole one of your parents or a fiscally responsible relative into co-signing for your credit account if you don't qualify by yourself. But be warned: If you don't pay your bill, the credit card company will require your co-signer to pay it.

*I've tricked myself into believing that I actually have a sizable disposable income. Things come up—friends going out for drinks after work, a weekend away with my girlfriend—and I have a hard time saying no. I figure that I am already in debt for $5,000, what harm will $20 more do? And so I just charge it. I never buy anything for myself, and all my money goes for incidentals like gas, movies, and beers. I don't want to change my lifestyle, I just want to have fun.*

Down that road lies trouble. There are some basic rules of good practice that all credit card users should follow.

Have a credit card with a very low interest rate. When you do not pay in full the amount you owe, your account accrues interest. Most issuers charge a variable percentage based on an underlying interest rate, such as the prime rate, the interest a bank charges to its best customers. The amount you are charged fluctuates according to a formula based on the prime rate.

Monitor your credit card purchases between bills so that you are not staggered by what you owe when the bill arrives. Hold on to those credit card receipts and keep a running tab or look at your statement online so you know when to apply the spending brakes. Let the first time you're shocked by your credit card balance be the last. Surprise is a terrible way to run your financial affairs. And don't plead ignorance about your credit card spending.

*When I start to get overwhelmed with credit card bills, I take a stand against impulse purchases. I take the card out of my wallet for a month or two—*

*no need to do anything so drastic as cutting it in half.
It's amazing how much it helps me cut back on my
spending.*

Stay out of debt. Pay off your balance every month. At the
very least, you'll end up paying a lot more for your purchases
than the original price. Worse, if you are able to afford only the
minimum payment each month, which covers only interest
charges, you may never be able to get out of debt. *Ever.* You may
not be able to get a loan to pay for graduate school. You could
have creditors writing you scary, threatening letters and generally
making your life miserable.

*I was a credit card junkie. As I get further from
college life, my needs and wants change. For instance,
I don't want roommates, so my expenses are higher on
my own. And I want nicer things that cost more, and
I'm responsible for paying for those things. I landed
in credit card hell for six months and paid dearly in
finance charges. Ever since I started paying in full every
month I am acutely aware of how my spending fluctuates, what I spend money on, and what I need to be
more careful about.*

Use a debit card. Debit cards are another way to eliminate
credit card abuse. Debit cards, the just-as-cute-but-not-as-racy
sister of credit cards, are linked electronically to your checking
account so that you don't run up any debt: you cannot spend
more than what's in your account. Debit cards, which often carry

the Visa or MasterCard insignia, can be used as an ATM card and are accepted at most businesses.

Many financial advisors are strong advocates of debit cards—particularly for debt-prone recent college graduates. But debit cards are not necessarily a perfect alternative to credit cards, which offer superior consumer protection. If you lose your credit card, or if it's stolen and the thief goes on an $8,000 shopping spree at an herbal-diet drugstore—hey, it's happened to me—federal law limits your liability to a mere $50. With a debit card, $8,000 is the price you pay. Plus, with debit cards you lose what's called "the float"—the twenty to thirty days that your money is in your bank account earning interest before you have to pay the credit card bill. That cushion also gives you time to return defective merchandise or dispute a transaction before you have to pay for it.

## Conquering Credit Card Debt

What if you find yourself in deep credit card debt? What then? The answer is to make a plan and stick to it. Do not apply for yet another credit card. Be constantly aware of exactly how much money you owe to discourage yourself from going out and charging even more. Pay as much of your outstanding balance on your cards each month as you possibly can. If you have debt on more than one card, pay off the card that has the highest interest rate first.

If you're having trouble keeping yourself from overcharging, cut up your credit cards, then call the credit card companies and tell them to close your accounts. "Make a list of everything you owe—car loans, student loans, credit cards—and then prioritize that list in payment terms and interest rates. Obviously the higher the interest rate, the higher the priority," suggests Bill Cullinan, president of the National Foundation for Credit Counseling. "Then determine how much in addition to the minimum amount you can afford to pay each month."

If bills are mounting and you're using credit to pay for groceries and basic utilities, then you may be able to negotiate with your credit card company for some financial relief. Most collection agencies are willing to reduce monthly payments to temporarily ease your burden.

But when frivolity and pure laziness are forcing you into the red, it is indeed time to make a lifestyle change. Spending recklessly is stupid. Do not persuade yourself that a luxury item is actually a necessity. When you're about to make an impulsive purchase, ask yourself: Do I really need this? And, even more important: Can I *afford* this?

We are a plastic society, says Suzanne Hunstad of IHateFinancialPlanning.com, a personal finance Web site, but it is imperative that you minimize your personal debt. "If you can see the cash—the green stuff flowing through your fingers or feel a lightened pocketbook—every time you make a purchase, then you will inevitably spend less. Don't jeopardize your long-term future for instant pleasure."

## Student Loans: Not a Life-or-Debt Situation

Unfortunately, many of us are saddled with significant debt even before we get a real job and think about how to handle it. We just know there are all these little coupons, and every month we have to send one off with a check. After four years of studying, reveling, and carousing, graduation comes and brings with it five-figure debt. It's payback time.

## Dealing with Debt: Helpful Web Sites

**www.cccsintl.org**
Consumer Credit Counseling Service provides budget counseling, educational programs, debt management assistance, and housing counseling.

**www.moneymanagement.org**
Money Management International provides financial guidance, free credit counseling, and debt management assistance.

**www.myvesta.org**
MyVesta—The Financial Health Center offers credit and financial assistance.

Half of college students graduate with student-loan debt, with the average debt around $12,000, according to the American Council on Education.

Student loan debt does not signal financial crisis and it does not have to interfere with your lifestyle. In fact, most graduates with student loans are able to go about their lives without much impact on their spending habits. The average percentage of borrowers' monthly income that goes toward that debt is 12 percent, according to the Sallie Mae Foundation, a provider of education loans.

First, congratulate yourself. You've made an investment in your future. You've earned a college degree that can ensure better job opportunities and higher earning potential in years to come. Student loans, along with mortgages, are considered "good debt"—real investments in your life that don't cost you a lot of interest.

Second, breathe easy. You'll probably have a grace period—a payment-free interval after you graduate and before any money is due—that typically lasts for six months. But don't exhale for too long. This transition time allows you to prepare for the repayment of your loan.

Use your grace period sensibly. Compare repayment options to determine the best option for you. Set up your retirement fund *before* you begin repayment. Create a budget with a little latitude so that your loan bills will not traumatize your checking account. And if you've received a monetary gift for graduation or even a signing bonus, prepay a portion of your loan with that money. Remember that paying off debt, especially debt that is not tax-deductible, is usually the wisest way to invest your money.

> *While I am hardly the recipient of a fat weekly paycheck, it was a big deal to pay off my student loan with no help from my parents. When I sent that last check in, I realized that I was truly on my own.*

Investigate money sources. In some cases employers might even help out with the student loans. There are many government programs that will assist you if you agree to sign on for a particular time frame. In addition, there are some teaching programs that offer debt-reduction incentives for recent graduates. Talk to your college's financial aid office or career center to find out more information on this.

Finally, get organized. Gather all of your loan documents in one place. Review these papers to make sure you understand your obligations and have worked the amount of money you owe into your monthly budget.

You definitely want to set up direct debit from your bank account to the lender or an online payment system. Automated bill paying ensures that you don't miss payments and that they won't be late, and it also works wonders for your self-control.

*Automated payments were critical to my repayment success. They provided me with much greater willpower than I would have been able to muster on my own. The money moved out of my account so quickly that I never viewed it as mine to spend. It went straight to Sallie Mae.*

There are practical, financial inducements to make automated payments, too. Some lenders knock a percentage point off your loan if you're willing to have the money deducted from your checking account. Others create incentives, such as cash back for example, to pay your loans on time, says Ray Loewe, president of College Money, a firm that specializes in advising parents on college financial planning. "You can ruin your credit pretty fast if you don't make your loan payments on time. And it takes a long time to repair."

Debt can be a huge financial drag, so you'll want to put any extra money you can toward paying down that debt.

*Understanding that the longer the repayment period, the more I would pay to my lender provided me with additional motivation to pay back my loan as fast*

*as possible. To do this I committed to paying 30 per-*
*cent more than the minimum payment each month and*
*applying income tax refunds, year-end bonuses, birth-*
*day checks from my grandparents, or any other 'found*
*money' to my loan. I was anxious to reach the point*
*where my paychecks were really my paychecks.*

## Payment Impossible

If only the government were as forgiving as Mom and Dad with short-term loans, we'd all be in great shape. Unfortunately, it's not. Student loans are not like other kinds of consumer debt—they will never be forgiven, even if you file for bankruptcy.

It may seem impossible to come up with the payments for your student loan, but luckily there are alternatives. You may be eligible through the Federal Family Education Act for a graduated or income-sensitive repayment schedule, where you pay less in the beginning while you are getting established and pay more later as your earnings increase. Under this plan your monthly payment is adjusted each year to reflect changes in your total monthly income and the amount of student loan debt.

Or you might opt for a graduated repayment plan where you pay the interest, not the principal, in the first few years, enabling you to begin repaying the loan at a lower payment than normal. Periodically the payment will increase until the full balance of the loan is paid off within a ten-year repayment period.

*I left college with $20,000 in loans. The initial*
*monthly payments were astronomical—nearly $350*
*per month. I couldn't swing it, so luckily I was able*

*to defer the principal payments and just pay the interest amount, which was much more reasonable. I'm still on that plan but try to pay a little extra each month toward the original amount. I'm more resigned to the fact that the loan is there and it will be for a while.*

Consider consolidating your student loans with a bank or a loan agency. Consolidating—combining multiple loans from different programs and different lenders into a single loan—enables you to lower your monthly payments by extending your repayment period. You may also be able to lower your interest rate. However, like other extensions, consolidation may result in paying a higher amount of interest.

Extending repayment over time, however, is not wise unless you've exhausted all other alternatives. "You're putting off the inevitable and making it worse," says Ray Loewe. "Extending the terms of your loan creates a monster problem because some day down the road you may want to buy a house and you'll still have loans hanging over your head. Pay off your debt as quickly as you can within reason."

If you find yourself in a grim financial state, there are drastic measures available, too. You may be eligible for a deferment, which allows you to temporarily stop your payment if you meet certain criteria. Deferments are offered for working mothers, graduate students, and military personnel, or even sometimes for those enduring economic hardship. There are other options, too. "Forbearance," for example, is a provisional postponement or delay in your payments based on the discretion of your lender.

## Cost of a $50,000 Loan at 8 Percent Interest

| Term of Loan in Years | Monthly Payment | Total Cost of Loan |
|---|---|---|
| 5 | $1,014 | $60,829 |
| 10 | $607 | $72,797 |
| 15 | $478 | $86,009 |
| 20 | $418 | $100,373 |
| 30 | $367 | $132,078 |

Remember that when you finally pay off your loan it will feel great and snipping the purse strings is a big step toward independence.

# April 15: A Day of Reckoning

At the end of the year your employer sends both you and the Internal Revenue Service a W-2 form that reports your income and the taxes that were withheld in the previous tax year. It's your responsibility to determine how much you owe for the entire year and pay the difference—or file for a refund check for the amount you overpaid—by April 15.

Chances are you've filed tax returns in the past for summer jobs or internships, but it's likely those forms were very simple. Unfortunately, it gets more complicated as you make more. You shouldn't fear taxes, even though it's understandable why they're intimidating. The tax code is riddled with mind-boggling jargon: deductions, credits, exclusions, enhancements, phase-outs.

Paying taxes is your duty for life, and there's no better time to begin to learn how to prepare and file a tax return than when you're young and things are relatively simple. Start with the basics and add to your knowledge as need requires. Don your green visor, get out your calculator, and have at it.

In your first year out of college, the standard deduction will probably be the organizing principle of your tax-paying life. "If you have a basic wage and you're taking the standard deduction, then you should be able to prepare your own taxes without the help of an accountant," says accountant Michael Dentamaro. "It depends on the complexity of your finances. The IRS forms will assist you. Read them carefully."

*Doing my own taxes is not at all the nightmare I thought it was going to be. The forms are intimidating, but if you just follow them logically, they're pretty painless. I was caught off guard, though, when I cashed a couple of savings bonds I had been given as a little kid by grandparents. They don't take taxes out when you cash them, so at the end of the year when you're expecting a refund, you end up paying about a third of what you got when you cashed the bonds. I was annoyed when I owed something like $700 to the IRS at age twenty-three!*

Software programs and online taxpaying services have made it much easier to pay taxes without the help of an accountant. It is inexpensive—most services charge about $20. And the best part is you'll get your refund more quickly than many paper filers will. Alternatively, if you owe the government

## Real World Realities: Tax Brackets?

You always thought of the money you earned during the year as one lump sum—affectionately known as your income. But the IRS puts income earners into categories based on how much money they make. That's because income tax is a graduated tax, designed so that people pay an increasing percentage as their income rises through various tax brackets.

This is important because the rate of tax you are paying on your highest dollars of income is called your marginal tax rate, and it can have an impact on your financial decisions. For instance, the higher your tax bracket, the more attractive investments like tax-free municipal bonds or home mortgages become.

Any W-2 forms or other information you receive about interest, dividends, and deductions have also been sent to the IRS, so look them over thoroughly. In addition to the W-2, you might also receive 1099s, like the 1099-B, 1099-DIV, or 1099-INT, which report income from financial transactions—in this case, capital gains, dividends, or interest income, respectively. These transactions get reported on the schedules that round out your 1040, the standard income tax form. Be sure to add these documents to your newly acquired filing system.

money, you can have it automatically withdrawn from your checking account.

If this is too overwhelming, you could always hire an accountant. But even if you opt for the hand-holding of a professional, it's unwise to surrender all your big money decisions to someone else. There is so much information about managing your personal finances—books, Web sites, magazines, newspapers, entire television channels devoted to money—that even the most numerically challenged can blossom into a shrewd manager of finances.

## The Big Plunge: Investing Your Money

So you're reading this chapter on money and you're following along pretty well. Budgeting: check. Taxes: got it. Credit cards: yup. Suddenly you come to this section, on investing, and your first instinct is to skip it altogether. Don't. This is important stuff.

I know what you're thinking. "I can't afford to invest. It's too risky. I can barely pay my rent, let alone come up with a couple hundred bucks to stick in the stock market. Investing is something for middle-aged people."

Amazing, eh? I read your mind. How did I do it? I know what you're thinking because a few years ago I was just like you. I had problems investing my money. Fear and ignorance were dominant among them. The stock market is intimidating, I thought. I didn't understand bonds or mutual funds. Who or what is Charles Schwab? I wondered.

Few people know about this stuff when they're just starting to earn a real living. Like most everything else, investing is a learned set of skills best acquired one at a time. If you start simply, then build a more sophisticated portfolio as you grow more knowledgeable—and wealthier—you'll find that investing is not only manageable but fun.

Besides, you'll easily get the hang of investing. And you're lucky enough to be investing at a time when there is plenty of literature on how to get started. There are twenty-four-hour television networks devoted to every movement of the stock

## Terms of Investment

*Appreciation*—An increase in the value of an asset such as a stock, bond, or real estate.

*Blue-chip stocks*—Stocks of experienced companies that have paid dividends in both good and bad years. Investments in blue-chip stocks are typically considered conservative.

*Capital gain*—The difference between an asset's purchase price and selling price; it's called a capital gain only if it's a positive number.

*Dividend*—Cash or stock payment to shareholders of a particular company used to distribute the profits of the company.

*Hedge fund*—A type of investment fund that pools money from investors and invests in a variety of markets. Hedge funds usually require a very high initial investment, charge a management fee of 1 to 2 percent, and take the first 20 percent of profits for themselves.

*Index fund*—A mutual fund that invests in stocks upon which an index is based. For instance, an index fund based on the Dow Jones Industrial Average invests in all the stocks included in that index. Index fund performance closely mirrors the performance of the index itself.

*Money market*—A mutual fund that invests only in money market investments. Most money funds allow limited check writing. An investment in a money market fund is not insured or guaranteed by the U.S. government.

*Standard & Poor's 500*—An index of 500 large, leading companies that represent the overall stock market. The index is market-value weighted, which means that stock prices are multiplied by the number of shares outstanding. The S&P 500 is the most widely followed benchmark for portfolio performance.

market. There are heaps of magazines, books, and Web sites specifically tailored for neophyte investors. Seek them out. They can help.

## Investment Basics

The two most important rules of investing are *start early* and *diversify*. Investing early in your life—as in *now*—enables you to get the largest return later. The earlier you start to save, the less you may need to invest. The aim is for the principal, your initial investment and the amount that earns interest, to compound—your interest earning interest—for as long as possible.

You can get ahead by stashing money now and letting the interest compound. Interest can compound annually, quarterly, monthly, weekly, or even daily. The more frequently your interest is compounded, the more your money will grow. Even if you have student loans hanging over your head, even if you have car payments to make, it's essential that you scrape together some money and invest it. Over the long term, your investment will compound and will amount to more than the interest on your loans.

Let's consider three individuals who plan to retire at age 65 and have $5,000 earmarked for their retirement investment (see page 214). Our first investor, Sally Smartiepants, invests her $5,000 at the age of 22, and by the time she reaches retirement, she has built up a nest egg of $301,200. Our second investor, Willie Waitawhile, waits until age 35 to invest his $5K and ends up with $87,247. Our last investor, Nellie Notsoswift, waits until age 55 to invest $5,000 and in ten years has accumulated only $12,699. (All calculations assume a ten-percent rate of return.) It's clear that the earlier you invest, the bigger the effect that compounding will have on your investment.

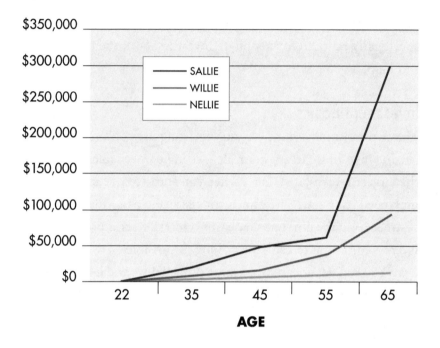

Even though you're earning money through the power of compounding, you must add to your investment gradually over time in order to secure a comfortable retirement. Even small increments can contribute significantly toward your financial bottom line, as the graph on page 215 demonstrates. Here the comparison is between two people. One invests $5,000 at age 22 but nothing more after that. The second invests $5,000 at age 22, then $2,000 a year thereafter.

The second important rule is to diversify your investments. This involves asset allocation: Blending your savings, stocks, and money market funds until your portfolio—your collection of investments—reflects your savings objectives and your tolerance for risk. In calculating your risk tolerance, consider your job security (Could you survive a corporate downsizing?) and need for

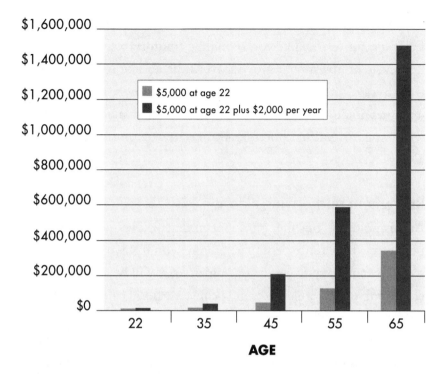

$1,600,000
$1,400,000
$1,200,000
$1,000,000
$800,000
$600,000
$400,000
$200,000
$0

■ $5,000 at age 22
■ $5,000 at age 22 plus $2,000 per year

22    35    45    55    65

**AGE**

access to a nest egg. (Do you plan to buy a house soon?) On a personal level, risk includes your psychological and emotional ability to endure the market's fluctuations. (Will you glue yourself to MSNBC and stay up at night fretting over the doings of the Dow?)

If there is a time to relish risk, however, your early twenties is it. Young investors can afford to lose a little money, especially if they are investing for the long haul and do not need to tap into a large sum soon. But youth doesn't last that long. And nobody—including the so-called financial Masters of the Universe—really knows what the market is going to do. Don't try to time the market—getting in when a stock is low and out when it peaks. And it's dangerous to invest solely in one particular stock, even that handsome little biotech start-up that your buddy promised would go through the roof.

Markets move up and down. It's what's known as volatility. Long-term investors like you should be comfortable with the natural cycle of investment growth over time and be willing to ride the waves of the market. Some days you go down, some you go up—you don't actually lose money unless you panic and sell. But over time, diversified portfolios trend upward, or at least they always have.

## Retirement and Savings Plans

At this point in your life, it's doubtful that you've spent any time pondering your retirement. You assume you'll leave the working world by age sixty-five and your older years will be a haze of big, comfortable cars, cruises to sunny climates, floral caftans, and impeccably groomed golf courses. Sounds good. But these fantasies will require some money and planning. You may be young, but you need to start building a nest egg now so that when you're ready for that fancy retirement resort lined with palm trees, it will be ready for you.

*I am only twenty-four but I'm saving for retirement—preferably, early retirement. I like to think of the working world as a terrible marriage: You'll eventually get out, but only after you've been robbed of your youth and idealism. Your best option is to go for a smooth, no-fault divorce as soon as possible—a smooth no-fault divorce being, in this case, early and fiscally secure retirement.*

With employer-sponsored retirement programs such as 401(k) plans, Keoghs, and 403(b) plans, saving money is downright easy.

## Finding a Financial Planner

In striving to be a serious saver, even if you're starting out with only a small sum to invest, your goal is to make sound financial decisions. When those sums become larger, your aim is to make consistently sound decisions. And sometimes you might need a little help from an expert. But to whom should you entrust your life savings?

Ask your friends, relatives, or colleagues to recommend a financial planner; word-of-mouth is a fine way to meet a trustworthy professional. There are also referral lines at various financial planning associations available online. These organizations will send you a list of qualified professionals in your area.

Contact the financial planners on your list and find out about them. Many will send you a packet of information about what they do and a synopsis of their investment style and strategy. Others may give you basic information on the phone. Most financial planners offer a complimentary initial interview, so make an effort to meet the advisors that appeal to you most. Be sure to ask specific questions about their background and approach to investing:

What are your qualifications? What do you specialize in?

Could anyone besides me benefit from your recommendations?

What is your approach to financial planning?

What services do you offer?

How much do you typically charge? How are those charges applied?

How will I pay you?

SOURCE: Financial Planners Standards Council (www.cfp-ca.org)

There are usually a bevy of investment options: mutual funds, stocks, and/or bonds. Investing money through your 401(k) plan gives you the benefit of tax-deferred saving. This lets you increase your take-home pay and decrease your current taxable income. You figure out how much money you want deducted from your paycheck, usually up to fifteen percent, and that money is drawn off in pre-tax dollars. That means you don't have to pay taxes on the income that you invested that year in a tax-deferred investment plan. And most employers match your contributions up to a certain amount. The combination of pre-tax investment and employer matching contributions allows you to add approximately two dollars to your 401(k) for every dollar allocated from your paycheck.

> *I never look at my paychecks and just get direct deposit with the 401(k) money already taken out. It's a psychological fake-out I play: I figure that I just grin and bear it and pretend that I never get the money in the first place. And I never miss what I never knew I had.*

Financial experts recommend putting in the maximum amount your company allows—especially in your early years of working. This period of compounding interest is most beneficial. Best of all, your investment is protected from federal and local taxes until you withdraw the money, presumably when you retire and find yourself in a lower tax bracket. But for unexpected needs, many plans allow employees to dip into their account balances before retirement, mostly through loans.

## Roth IRA (Individual Retirement Account)

Created as part of the Taxpayer Relief Act of 1997 and originally named the American Dream IRA, the Roth IRA is one of the best investment vehicles around. Your contributions are pre-tax up to certain income limits, and the money compounds tax-deferred; in other words, no taxes are deducted from your initial investment, which allows the compounding effect to be maximized.

"Young people aren't typically thinking about retirement," concedes Mary Kline-Cueter, a certified public accountant, "But if you can start to save in a Roth IRA tax-free, when you're older you'll be thrilled about how that money doubled and quadrupled over time."

In a traditional IRA, investment gains are tax-deferred but you do pay taxes when you withdraw. But with the Roth IRA, you don't owe Uncle Sam any money on withdrawals—as long as you are at least 59½ years old and have had the account for five years. You will not, however, pay a penalty if you withdraw earlier for particular purposes such as buying your first home or paying for your children's college education.

The great advantage of the Roth IRA is the ability to have investment earnings avoid taxation. The disadvantage is that you don't get a deduction when you contribute to the Roth IRA, and you qualify for a Roth only if your annual income is below $100,000—unfortunately, a feat too easily accomplished by the new graduate.

## Traditional IRA

Similar to a Roth IRA, the traditional IRA allows you to save money for retirement while allowing the savings to grow tax-free.

## Good Reads

In addition to the books mentioned in this chapter, you might find these helpful:

*Your Money Matters: 21 Tips for Achieving Financial Security in the 21st Century,* by Jonathan Pond (The Berkeley Publishing Group, 1999).

*Right on the Money: Taking Control of Your Personal Finances,* by Chris Farrell (Villard Books, 2000).

*Debt-Free by 30: Practical Advice for the Young, Broke, & Upwardly Mobile,* by Jason Anthony and Karl Cluck (Plume, 2001).

The IRA converts investment earnings—interest, dividends, and capital gains—into plain old income. Again, contributions are limited, but funds in an IRA may be invested in a variety of stocks and bonds. And many people, especially younger people, can deduct their IRA contributions from their gross income.

You may withdraw from a traditional IRA at any time, but the IRS imposes a 10-percent penalty on withdrawals made before the magic age of 59½. The Roth IRA is far and away the better option.

## Mutual Funds

Mutual funds are an ideal way to get started playing the market. The fund combines lots of people's money to create a pool for a fund manager, who has studied the intricacies and nuances of the market for years, to invest in a selected portfolio of bonds and stocks. Stocks take a lot of work, but with mutual funds, money managers do the work so you don't have to.

There are many mutual funds to choose from. Some specialize in a particular sector like technology or pharmaceuticals. Others pride themselves on aggressive, high-risk, high-reward investments. Still others are socially conscious and invest in eco-friendly companies. There are index funds—a personal favorite—that purchase shares of all the stocks in a predetermined stock index, such as the Standard & Poor's 500.

"With mutual funds, you have automatic diversity which offers safety and growth potential. And you get professional management," says Jeff Wuorio, author of *Got Money?: Enjoy It, Manage It—Even Save Some of It—Financial Advice for Your Twenties and Thirties*. "Look for one that's reasonably aggressive. You're young and you have a long time frame to invest."

This requires some research on your part. Look into the funds to see what they invest in—technology or international companies, for example. Start deciding now how you want to invest. No matter which you choose, you should opt for what's called a "no-load" mutual fund, one that does not charge fees for moving money in or out.

## Bonds

A bond is a debt security, an IOU. When you purchase a bond, you are lending money to a government, municipality, corporation, federal agency, or other entity known as the issuer. In return for the loan, the issuer promises to pay you a predetermined rate of interest during the life of the bond and to repay the face value of the bond—the principal—when it matures. You are taxed when these are paid out.

The bottom line with bonds is this: low risk, low return. If you want to retire before you're too old to move, don't let that same formula describe your youthful investing strategy. Take a chance on the market sooner rather than later, and chances are you'll be surprised and amazed by the stash of cash you'll have waiting for you when you *choose* to retire.

# chapter six

# it's the only body
# YOU'LL EVER HAVE

MOST YOUNG PEOPLE are relatively healthy without having to work too hard at it. That's one big reason our middle-aged peers speak wistfully about being twenty-two again. We're famous for believing that we're invincible and indestructible. We think we'll live forever, so we take risks and court danger. We don't always get around to seeing the doctor when we know we should. We balk at buying health insurance. We might drink too much. We regard the Surgeon General as Chicken Little and never read, let alone heed, his warnings. When we drive, we treat the speed limit like the opening bid in a negotiation. We practice birth control like we used to practice the piano: inconsistently. We get too little sleep and eat too much junk food.

But since we're immortal, none of that matters, right? Get real—that's also why we're regarded by those same wistful middle-agers as naïve.

I, for one, had always taken my health for granted. Aside from an occasional head cold or a biannual bout with strep throat, illnesses were few. I knew I wasn't in immediate danger of having a heart attack or getting cancer, at least statistically. And I've always been in pretty good physical condition.

Just my luck. I'd had twenty-one years of near-perfect health and full coverage on my parents' health plan; then, just three weeks into living on my own, I woke up with a terrible pain in my side. I knew I needed medical attention but I didn't have a doctor. I didn't even know where a hospital was. This had never happened before and I didn't know what to do. I found a phone book and madly searched for the emergency room number. Here's a fact: There is no emergency room listed under "emergency" or "room" in the phone book.

I did finally find the name of a hospital and a friend to drive me there. When I arrived I expected an instant greeting from a handsome Croatian named Luka or a cute resident named Dr. Carter. Instead, I was handed a clipboard, pointed toward a plastic chair, and told to fill out approximately three hundred forms. All the while, the pain was growing worse and worse. After many rotations of the clock, a very young doctor looked at me briefly, posed some terse questions, then scribbled a few words on my chart and moved on. A few minutes later the woman behind the glass panel handed me an unreadable prescription and sent me off to the pharmacy. Weeks later I received a hefty bill.

I survived all this—the illness and the bill—but I learned valuable lessons about health insurance and medical care that I'll share now with you: They're complicated and they're costly.

While your twenties are likely to be a time of good health and a strong body, you need to put in a little effort now to make sure that blissful condition continues. This chapter is about taking good care of and protecting your health. It's about selecting adequate health insurance, maintaining a proper level of fitness, watching the foods and liquids and perhaps chemicals that you ingest, and controlling your stress level. It's about feeling safe and secure in your new surroundings. And it's about seeing a doctor regularly and dealing with health issues now, so that they don't lead to life-or-death problems.

## Health Issues for the Healthy

You may discover that your health improves dramatically after you graduate. A lot of people do. College is no health spa: pulling all-nighters writing term papers, trolling the pasta bar at the dining hall, the contagious laziness of dormitory life, and too many rounds of beer pong.

> *In my first year out, the regularity of my new schedule helped motivate me to exercise more and eat better food. I stopped drinking during the week and had no need to stay up as late either. Having excellent health insurance through my job, I had my first physical exam in three years and went to the dentist for the first time in four years. I lost ten pounds and my skin cleared up. Getting out of the college atmosphere and routine saved me.*

Now your health is your own responsibility. Let that sink in a minute because that's the key point here. Your family doctor is many miles away. There's no twenty-four-hour infirmary a few yards from your dorm.

Remember: It's the only body you'll ever have. Don't be

## Real World Common Sense:
## Stock Your Medicine Cabinet

Some day, some time, you will almost surely slice your finger cutting a bagel, come down with the flu, get a splinter in your heel, or just plain have a headache. Be prepared for the inevitable.

Since you're building a medicine cabinet from scratch, it's good to start with the basics: aspirin or ibuprofen. You may want to stockpile other drugs like decongestants, cough suppressants, and antihistamines. Experts also recommend keeping medical supplies on hand: a thermometer, special medicine spoon, bandages in assorted sizes, antiseptics like hydrogen peroxide and rubbing alcohol, tweezers, and antibiotic ointment.

Be sure to throw away items that have expired or are not potent enough to offer relief. Check expiration dates. If medicine appears discolored, chuck it. Prescription medication should remain in its original container and be stored in a location that is cool and dry, not in the bathroom, as the humidity can decompose and alter the effect of the drugs.

passive and don't skimp—keep up-to-date with your doctor's visits, exercise regularly, play it safe. Don't wait until you get sick to find a doctor and deal with the hassle of health insurance. It's also smart to get a big check-up just before going out on your own, when you still have college health insurance or at least parents willing to pay.

## The Common Cold

The health problem you're most likely to confront in your first year out of school is the common cold: post-nasal drip, hacking coughs, aching head. In fact, the average adult endures two to four of them each a year. You've probably nursed yourself back to health from one of these babies with a little chicken soup, orange juice, and a Blockbuster video or two. But that was then, when parents hovered over you or the infirmary took you in.

In the Real World, colds are just as miserable but sympathy and TLC are harder to find. Offices, like dorms, are breeding grounds for germs and other health threats. And during flu season —December to early April—expect coughing, sniffling, and sneezing to emanate from surrounding cubicles as colds and flu make their appointed rounds.

*Whenever my coworkers get sick, I get sick, too. It's like a cruel joke. My office has instituted an informal policy—if you've got a cold and you might give it to others, stay home. Do not come in to the office. We don't want any martyrs—we'd rather shoulder a heavier workload for a day or two than get sick.*

Colds usually cure themselves, but there are some preventive measures that can help protect your immune system. Get a flu shot—at the end of fall, as it takes about four weeks to develop the protective antibodies. Load up on vitamin C, found in citrus fruits and tomatoes, even when you're not sick. Vitamins A and E, found in dark green vegetables, deep yellow fruits, and oils and nuts, are especially good for your immune system, too. Avoid sick friends and coworkers, as the incubation phase for most colds is two to five days but people are contagious from the onset of a runny nose. Get enough sleep—experts say that the average twenty-two-year-old requires seven to nine hours per night. Eat well. Make maintenance your mantra.

## What's Up, Doc?

"I had been out of school for about eight months when I came down with a horrible case of tonsillitis. I was miserable and woefully unprepared," says Jake Simons, a UCLA grad. "I had insurance and a primary care physician that I had picked based on his proximity to my office. The problem was that I lived a long way from there—not to mention the fact that I was a new patient and therefore had very little leverage in making an emergency appointment. It turned out that my doctor was on vacation so I was sent to another location. I had been unable to sleep for days, and this cruel and unusual punishment was almost more than I could bear."

Learn from Jake's dilemma that it's much better to take some time to figure out the key details of your health plan and doctor information when you're healthy. Who is your doctor? Where is she located? What happens if you go to another doctor? What's your emergency room coverage? And it's wise to pick a primary care physician who is close to home, not work, because if you're really sick, chances are you won't be coming from the office.

## Stress

In today's world, speed is the deal: fast food, fast cars, fast track. People tend to wear stress like a badge of honor. Remember the frazzled girl in college who talked obsessively about how many hours she'd studied for her midterms, or the insufferable guy who recounted how many papers, down to the precise word count, he had to write within the confines of finals week? In the Real World, it's much the same. The common refrain of the active, on-the-go twentysomething: We're so-o-o-o busy and feeling so-o-o-o stressed out.

Arrange a get-acquainted visit with your prospective doctor. Ask whether she has another doctor cover for her when she is away. Ask about hospital affiliation, too, because that's where you'll be sent if you get sick. Afterward, ask yourself: Am I comfortable with this person?

"It's easy to say, 'I'm young, I'm healthy. I don't need to go to the doctor, there's nothing wrong with me,'" says Chris Cooper, a financial planner. "But you need to have developed a relationship with a doctor in order to have fast health care. You want the doctor to be there when the time comes—say you need a prescription, or there is something wrong with your body's plumbing."

You know your body better than anyone, so it's important to keep your doctor abreast of your health problems. Give your doctor a thorough medical history, including past physical and emotional problems, drugs you are taking, and other matters that might affect your health, particularly when health problems are recurring.

All that bluster is likely to be true. Sure, you've experienced stress before. But nothing like this. In your first years out of school you'll undergo dramatic life changes, a shake-up in your very existence. You'll start a new job. You'll take on responsibilities at work that will sometimes overwhelm you. And you'll probably be under pressure in your personal life, too.

"Try not to obsess about the things you have no control over," says Dr. Dori Winchell, who specializes in coping with life changes. "When you think about the pile on your plate and the 'What if,' the 'How can I,' and the 'What if I don't live up to,' that's when you get into trouble. That is when stress becomes overwhelming. Learn to trust yourself."

*I moved to my city without a job, so I was paying rent and paying bills without receiving a paycheck. It was stressful to be spending a lot of money and not be earning any. On the job front, I was sending out ten résumés a day but no one was getting back to me. I thought I would never get on my feet. It seemed hopeless. I couldn't eat, I couldn't sleep. I was always in a bad mood.*

It's natural that you might feel stressed during this transition and experience headaches, difficulty sleeping, or feeling frustrated with things that normally don't bother you. "Your life up to this point has been focused on school and academics. Now you might be feeling, 'What do I do with my life?'" says Dr. Eric Barker, a pharmacist who specializes in depression. "You need to find an activity to be engaged in. Maybe you were a musician in college, or you played sports or did yoga. Explore those outlets and hobbies as you settle in to your new life. Try to rediscover the things that used to give you pleasure."

Stress happens, so learn to handle it and control it. Maybe hanging out with friends will take your mind off things for a while. Go to the gym and work off steam, or treat yourself to some serious nothing.

*One thing that I've started doing is taking a couple of vacation days each year and I do nothing. I don't go away, don't plan a bunch of activities, and I don't save it for my Christmas shopping. I turn off the TV, turn off my cell phone, and veg out. I give myself a total free day. It's better than weekends since I'm the only one with the day off. It's a great stress reliever.*

Stress becomes a problem when it starts to affect how we cope with our day-to-day routine and more serious feelings of depression take over: feelings of low self-worth, lack of interaction with friends, lack of enthusiasm. You may experience energy loss, little control over appetite or weight, and concentration problems. Stress and depression are common accompaniments to major changes in life. Don't be afraid to ask for help in coping with them.

"When your ability to function is compromised—you're missing work because you don't even want to get out of bed in the morning—that's an indicator for the need for clinical interaction," says Dr. Barker.

## Drinking and Drugs

Many of us engaged in the requisite collegiate drinking fests. Some of us gave mind-enhancing drugs a try. We dabbled freely in the safe confines of college, largely isolated from danger, and graduated more or less unscathed. But things are different now. In most of the Real World, illegal drugs and public drunkenness are not only frowned upon, they are prosecuted as criminal offenses.

Being the drunken fool with the lampshade on his head during college may have amused your buddies, but forcing your new roommate into playing nurse on weekends as you hork into a toilet is not a good way to keep your friends or your sanity. As a card-carrying adult, it's time to grow up.

*Excessive drinking was a rite of passage at college,*
*but hitting the bottle is less and less appealing these*
*days. The older I get, the more drinking takes its toll on*
*my body. Even a leisurely Sunday evening trip to the bar*
*can lead to a bleary-eyed Monday morning at work. I*
*don't want to grow a gut from beer consumption. And*
*I don't want drinking to interfere with my life.*

Believe it or not, it's possible to go out, have a drink or two, and have fun without getting sloppily smashed. "If you're a moderate drinker, keep it that way," says Ames Sweet of the National Council on Alcoholism and Drug Dependence. "It can be very easy in the working world to get caught up with drinking as a way of relating to people—the luncheon meeting, the networking reception, the cocktail party. Alcohol is a part of almost every social situation and the pressure to drink is severe."

Plus, intoxication can lead you to do stupid things like make out with a not-so-discreet coworker, which can put your professional reputation at risk. Hangovers are a lot worse in the Real World, too. As you get older, your body doesn't bounce back as well as it used to: It takes three hours to eliminate the effects of two alcoholic drinks, according to the National Institute on Alcohol Abuse and Alcoholism. You can't skip work the way you could a psychology class. And coworkers do not look kindly on your calling in sick knowing that your party-animal tendencies are increasing their workload.

Be careful. Be realistic. Learn to heed your inner tolerance for alcohol so that you're always capable of making decisions for yourself. Drinking and drugs lead to reckless behavior and a release of inhibitions that can be just plain dangerous: roaming city streets inebriated, going home with a stranger, taking a stranger home with you, driving while under the influence, damaging property, and passing out in sketchy places. Don't be blind to the threats in the Big Bad World, and don't abuse your body.

## Safe Sex

Way back in seventh-grade health class, in between self-conscious titters and nervous snickering, you learned about the reproductive system and about various methods of birth control. You learned about sexually transmitted diseases like AIDS. And unless you went to Puritanical Public School in Chaste Town, USA, you learned about the importance of practicing safe sex.

Sex is no less dangerous now. Your "youthful" indiscretions can have serious consequences. Sexually transmitted diseases are a lot more common than you'd think. According to Planned Parenthood, by the age of 24, one in three sexually active people will have contracted a sexually transmitted infection, and the greatest proportion of AIDS cases in the United States has always been among people in the 25–44 age group.

> *I've had plenty of casual sex, but nothing unprotected. It's just not worth the risk. Especially if I'm not in a committed relationship with the person I'm sleeping with, I always make sure we're using a condom. I wouldn't begin to know how to deal with the consequences if something happened. But I guess you can never be 100 percent sure.*

Use a latex condom. Since most sexually transmitted diseases are asymptomatic, it's hard to discern whether your prospective bedmate is infected. No matter how alluring that musky-scented stranger seemed at the bar, when he or she is in your bed, you'd better practice safe sex.

"When you're young and your hormones are raging and you're having a good time, you think you're invincible," says Joel Zive, a pharmacist who specializes in HIV prevention. "But in this day and age, you must understand the dangers associated when you decide you want to be intimate with someone."

*I was going through that post-college dating phase where I was going out a few times a week, sometimes with different guys, and not being as careful as I normally would. Plus, I didn't have very much money and I had no health insurance. My social life ended up being very stressful. I knew that if anything did happen—pregnancy or an STD—I wouldn't have the money to fix it.*

Take charge of your sexual health. Women should see their gynecologists on a yearly basis for breast examinations and pap smears. Men should see their doctors on a yearly basis as well. Talk to your doctor about HIV testing and the different methods of birth control.

Do yourself a big favor: Enter the adult phase of your life knowing that you have a clean bill of health. Go to the doctor or health clinic and get tested for various STDs: syphilis, chlamydia, human papillomavirus, herpes, gonorrhea, hepatitis. Many STDs are curable, but left uncared for, they can cause long-term health problems.

## Satisfy Your Soul

Spiritual health is another consideration. Maybe your connection to an organized religion has long been an important component of your life. Or it may be an attachment you once had and dropped—or one you acquired in college. Now, perhaps for the first time, you have the freedom to pursue a faith or practice entirely as you wish. You are finally free to decide whether religion and spirituality will play an important role in your life.

Spiritual satisfaction is its own reward. But participation in religious activities may have other potential benefits as well. It can give your life a point of focus, a special meaning, and a schedule and structure for your weekends. Religious activities are an escape from the highly competitive business atmosphere in which you spend your workweek, or simply a good place to meet other people like you.

Most faiths have activities and events organized specifically for young people. Look through your local Yellow Pages or ask friends and other family members to help you find churches in your neighborhood that have a young population. In smaller cities or towns, newspapers may even publish schedules of church events. Attend services and try to meet with a member of the clergy or your religious community. If you're new to a church or to the practice of religion entirely, find out what a church's members believe, what its goals and priorities are, and then ask yourself: Is this for me?

Organized religion isn't for everyone. You might wish to explore your own, very personal version of spirituality. Perhaps you find inspiration in hiking in the mountains. Or you find comfort in spending time with your family, or in a yoga or meditation

class. Try to make time for the activities that bring you solace; we
all deserve a little Nirvana here on Earth.

## Health Plans and Insurance

Is it possible to get by without health insurance? Sure. After all,
nearly 39 million Americans live without it, according to the U.S.
Census Bureau. Of course, they should be very careful when
crossing the street.

It's tempting not to buy health insurance when you're looking
for a job or waiting for your employer-sponsored health plan to
kick in. It's just one more cost, you think, and when you are feeling
broke it can seem like an easy way to save money. But unexpected
situations come along—an allergic reaction to shellfish, a sprained
ankle from a pickup basketball game, a car accident—and a couple
of doctor's visits or nights in the hospital later, you're saddled with
massive medical bills. Then that shortsighted belt-tightening will
seem like a financial blunder.

Playing the insurance game is all about balancing the worst-
case scenario with what you're comfortable paying. If you're a
healthy twentysomething, chances are that things will be fine—
for now. But if the worst does happen, the only person signing
your cast will be your loan officer.

### Picking a Health Plan

Health insurance is based on the concept of sharing financial risk
and benefits. Insurance is most cost-effective with larger numbers
of people participating in a plan. The money you pay for health
coverage, which goes by the stage name of premium, is combined
with the premiums of other members to form a pool of money

that goes to pay the medical bills of those who need health care—sometimes you and sometimes not. Typically, the more people who are enrolled in a plan, the bigger the net collection and the more so-called "paying power" it has to negotiate or provide better services for its participants.

> *I've realized how lucky I am to have good insurance through my job. I'm not a young kid anymore, even though I still think I am. I still do the same dumb stuff I did when I was a freshman in college. I drink beer while playing a pickup game of softball. I play basketball in running shoes and think I can still bench 300 pounds like I am an eighteen-year-old. I'm not that old, but I feel like my body doesn't recover so well and my injuries are more intense and longer lasting.*

If you too are lucky enough to be offered health coverage from your first employer, carefully read through the terms of your benefits package. Don't feel like an idiot if the maze of managed care, HMOs, and constantly changing corporate policies confounds you. It confounds a lot of people who've been around much longer than you. It's one of the most important parts of our lives, but most Americans know far less about health care options and health insurance than they should. It's worth your time and money to get educated about your health care options.

> *I've been out of college for over a year now and I've yet to see a doctor. I have health insurance through my job, but the whole thing seems like such a hassle so*

*I haven't bothered. I guess you could say I am electing not to think about it, which may be destructive, but may be more affordable as well.*

There are two basic kinds of heath insurance plans: fee-for-service and managed care. Fee-for-service plans generally assume that the doctor will be paid for each service provided to the patient. Patients may see the doctor of their choice, and claims are filed with your insurer by either the medical provider or you, the patient. Managed care plans, the bulk of employer-sponsored health insurance, provide health services to their members and offer financial incentives to patients who use the providers in the plan. Managed care helps to lower costs but usually provides participants in the plan with less personal control in choosing providers and more rigid definitions of covered services.

Prioritize your health care needs. If you rarely get sick, save for a head cold now and then, you might opt for a low-cost plan that limits your choice of physicians. On the other hand, if you're constantly plagued by mysterious illnesses or prone to histrionics, you might prefer a plan with more freedom of choice even though it might cost a bit more. Talk to your friends and colleagues about their experiences with the company health plan.

*I've never had a problem with my health insurance. I have a great doctor who knows me by name. My pharmacy is really easy to use. It's always been convenient. Isn't that the way it's supposed to be?*

Know the right questions to ask about your company's health insurance plan. On money: What is the monthly premium? What deductibles (the portion of health care costs you must pay up front) will I have to pay out-of-pocket before insurance starts to reimburse me? On user-friendliness: What happens if I want to use a doctor outside the network? How easily can I change primary-care physicians if I want to? Do I need to get permission before I see a specialist? On the medical nitty-gritty: What are the procedures for getting care and being reimbursed in an emergency situation? If I have a pre-existing medical condition, will the plan cover it? Are prescription medicines covered by the plan?

> *I had been out of college a couple of months when I tore my ACL, a ligament in my knee. I had to get an MRI, surgery, plus a year of physical therapy. While my insurance covered some of it, I was still stuck with about $3,000 in medical bills. I had to get a second job to pay for it. I wish I had chosen my plan a little more carefully before this happened.*

"There is no right answer here—it's all just personal preference," says Joe Luckok of the Health Insurance Association of America. "At twenty-two you're in prime health, so you just want to make sure that the plan covers all your basic medical needs. But if you have a preexisting condition, like diabetes, then you'll want to make sure that those needs are met. And if you're a young woman and intend to see a gynecologist once a year, then you'll want to have as much freedom as you can on that. If you plan on getting married or having children right away, you want to know if it's easy to change your policy to a family plan."

Sometimes there are hidden benefits in your health plan.

## Some HMO Details

Health-maintenance organizations, popularly known as HMOs, emphasize preventive care. HMOs offer richer and deeper benefits and have lower out-of-pocket expenses but have a closed network, which means you must use preselected or "in-network" doctors. You also need a referral to see a specialist, whether it's a podiatrist, a gynecologist, or an optometrist. Even so, many young people find HMOs user-friendly—which is fortunate because they're also the most cost-effective plan for employers to offer.

"For me, HMO is the way to go," says Sam Mackenzie, a St. Lawrence grad. "I have all the specialists you could ask for at one simple price. I've gotten X-rays, STD tests, physicals, allergy tests, special orthotics for my feet, and a million other things for only $10 a pop. I pay $25 per month for this privilege but I am psyched to have such a net to fall into. Paying out of pocket seems like financial suicide to me."

Many HMOs offer an option known as a point-of-service plan, or POS. The primary care doctors in this plan typically make re-

Your plan may include massage discounts for people with back pain, or free mental health sessions. Many plans pay for preventive health care such as diet and exercise advice, immunizations, health screenings, and genetic testing for you and your partner if you know that certain diseases run in your family. Your plan may offer you the use of an "advice nurse" for twenty-four-hour over-the-phone consultations. Others may reimburse you for alternative medical therapies such as acupuncture and chiropractic treatment. It's worth reading into the details to see what is and what isn't covered.

ferrals to other providers in the plan. But in a POS plan, members can refer themselves outside the plan and still get some coverage. POS plans also tend to cover more preventive care services and may even offer health improvement programs like workshops on nutrition and discounts at health clubs.

Preferred provider plans, or PPOs, offer more choice, but the cost is generally higher. There is a limited network of providers to choose from when you enroll. If you choose to see those doctors, there is a reasonable co-pay—typically $10–$15 per visit. Most PPOs do not require you to select a primary care physician, but you are encouraged to develop a relationship with a doctor. You can self-refer to a specialist in a PPO, and coverage is offered for out-of-area treatment.

SOURCE: Sorting Out the Details of Private Health Insurance (http://insurance.yahoo.com and www.insure.com)

## On Being Self-Insured

If your employer-sponsored health insurance doesn't kick in right away, or if you've opted to take the summer off to drive cross-country, invest in some basic coverage like temporary insurance to protect against unforeseen calamities. With low premiums and high deductibles, short-term policies are designed to be a low-cost safety net in case of serious injury or illness, not a comprehensive day-to-day health insurance plan. In other words, short-term insurance is intended to pay for major hospital and medical expenses, not routine visits to the doctor's office or trips to the emergency room.

"Young people don't need a Cadillac policy—one that covers everything. You need to think about the most likely things that you'll need covered," advises Joe Luckok of the Health Insurance Association of America. Thankfully, since recent graduates are generally healthy, we're less expensive to insure.

Benefits are limited and there are strict eligibility requirements to qualify. While some plans offer coverage for up to a year, most short-term policies offer between one and six months of coverage. With short-term health insurance plans, you have the freedom to go to any doctor or specialist you like.

You might consider a negotiation with your parents about short-term coverage. For example, you pay for a short-term plan to cover your ordinary health care costs while your parents pay for "catastrophic" coverage that kicks in when something really expensive comes along.

> *I have two brothers, and each of us spent some time after college without health insurance. Our parents were happy to work with us on short-term coverage. They knew it was in their interests as well as ours. They wanted us to be on our own financially, but they also knew that if anything terrible happened to us, they weren't going to let us suffer. So we worked together to split the cost of relatively inexpensive policies that had a high deductible but provided coverage up to a million dollars in case of a catastrophic illness or accident. We paid our routine medical costs; they helped with the catastrophic coverage. They had the comfort of knowing we were covered in case of something out of the ordinary.*

## Real World Realities: Disability Insurance and Risk

Disability insurance, typically included in your employee-sponsored health plan, protects you if you become injured and disabled or seriously ill and cannot earn a living. This type of insurance, typically offered through your employer's health plan, wards off financial ruin and is a must-have for the twentysomething set.

"Young people are more apt to waive disability coverage because they don't want the extra few dollars coming out of their paycheck each month," says Suzanne Hunstad of IHateFinancialPlanning.com, a personal finance Web site. "But it's wise to consider all the forms of risk you face. You have to take care of yourself."

A debilitating illness or injury can happen to you, and a disability income policy is the best way to ensure a continuing income in the event of a serious injury.

The appeal of a catastrophic policy like this is its low premium. Of course, the flip side is the high deductible. That means you pay all your medical costs until they reach the deductible amount. It's little more than a backup, and it's temporary; but for a small cost, there's a good return in peace of mind for both you and your parents.

COBRA is yet another option for those without employer-sponsored health insurance. Named after the Consolidated Omnibus Budget Reconciliation Act of 1985 from which it sprung, COBRA was designed to protect people who change or lose their jobs and are threatened with the loss of employee benefits. But it can also help recent grads who've relied on their parents' health plans but are now ineligible because they reach the policy's age limit or are no longer full-time students.

Another option may be the health insurance plans that some college alumni associations offer to graduates. As a last resort, you can visit local clinics for free or low-cost medical care, but this won't protect you if you have to be hospitalized, and you might have to prove your low-income status.

## Dealing with the Insurance Company

Don't be deterred by the bureaucracy of your insurance company; getting the most out of your health plan is worth the bother. For even the simplest inquiry, you will fill out mounds of forms and endure some excruciatingly long phone calls with many agonizing hours spent on hold listening to stirring renditions of classic Air Supply tunes.

Doggedness and thorough record keeping are the keys to success in wrangling with your insurance company.

> *Breast cancer runs in my family, so I realized that it was important for me to start getting mammograms right away. The problem is that most insurance companies don't cover them in women under thirty-five and it's a very expensive test. But I had made up my mind that my health is worth it. So I wrote over twenty letters to the insurance company, my doctor, and my company's human relations department. I faxed my health history and my mother's health history. And I probably spent about ten hours on the phone dealing with this issue. In the end, my insurance covered it.*

## Real World Common Sense:
## Should You Buy Life Insurance?

If you die, life insurance protects people who rely on your income. Once you join the working world, it seems there's always someone trying to sell it to you—maybe even a classmate of yours who's gone into the insurance business. They'll make it sound like you're being irresponsible by not buying life insurance when you're young and it's cheap.

But most of us have little need to have our lives insured at this time, and life insurance is rarely the best investment we can make with our extra dollars. Never buy a life insurance policy until you've studied it and talked it over with people you trust. Life insurance may be a good idea at some point in your life, particularly when you have someone else depending on you—a spouse or children—who would be in dire straits in the unhappy event of your death. But be sure this is clearly the case before you buy.

If you think your insurance company is shortchanging you, speak up. Insurance providers aren't infallible. They're certainly not in the business of being cooperative or generous. They don't want to pay a dollar more than the policy requires, and even that can be an effort. So prod them. Nudge them. Bug them. Call every day if you must. And make sure you keep a record of who you talked to, when, and what they said so that your hours on the phone are not wasted.

Persistence pays off, says financial planner Christina Povenmire. "Getting answers from your insurance company can be hard. And there are a lot of people who just pay the claim and give up. But if you're having a problem, try to find someone, a human resources representative or even your primary care physician, to intercede on your behalf. Many times, it's just knowing the right person to talk to about a specific issue."

## Food, Glorious Food

Many things will amaze you about life after college, but few will affect you on a day-to-day basis more than just how difficult it is to eat healthy and well-balanced meals. Welcome to the Real World, where desk jobs abound and deli sandwiches are a way of life. Having a job and living in the city are full-time temptations to eat the wrong things. Someone is always calling out for pizza. There seems to be chocolate jumping off everyone's desk and into your hands. A gaggle of coworkers is usually going out for drinks—and nachos or Buffalo wings or chips—at the end of the day. Then there's March, when everyone's daughter or little sister has sold them a lifetime supply of Girl Scout cookies. You know what these foods do to your waistline but you find yourself eating them anyway. Every day.

> *I really hoped that living on my own would force me to learn how to cook, but it hasn't. I cook when I have time. It's hard to find the motivation to cook something nice for yourself. It's like putting on a performance when you're the only audience member. I get home from work and I'm exhausted and I'm starving. So I usually just get takeout.*

Weighty problems creep into life after college. Your metabolism, the energy your body uses to operate, is slowing down and

## Experimenting in the Kitchen: Helpful Web Sites

---

**www.foodtv.com**
Recipes, wine reviews, forums, and schedules

**www.epicurious.com**
Recipes from *Gourmet* and *Bon Appetit* and an extensive recipe archive

**www.allrecipes.com**
Recipes, meal ideas, and cooking advice

---

you simply can't eat the same amount of junk food you did as a teenager and maintain your same body weight.

You're developing eating habits for your adult life. Let's face it, there's more to life than surviving on Ramen noodles and Dr. Pepper. Luckily, learning to prepare some tasty and healthful dishes can be fun.

## Good Eats? Good Luck!

I was never deprived of sugar as a child. I was raised, after all, by a certified chocoholic. So when I arrived at college, the first time I was truly away from adult supervision of my eating habits, I indulged at the dining hall. I dined on Krispy Kreme donuts for breakfast, chicken nuggets for lunch, pepperoni pizza or pasta for dinner. And an apple here and there. Why not eat dessert first? Why shouldn't a sundae for lunch suffice?

The appeal of institutional food wore off and five pounds wore on a bit into second semester. I realized I had to be more disciplined about food—or become a beach ball. After college, I had to face new challenges to that discipline from a new wave of junk food attacks.

You may find yourself going through a similar post-college cycle. For most of us, this is the first time we are responsible for buying and making our own food. It can be a difficult adjustment; good nutrition never seems to be a match for ease and convenience. You may find yourself skipping meals, chowing down on a foil-wrapped frozen burrito or a square-shaped processed dinner, or getting by with the cheapest and easiest dishes—none of which is good for you over the long haul.

> *Meals were hellish in my first year out. I took to buying a huge pack of chicken drumsticks at the local supermarket for just $3.25 a pack, and then having Shake-n-Bake and a raw head of lettuce—just 67 cents a head—every weeknight for dinner. Lunch you would usually find me at the hot dog cart outside my office. But after a year of mad saving and scrimping, I amassed a respectable cash cushion that both allowed me to eat out more often, cook better stuff for myself, and in general, not occupy a spot on the culinary chain one step removed from a railyard hobo.*

And if you have roommates or work at an office, eating healthy becomes that much more difficult. Invariably, people around you will be eating at all hours of the day and night. And most of what they are eating is probably not that great for you. Under these conditions it is difficult to form healthy eating habits.

# FOOD GUIDE PYRAMID
### A Guide to Daily Food Choices

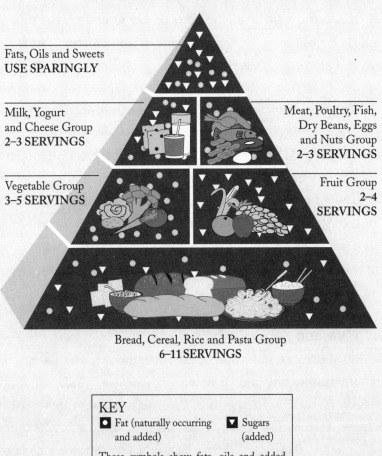

Fats, Oils and Sweets
**USE SPARINGLY**

Milk, Yogurt
and Cheese Group
**2–3 SERVINGS**

Meat, Poultry, Fish,
Dry Beans, Eggs
and Nuts Group
**2–3 SERVINGS**

Vegetable Group
**3–5 SERVINGS**

Fruit Group
**2–4
SERVINGS**

Bread, Cereal, Rice and Pasta Group
**6–11 SERVINGS**

**KEY**
◗ Fat (naturally occurring ▼ Sugars
and added) (added)
These symbols show fats, oils and added
sugars in foods.

SOURCE: U.S. Department of Agriculture, U.S. Department of Health and Human Services

> *My roommate is vegetarian—vegan, and con-*
> *stantly on a diet. She subsists on weird foil packets of*
> *plant enzymes, strange teas, drops of plant extract, gin-*
> *seng smoothies, and vitamins. She occasionally supple-*
> *ments this with small amounts of real food. I try not to*
> *get sucked in to her weirdness when I eat at home, even*
> *if that means I just skip dinner.*

Skipping meals is not the answer. Nor is it necessary to give up all those tasty enemies of good nutrition. Discipline, not abstinence, is the goal. Twizzlers and potato chips are best in moderation. Go easy on butter, oil-laden salad dressings, and sour cream. Try to avoid processed foods, convenience foods, and ready-made dinners. Stay away from prepared frozen entrees or anything that pleads Just Add Water or begs Pop into the Microwave. That stuff is usually full of salt and loaded with fat, not to mention overpriced.

## DIY Nutrition

Healthful diets contain nutrients and calories and a balance of carbohydrates, fat, and protein. Try to eat a variety of foods from the five major food groups every day, advises the American Dietetic Association. Eat two to three servings a day of dairy, milk, cheese, or yogurt. (Sorry Ben and Jerry's fans, ice cream is not counted in this category—it's a bona fide sweet.) Aim for three to five servings of spinach, green beans, carrots, tomatoes, or other vegetables. Juice works, too. Eat two to four servings of fruit. Try to eat two to three servings of meat, fish, or poultry. (For vegetarians, cooked beans, peanut butter, nuts, and eggs are great sources of protein and serve as stand-ins for meat.) Eat six to eleven servings of grains—pasta, rice, noodles, bread, cereal.

"Most young people don't get enough fruits and vegetables, which are low calorie and chock full of nutrients," says Dr. Keith Ayoob, spokesperson for the American Dietetic Association. "Fortunately, fruits and vegetables are fast, inexpensive, and everyone likes at least a few. Think beyond apples and bananas. Think grapes—they're the perfect impulse food—or tangerines and clementines. Grab a container of cherry tomatoes or a package of baby carrots.

"Young people are also lacking in dairy products, and now is the time to add some calcium into your bone bank to prevent osteoporosis. Bring yogurt to work as a snack. Get a latte instead of a coffee. Eat cereal with milk."

Winning the food war is not easy. It requires conscious effort. You have to think about what you eat and plan ahead. "Once or twice a week you're going to have to head into the super-market and do some food shopping. Establish a pattern now," says Dr. Ayoob.

*During college, I battled with my weight. But now that I've started having to go to the grocery store and make decisions on what I am going to be eating for the next two weeks, I put a lot more thought into my diet. While my job forces me to work late hours and order dinner in, I have become savvy at ordering healthy meals from restaurants and avoiding the stuff that is bad for you. I know a lot of people I work with make common mistakes, such as ordering a Caesar salad and thinking they are being healthy or skipping lunch and then eating a big dinner. I always have some fruit or*

## Real World Realities:
## Caloric Content of Tasty Temptations

It is possible to squeeze the food of your social life—pizza, beer, chips—into a healthy diet. But do not make it your complete dinner. Watch how much you drink and eat at bars. Be aware of the cost—in both dollars and calories—of eating out. Try to limit your indulgences to once a week instead of every day.

Below is a list of commonly consumed "foods" and the nutritional damage they do. Food for thought: Twentysomething women should be eating a daily diet of about 2,000 calories with about 60 grams of fat, and twentysomething men should be taking in around 2,800 calories with 85 grams of fat.

| | |
|---|---|
| Slice of pizza (cheese) | 183 calories; 10g fat |
| Deli sandwich | 671 calories; 34g fat |
| Bagel (plain) | 170 calories; 0.8g fat |
| Candy bar | 250 calories; 12g fat |
| Can of soda (12 oz.) | 150 calories; 0g fat |
| Nachos (1 oz.) | 140 calories; 7g fat |
| Donut (plain) | 190 calories; 10g fat |
| Pint of beer (12 oz.) | 146 calories |
| Glass of red wine (4 oz.) | 85 calories |

SOURCE: Calorie Control Council

*granola bars with me. I have also found foods that I love that are also good for me, such as sushi and vegetable soups.*

There are some simple ways to improve your eating habits. Eat breakfast before you leave for work, where it's cheaper and probably more nutritious. The commuter breakfast—a large glass of OJ and a banana or a half a bagel—will suffice. Pack your own lunch—you have more control over portion size that way. Try an individual-size can of tuna, or turkey cold cuts on whole-grain bread. When the afternoon craving hits, munch on a handful of nuts or a slice of cheese, both sources of so-called heart-healthy fats.

## Add Color

"The real aim is to add color to the plate with fruits and vegetables because this is where lifelong habits can form," says Janet Helm, a registered dietitian. "In college, so much of your eating was beige: bagels, frozen yogurt, bread. So now you want to eat a wider variety of foods. Break out the cookbook and learn some basic dishes. Pick up some staples at the grocery store like brown rice or couscous and some convenience items like precut vegetables and frozen chicken breasts and build a meal."

Marinate meats in lemon juice and garlic or even bottled Italian salad dressing, Helm recommends. Also try grilling, baking, roasting, or broiling fish—it's delicious and good for you. Make egg-white omelets and stuff them with meats and cheeses and spinach. Pasta is a good standby, and easy to spice up with various sauces like pesto, white or red wine, and mushrooms. Make your own pizza and top it with fresh vegetables: onions, mushrooms, peppers, and tomatoes. Frozen vegetables are nutritious and versatile.

For snacks and side dishes, make a huge salad with unusual ingredients like cheese, olives, meats, and tropical fruit. Sauté vegetables in a small amount of oil and add spices to taste. Spice up fresh or low-sodium canned vegetables and other foods with herbs and lemon juice. Whip up a fruit smoothie with frozen yogurt and frozen or canned fruits packed in their own natural juices and ice cubes. All easy, all good.

## What's Cookin'?

Did you learn how to cook when you lived at home? That used to be one of the rituals of childhood, at least for girls: Your mother taught you how to cook and iron and sew and all those other things most of us never learned. Family life changed. Most of our parents have demanding jobs and too little time to teach us domestic skills.

Now we're on our own and we don't know how to cook, at least not well. But we're beginning to sense the need and to acquire some interest in cooking for ourselves. It turns out it's not so hard. In fact, it can be a creative outlet, a cost-saver, and a way to make things just the way we like them.

Cooking is a skill that will grow as your life progresses. You don't have to learn everything at once. And what you cook doesn't have to be gourmet, but it should be appetizing and somewhat nutritious. Plus, being a good cook impresses people—everyone from your grandma to hot dates.

Forget the Naked Chef. Nigella who? In your first years of cooking and experimenting in the kitchen, you'll have little need for grueling goulash or feisty flambé recipes. Learn to prepare a handful of simple dishes, meals that you enjoy eating week after week—roast chicken with herbs, spaghetti with marinara sauce, chopped salad. Take it one dish at a time, building a repertoire of healthy recipes that are easy to prepare and simple to clean up.

For those Thursday nights when you simply can't lift a finger in the kitchen and Must-See TV is luring you to the couch, it's

## Good (Cookin') Reads

*The Joy of Cooking,* by Irma S. Rombauer
(Simon & Schuster, 1997).

*The New Basics Cookbook,* by Julee Rosso and Sheila Lukins
(Workman Publishing, 1989).

*Help! My Apartment Has a Kitchen Cookbook,* by Kevin Mills,
et al. (Houghton Mifflin, April 1996)

---

handy to have homemade reheatable meals on hand. You can make a pot of hearty vegetable soup and it will last for a week. Prepare a vat of tomato sauce or a gigantic lasagna dish; both are freezer-friendly. A pot roast or a ham can get you through several nights of eating for only one night of preparing.

> *In my first months out of college I ate a fast-food-heavy diet. These days, however, I cook like a fiend. Eating at home is much healthier than eating restaurant food. I just make a few simple dishes for during the week, and every Sunday night I usually try something new and exotic like a Thai dish or some special Italian feast.*

Developing good eating habits requires good cooking habits. You'll be an expert in no time: making a dish again and again, seasoning to taste. As your cooking skills improve, you may wish to take on more labor-intensive recipes. Try your hand at foreign cuisine, or even bake your own bread.

*(continued on page 258)*

## Easy-as-Pie Recipes

My grandmother, one of the best cooks around, has some quick and easy recipes that require basic ingredients and very little preparation time. Here are four to get you started.

### Chicken with Sour Cream and Mushrooms

½ to 1    cup sliced mushrooms
2    tablespoons butter
2    tablespoons olive oil
     Salt and pepper
2–4    boneless chicken breasts
½    cup dry white wine or cooking sherry
⅔    cup sour cream

Sauté the mushrooms in the butter. When they are brown and starting to look a little dry, add the olive oil. Salt and pepper the chicken breasts to taste, then brown them in the pan with the olive oil and mushrooms. Add the white wine or cooking sherry. Cover and cook on low-to-medium heat for about 15 minutes. Add the sour cream. Serve with spinach, rice, or noodles.

### Rice Pilaf

1    cup rice
2    tablespoons butter
3    tablespoons broken vermicelli
2½    cups chicken, beef, or vegetable broth
     Salt (optional)

Wash the rice and let drain. Melt the butter and lightly brown the rice. Add the vermicelli and gently stir until lightly brown, which will take only a few seconds. Remove from heat. Add the broth and salt to taste (if using). Cover and bring to a boil. Immediately reduce the heat to low and cover. Cook for 20 to 25 minutes, or until the liquid is gone. Remove from the heat and let stand for 5 to 10 minutes. Stir with a fork and serve.

## Linguine with Clam Sauce

8   ounces linguine or angel hair pasta
3–4  tablespoons olive oil
1   onion, chopped
1   cup sliced mushrooms
2–4  chopped garlic cloves
1–2  cans clams and clam juice
½   cup white wine
3   tablespoons minced fresh parsley
½   cup coarsely chopped walnuts
    Salt and pepper

In a large pot of boiling water, cook the pasta according to the package directions. Meanwhile, heat the olive oil in a large skillet and sauté the onion, mushrooms, and garlic. Add the clams, clam juice, and wine and cook for 3 to 5 minutes. Add the chopped parsley and walnuts. Season to taste with the salt and pepper. Drain the pasta and toss with the sauce.

## Chocolate Cherry Cake

Cake
1   package devil's food cake mix
1   20–21 ounce can cherry pie filling
1   teaspoon almond flavoring
2   eggs, beaten
Icing
¾   cup sugar
3   tablespoons butter
3   tablespoons milk
¾   cup semisweet chocolate chips

*To make the cake:* Preheat the oven to 350°F. Combine all ingredients and stir by hand until well blended. Pour into a greased 9" x 13" pan or a 15" x 10" jelly roll pan. Bake 9" x 13" for 25 to 30 minutes. Bake 15" x 10" for 20 to 25 minutes.

*To make the icing:* Combine the sugar, butter, and milk. Bring to a boil, stirring constantly. Add the chocolate chips and stir until smooth. Pour over the warm cake.

Invest in some basic cooking equipment. Again, you can do this one piece at a time. Your equipment will expand as you get better and more comfortable in the kitchen. Every novice cook should have a set of pots and pans, including a nonstick skillet, available in any discount department store or your mother's cupboard. You'll need a good, sharp knife or two. Cookie sheets and cooling racks. And enough flatware and plates to serve dinner for people. Then there are some more sophisticated appliances that are worth the investment: a small microwave, a wok for stir-frying, and a food processor or blender.

Kitchen equipment is like anything else: You get what you pay for. Think about buying better-quality pieces, even if it means acquiring fewer at a time, because you'll use them almost every day and cheap equipment will haunt you for years. One good knife that keeps a sharp edge is better than a shiny set of knives that are chronically dull. A solid pan that conducts heat evenly is more valuable than a full set of cheap tin.

Think of the task of building a well-equipped kitchen not just as one piece at a time, but one good piece at a time. And remember your kitchen when friends and family ask what you want for your birthday or holiday gifts.

## Staying Fit

Perhaps you've always been svelte, blessed with an enviable metabolism. Perhaps you never had to make an effort to exercise, but somehow always managed to stay in shape. Perhaps you were one of the lucky ones who never packed on the dreaded Freshman Fifteen. I hate you.

Most of us have no such luck. And when college is over,

we're faced again with frightening forces insidiously seeking to load fat where muscle ought to be. In the Real World it's easy to evolve into a desk-bound, slothful, indolent creature with a cramped schedule. Most of us spend much of our working day sitting at a computer doing things that require little energy and burn few calories. You keep meaning to work out, but there are many days when you don't have the time to make it to the gym during lunch and by evening the last thing you want to do is exercise. You'd rather watch television or relax. There are so many good excuses for not exercising.

Rethink the concept of physical activity. "If your schedule is so demanding that you don't have any time to devote to exercise, think in bites of ten minutes at a time," says Kathy Stevens, a fitness consultant. "Walk from here to there rather than take your car. Take the stairs. Go for a walk during your lunch hour. Do calisthenics before you shower in the morning. Clean your house. This may sound utilitarian, but any movement keeps you healthy. Most of us just need to move more."

*I really like exercising with my friends. I've found someone I can run with, ski with, and play tennis with. It's easy to enjoy these things with people you don't know too well if you're both enjoying the activity. It's great motivation to stay fit, too.*

There are more than aesthetic reasons for staying in shape. Exercise helps you sleep better at night. Exercising relieves stress and purges pent-up energy. It leaves you feeling much calmer. Aerobic activities like walking, running, and bicycling make your heart beat faster, which helps keep it healthy. Weight-bearing activities are good for your bones—and help prevent osteoporosis. Exercise also improves your strength, flexibility, and muscle tone.

Experts say that adults need thirty minutes or more of light to moderate exercise about five times per week. "It's a commitment that you have to make—you can't just diet and exercise for two months every spring so that you'll look good in a bathing suit," says Neil Sol, who has a Ph.D. in exercise physiology. "Go in with the mind-set that this is for your lifetime. You don't have to pull it off on your own. Exercise with a buddy or invest a little money in a personal trainer. You've got to start young."

## Off to the Gym

The natural response of recent college graduates eager to stay in shape is to join a gym or fitness club. Your gym or health club should be your sanctuary, your haven away from the demands of coworkers, roommates, bosses, or significant others. To ensure that you choose the perfect refuge, you should tour prospective gyms in your neighborhood to check out the scene.

Perhaps you're eager to lock eyes with someone amidst rows of free weights. A posse of spandex-clad muscled men eyeing the pony-tailed sylphlike Stairmaster bunnies is the sure sign of a pickup scene. Or perhaps you're aiming for a Rocky Balboa sweat-laden cave complete with punching bags and imposing barbells. Or maybe you're looking for a sleek health club with spa and other luxury services.

Whatever your pleasure, many health clubs offer a one-day to one-week trial membership for free, so try out several in your area. It's best to join a gym that's located a quick walk or drive from your home or office—the easy commute will be added incentive to actually go. And make sure that it has convenient hours.

> *Continuing my exercise routine was not just a top priority coming out of school, it was my religion. My search combed a number of the gyms in my neighborhood. If I was going to have to pay to work out, I wanted to have all the weights and machines that I like. I went for the basic, no-frills gym. I wasn't looking to pick up girls, meet people, or socialize. Nor did I care what the lobby looked like or if the lockers were oak.*

Go at a time when you would regularly visit, to see how long you have to wait for a treadmill or if the inner/outer thigh machine has lines as long as Disneyland. Too many "out of order" signs may indicate that the maintenance folks may be a tad slow getting around to fixing errant recumbent bikes. Take a group class to see if the instructors are challenging. Can you grow to love the drill sergeant who teaches step aerobics? Will the flaky yoga lady's incense give you a migraine?

> *I don't love to exercise, but I found that the more expensive a gym was, the more often I went and the more I got out of it. Since I was paying a small fortune every month for it, I made myself go every day. Plus, really nice gyms—with sauna, Jacuzzi, Pilates classes— did so much for my mental health and stress level that they were worth every penny.*

Even if you can't afford to join a club or don't want to spend money on that instead of something else, there are cheaper alternatives. The YMCA and YWCA are both relatively inexpensive places to work out, and there is usually one (or more) in decent-size cities.

## Exercise for Life

Perhaps a standard health club isn't for you. Or you realize that you simply won't go regularly enough to justify the expense. Remember, even if you go sporadically, you will pay frequently. Investigate other ways to stay in shape in your city or town, like a public pool, ballroom dance lessons, a climbing wall, or a running club.

> *I tried the gym membership route and found that tiresome. What I really disliked was exercising without a purpose; there were no matches to win or coaches to impress. What finally made exercising click for me was entering a road race during my first year out. I found that it set a goal for me that I could train for. It also became a bit more competitive when some of my peers in the office also starting running road races. There was the issue of personal pride, but it was all in good spirit.*

Most cities have leagues for various team sports—soccer, swimming, basketball, rugby, softball. These provide you with great opportunity for exercise, an outlet for pent-up stress, and a social circle outside of work. Such leagues usually accommodate players of all skill levels and offer competitive matches complete with referees and uniforms as well as team training and the chance for weekend practices. It's a very cost-effective way to have fun and get exercise.

> *When I first graduated, I really missed the camaraderie of being on a sports team, but luckily I saw an ad in the paper for my city's Ski and Sports Club. It's*

*been a fun way to meet people and be a member of a team. I have played Ultimate Frisbee and Coed Softball with the group. I also go running and biking a lot— both very cheap forms of exercise.*

"It's important to find the kind of physical activity that you like to do—whether it's hiking, aerobics, or kick boxing," says Tom Ivicevic, spokesman for the Aerobics and Fitness Association. "Do it often enough so that your body gets the maximum benefit."

"In your twenties, exercise lays the groundwork of cardio-vascular strength and bone strength as an insurance policy for your body later in life," says Peg Jordan, author of *The Fitness Instinct*. "Try to sneak fitness in the back door. You might play tennis once a week or shoot hoops once in a while but realize you lack stamina and endurance, so you then might want to strength train a couple times a week and work out, too, so that your game improves."

Adds Jordan, "Most young people start exercising because they're sick and tired of being exhausted all the time. Their high-sugar, high-fat diet takes a toll. Exercise helps you shore up energy and stamina."

## Security and Safety

For most of us, graduation means leaving behind a pastoral campus complete with well-lit grounds, a protective administration, and a round-the-clock security force. College, like home, was populated by people who cared about us. A rather cozy, cuddly existence.

Your first job out of college may take you to a place that is very different from your home or school, often to a large city.

That's part of the excitement. The big city is exhilarating, stimu-
lating, and edgy. But the big city also has crime and a cast that
includes some strange characters.

Don't cower in your apartment as soon as the sun goes
down. Instead, convert your fear into a healthy awareness of
your surroundings. Arm yourself with information to enhance
your personal safety at home, at work, and on the street. Buy a
decent city map—those glossy ones that fold up easily will do
nicely—and familiarize yourself with street names and major in-
tersections. Particularly important for the directionally challenged: Learn the names of neighborhoods and the location of
major landmarks.

Learn the bus and subway lines—which colors, letters, and
numbers go in which directions. Be aware of when the subway
shuts down at night and when trains become less frequent. Find
out where taxis are likely to be at night. Have at least a vague
sense of how long it takes to get from place to place.

*One night I was coming back from a late party
and I got on the wrong bus. I ended up across town. At
first I thought I could just walk back home—I am over
6 feet, and not easily intimidated. But then I realized
that it just looked a little too scary. Sometimes even if
it's less convenient to go back the long way, I have to
think about safety first. You can't cut corners.*

Talk to longtime residents of your city, coworkers, and
friends to learn about sketchy neighborhoods. Most local newspapers have a weekly section that has a listing of all the crimes,

## Real World Common Sense: Prepare for a Lost or Stolen Wallet

Getting mugged is scary. Then there's the added annoyance that comes with replacing what you've lost: driver's license, credit card, insurance cards, and everything else.

Take some steps now to minimize the inconvenience of loss. Keep records of your credit card numbers so that you can cancel these right away. Have your bank account number handy and notify your bank that your card is in a stranger's hands. Right now, take a few minutes to lay all of your credit cards on a photocopy machine and make a copy or two. Then you'll always have a visual record of what's in your wallet.

Split your belongings up by putting some cash in your wallet and some in your pocket. You don't want to be mugged and stranded. And if you take prescription medicine, don't carry it all with you. Put the pills you need for one day in an envelope or pillbox.

thefts, rapes, health-code violations, and the like that happened during the past week. It's a treasure trove of information. Browse it regularly to stay informed of the darkest happenings in your area and get an idea of where it's safe and where it's not.

## Muggings and Assaults

Common sense is the surest key to crime avoidance. Let's review. Avoid dark, deserted, or dangerous streets, even if it means taking the long way around. Stay away from large bushes or doorways where someone could be lurking. Walk away from possible dangers; be leery of groups of people behaving in a threatening way. Be especially careful around automated teller machines at night—hotbeds for muggings and knifings.

Invest in self-defense classes if you need more assurance. These courses, typically tailored for women, are often offered by local law enforcement agencies. You learn how to avoid an attack and how to escape an attacker.

> *When I first moved to the big city, I looked into acquiring mace or pepper spray, but then decided against it. Instead, I took a free self-defense course offered by my local police department. I also rely on common sense. I never walk anywhere late at night by myself—I take a cab instead. I always carry my cell phone with me. And I always let a friend know where I'll be.*

Use your head. Anyplace is unsafe if you aren't on the lookout for your safety. Carry a cell phone whenever you go out, and have emergency numbers programmed in. Go places with friends whenever possible, and pay attention to what's going on around you at all times. Keep to busy areas—especially when you're new in town and unfamiliar with alien streets. At night, always walk in well-lit areas.

Avoid walking or running alone at night, and leave the Walkman at home, or at least keep it at a very low volume. Your ability to hear someone coming up from behind you is severely limited with a blaring Walkman. Carry an ID and a small amount of money for bus fare if you're out and about somewhere unfamiliar, just in case.

Unfortunately, you can be extra careful and bad things can still happen to you.

> *One spring afternoon I was walking through a very nice and very busy neighborhood in my city. There were a lot of people around and the sidewalks were pretty crowded. Suddenly, a man stepped out from the alley onto the sidewalk and pulled a gun from under his jacket and held it to my chest. He asked me to give him my bag. I reached into the bag and told him I would give him my money. I only had about five bucks on me. I gave it to him, he rummaged through my bag looking for anything else valuable, and he let me go. As I crossed the street, I watched him rob two women who were walking behind me. I called the police and gave my report right away. It definitely freaked me out. I have been more aware since then of my surroundings and never hesitate to cross the street—or walk in the middle of the street if it's dark—if I feel uncomfortable.*

If someone tries to hurt you or you think someone is going to hurt you, run away or scream to get attention. If you're accosted, give the mugger what's demanded. Don't fight back. Don't resist or struggle for your bag or wallet. You're probably no Schwarzenegger, and most times all that the mugger is after is your stuff. Don't try to coax the mugger out of committing the crime. Your charms and sweet talk will probably be lost on the thief. Try to end the contact as quickly as possible.

If you've had the misfortune of being mugged, call the police and file a report. Even if the police don't investigate, they will give you a case number—proof that you've been the victim of a crime, which you will likely need for insurance purposes. Homeowner's and renter's insurance will generally cover loss of property in a mugging.

Then be sure to call every financial institution that you do business with—credit cards, banks, insurance—and alert them of the incident. They will cancel your accounts. "Identity theft and card theft are big problems," says Jean Salvatore of the Insurance Information Institute. "Let the groups know that your card is missing so that if something doesn't look quite right, they'll notify you. Also, make a list of everything that was taken and its estimated value. Receipts are helpful in processing your claim."

## Break-Ins and Theft

It is scary and unnerving to find that a stranger has been in your home—pawing through your possessions, prowling through your rooms.

> *One night I returned home from a basketball game to find I had been burgled. Apparently, the thieves jimmied the lock to my front door. I lost every electronic thing I owned—TV, VCR, stereo, laptop. My crunchy, overeducated roommate came home and fell asleep on the couch, thinking that the missing items had just 'been moved' by me—for some manic late-night audio-visual spree, I suppose. After that, I realized I needed a dead bolt on my door. And a new roommate.*

Take measures to feel safe and secure in your home. You should "case" your house or apartment, just as a burglar would, to determine the easiest entry. Then consider how you can make it more break-in resistant. Lock your apartment when you're not home. Use a dead bolt on your front door when you are.

Your entranceway should be well lit. A peephole in the door is safer for identifying visitors than a door chain. Don't hide your keys in so-called "secret" places outside your home—under the doormat, in the front light, in a fake rock, in the planter. You're not fooling anyone; thieves usually know where to look.

Don't leave windows or doors open when you're out if you live on the ground or a low floor. Keep your curtains closed to avoid showing off your belongings to prospective thieves. If you live on an upper floor, watch out for access from your fire escape.

> *I came home one evening and noticed that the drawers and cabinets were open and papers were scattered around the house. I thought my roommate had messed up the place so I cleaned up, shut the drawers, and closed my window. Then it hit me that we might have been broken into. I immediately ran to check my jewelry and noticed that my gold necklace and my gold ring were missing. I called the police and they came and filed a report. Unfortunately, I had cleaned the house— big mistake. I had erased all the fingerprints. They told me that it was unlikely that we would be able to get our items back. Then they recommended that we always leave our windows shut and advised us to get window guards. It was a rotten experience.*

If you come home to a broken door or shattered window and you think you've been burgled, do not enter your apartment or touch anything. Go to a safe area and call the police. Advise your landlord about the break-in, too.

I know this might seem like simple common sense; in fact, there's probably not much in this chapter that you haven't heard before. What's different now, and why it's so important that you have this information on hand, is that *you're* the one responsible for your own health and safety, just as you're now responsible for securing health insurance, eating balanced meals, exercising, and taking care of yourself when you're sick.

It's not an impossible feat, just one that doesn't come automatically. Take control of your lifestyle now when you're young and it's easier to be reasonably fit and in good shape. You'll be happier and healthier for it.

# chapter seven

# getting
# A LIFE

COLLEGE IS A READY-MADE PARTY, the perfect social incubator: thousands of bright and attractive people, all the same age, hanging out; plays, concerts, and performances happening every weekend; beer galore; social gatherings erupting spontaneously.

In the Real World it's a different story. Even for people who've always been reasonably popular, never short of friends, it's not necessarily easy to get a life after getting a diploma. With a hectic schedule, there's none of the free time that seemed so abundant in college. And many urban dwellers, flat broke, are reduced to socializing mostly in dive bars.

When I first moved to the city and started working, I spent a lot of free time hanging out in smoky, noisy watering holes, gorging on free wings and guzzling cheap beer. It felt comfortable, a little like college. Besides, it's what all my friends were doing, and I was barely a year into the Just-Turned-21-and-It's-Legal-for-Me-to-Be-Here High.

Any bar I went to on any given Saturday had hordes of people my age at varying stages of sobriety. Without fail, I'd see a posse

of denim-clad ladies in the corner monopolizing the karaoke machine. And I couldn't avoid the baseball-capped band of brothers
hounding the midriff-baring bartender with the belly-ring.

But I soon grew tired of the pickup scene. It seemed the lads
who were eager to procure my phone number were always the
ones I would never want to have it—the *über*-suave man who
could turn an ordinary cocktail napkin into a paper pterodactyl,
or the bleary-eyed one I met who thought the Hutu rebels were a
rock band from the 1970s.

I felt like a parody of the bespectacled, nerdy high school girl
adrift in a cruel, cold world. I was bored and lonely and frustrated. Why was happy hour anything but? What was I doing
wrong? Why was it so hard to meet interesting people?

This chapter is about making a life beyond work: finding
friends, meeting dates, and maintaining relationships with family.
I also suggest creative ways to entertain yourself and even plan a
vacation—all on a budget, of course. After all, adulthood isn't just
about health insurance and retirement plans. You'll eventually get
a life, but not without some false starts and memorable evenings.
So let's go—there's fun to be had.

## Finding Real Friends in the Real World

Friends are those dependable folks who drive you to the airport for
your predawn flight. They move your furniture with only minimal
griping and help you paint your decrepit apartment. Friends cheer
you on at your neighborhood pub's open-mike night and take you
home when you've had one too many. Friends are always on your
side no matter how slightly, or deeply, you've been wronged.

But finding real friends in the Real World is tricky. More

than one million people graduate from college every year in the United States. These new graduates, like those before them, disperse to cities and towns all over the country, get jobs, and start lives. Simple math would suggest that any American city should be teeming with thousands of eligible, young, college-educated singles. These people presumably share interests, read books, attend parties, and want to meet new people. And yet often it seems impossible for these strangers to get together.

> *After graduation I moved to a new city for what I thought would be a great job, but things didn't really work out as I had planned. I had counted on mostly meeting new friends through work, but when I got there I found people were older and already had established friends, or at least didn't seem that interested in socializing after work. My social life bombed. It was frustrating—I was used to the lively surroundings of my university campus.*

Carving out a social life takes time, and meeting new friends requires effort. But of all the chores you'll undertake in your first year out of college, it should be the most enjoyable. Odds are there are plenty of fun, smart people in your midst. And, as a bonus, if you enrich yourself during your quest for companionship, you'll be a more attractive friend yourself.

## Freshman Orientation All Over Again

Twentysomethings face a lot of uncertainty beginning new social lives, says Dr. Dan Jones, who specializes in young adult transitions. "In college you had a circle of friends that you shared your complaints about your parents with, you shared your heartbreaks and goals for the future. In the real world, the system is not set up that way and you don't have that instant intimacy with people. It's a lot harder to meet a best friend or a confidante."

*Meet people? Intriguing concept. I suppose I haven't made any new, good friends since college. I work hard at maintaining my good, real friendships from high school and college. These are my best friends. I don't want an arbitrary friend just for the sake of hanging out with someone; then again, it would be nice to meet some new people. The working world is not conducive to forming friendships.*

And so goes the lament of many recent college graduates. It's lonely to realize that your best friends don't live down the hall anymore. You may live and work in a new place with no family or old friends around. Or your friends from college may be so busy in their jobs, as you are in yours, that you can't rely on them to complete your social life.

*The worst thing about graduating: empty time. Although it was great to have some space of my own and I absolutely loved the absence of papers and exams and assignments, I found myself getting home from work and wondering: 'Where is everyone? What am I supposed to do for the rest of the day?'*

The best response to the problem of feeling alone is to be proactive. Don't wallow in your aloneness, complaining that it's hard to meet people. In the Real World there's more to it than pre-arranged mixers and social gatherings tailored for young singles. Now you have to work at it.

> It's hard leaving college, where you live and breathe for your friends, to transition into this awkward stage of being alone and trying to meet people. But friendship is worth the effort. Friends give me great perspective and advice. And having people who are on my wavelength, make me laugh, and are easy to be around is priceless when I've had a hard day at work or a fight with my boyfriend.

Just remember that there are lots of other young people out there seeking the same thing you are, and lots of ways to meet them.

## Get Out of the House

The immediate cure for loneliness is simply to be around other people. If you're serious about meeting others, go to everything you're invited to—it doesn't matter if you are not all that inter-ested in a documentary on Iranian folk music or an exhibit on stamps of the nineteenth century. The important thing is to put yourself in a position to see and be seen.

> Braving the proverbial dating scene is one thing, but I have found it difficult to meet just plain old friends. So I've learned to put myself out there more. If I'm having a fun, spontaneous chat with someone in

*line at the post office, it's not hard to take it a step fur-*
*ther and say, 'Do you want to grab a cup of coffee*
*later?' People are receptive to friendliness.*

Spread yourself around. There are thousands of places where potential friends and dates lurk: at the grocery store, on jury duty, on vacation, at the beach, at a sporting event, or at a concert. Future lifelong friends are hanging out at the laundromat, at an alumni gathering, at a friend's wedding, at a bowling alley. You might meet someone at a coworker's party, at an art gallery, at the driving range, at the mall, at the car wash, at church, at a lecture, at the bus stop, at the bookstore, at Starbucks, in the cast of a play, or while waiting in line at the movies. But they're not in your apartment. Go find them.

## Take a Class

Maybe there's a second language you always wanted to learn but could never fit in into your course schedule. Perhaps there's an art or craft you've always wanted to master: photography, knitting, pottery, watercolor or oil painting, or gourmet cooking. Investigate these possibilities at junior colleges or YMCAs or through adult education programs at universities.

*When I was feeling like I really needed to meet*
*new people, I signed up for a belly dancing class, a Chi-*
*nese cooking class, and I joined a book club. I've met a*
*few people through those means. And it was easier to*
*strike up a conversation with people when you're both*
*learning something new.*

"You have to be willing to make an effort to find people of like mind," says Dr. Jones. "Don't be passive about it. Look around. Most communities have soccer leagues, softball teams, or bird-watching clubs." Classes, clubs, or some friendly athletic competition—whatever gets you out and about is good for your social life.

## Moonlight

A part-time job is a practical way to expand your circle of friends and earn some extra income. If improving a lackluster social life is a primary consideration, choose your second vocation carefully. Look for businesses or organizations that employ a lot of young people or attract a diverse crowd: Learn to be a bartender, work weekends at a bookstore or health club, pitch in hours at a community theater.

> *I was really strapped for money in my first year out of school. Nonprofits don't exactly pay particularly well, so I took a night job at a restaurant. It was really fun to mingle with completely different people, and I met some very interesting ones. Needless to say, restaurant workers lead very different lives than the typical 9-5'er. My advice for some instant change in your social life: for a sensory boost, start working at a restaurant.*

Of course, a second job isn't everyone's idea of a fun night out. But if you have the time and the energy, you just might find that it's easy to love your second job as a less-demanding post that helps pay the bills or funds your shoe-shopping habit—*and* expands your social horizons.

> *I am a super social person, but when I moved to Seattle after college I was really disappointed that I was not meeting new people. I would walk down the street smiling at strangers and all I got back were disaffected scowls. I was really lonely so I decided to take a second job—something totally different from my day job—as a waitress at a vegetarian restaurant three nights a week. I met a ton of young, single people who like to go out. While I wouldn't say that my new friendships are philosophical, we definitely have a lot of fun.*

## Volunteer

In college there were always organizations we could join to get involved in community service or social advocacy. All we had to do was read the bulletin board at the Student Center to find the tutoring assignment in a local school or weekend trip to help rebuild the Appalachian Trail. Now, though there's no central place to hear about these life-enhancing opportunities, and many of us still feel the urge to improve ourselves or help others in ways that don't relate directly to work.

When the work-a-day routine and the tired bar scene get you down, volunteering and social service are good ways to refresh your spirit, to feel good by doing good. Focus your energy on something you enjoy and feel passionate about, then figure out a

# Giving Back: Helpful Web Sites

## www.VolunteerMatch.org
VolunteerMatch, a nonprofit, online service, helps you find a great place to volunteer. Volunteers enter their ZIP code on the Web site to quickly find local volunteer opportunities matching individual interests and schedules.

## www.Idealist.org
Idealist is a project of Action Without Borders, an organization independent of any government, political ideology, or religious creed. At this site you will find nonprofit and community organizations in 153 countries, which you can search or browse by name, location, or mission and thousands of volunteer opportunities in your community and around the world, and a list of organizations that can help you volunteer abroad.

## www.CityCares.org
CityCares expands and supports an innovative alliance of volunteer organizations working to build community through service and civic engagement from Atlanta to Boston to New York to Chicago to L.A. to Washington, D.C.

---

way to make a useful contribution to your community. Maybe there is an organization you believe in—a political campaign, a homeless shelter, a worthwhile charity. You have the skills, time, and imagination to make a socially valuable and personally rewarding contribution.

Many organizations in need of volunteers are flexible and therefore make it very easy for you to donate your time. Approach the group you're interested in working for and pitch an idea. If there's already a volunteer program in place, even better. Show up and participate.

> *I've heard that many people graduate and become really lonely, but that wasn't the case for me at all. I joined a volunteer teaching program when I graduated, so when I moved from college to Phoenix I instantly had friends. We had a great group my first year in the program, and we are still very close and very present in each other's lives. The program snowballs, too. Alums and new volunteers manage to find each other, and I have met some really cool people that way.*

Beyond the altruistic feelings that come with volunteering, there are other reasons to get involved. It looks great on your résumé. And it's a surefire way to network and meet people who are at least interested in the same things you are.

## Scoping for Dates

In the Real World, the trick to finding love, or at least a relationship that lasts longer than twenty-four hours, is a willingness to take risks. There is no boy-meets-girl—or girl-meets-boy or boy-meets-boy or girl-meets-girl—mystery involved. Romantic relationships have begun and developed in the same way for many, many years. The rituals of real love remain steadfast: flirtation, conversation, then passion. And sometimes, even coupledom.

*I love to make the first move. If I am drawn to someone because of his intelligence or looks or humor or some commonality, then I often like to make a connection. One of my best relationships ever was with a guy I met on a plane.*

But be careful, and above all play it smart. The most common mistake made by singles looking for a good time is thinking that the only way to meet people is at bars and clubs. The second most common mistake is thinking that inebriation somehow increases your chances of meeting Mr. or Ms. Right. Toss the beer goggles; college is over.

*It's not hard to meet people, but it is difficult to meet quality people. The bar and club scene in my city is a lot of fun, but it is a terrible environment to meet anyone of substance to potentially date. It's too loud for conversation, and most people have an agenda for the evening anyway, and it rarely involves just talking.*

The foolproof way to attract an interesting person is to be one. Have opinions. Read books. Try new things. Single women who preoccupy themselves with the subject of men and love and lipstick are still single for a reason. The same goes for the preening, flexing studs who never have an original thought on the way between the gym and the bar. An obsession with notches on the bedpost is the natural antidote to good relationships.

> *I get asked out on dates by people I meet in bars once a week or so, but nothing substantial has ever come out of it. Establishing a real connection is very difficult. It seems like everybody I meet is looking to settle down these days. Looking for their future husband or wife. I even had one guy tell me that I could not be his girlfriend—we couldn't even date—because he didn't think I was his soul mate.*

Speaking to a stranger can be daunting, but don't let that stop you. Casual conversations can lead you to new friends—or to one very special one. Don't stalk and don't accost. Don't give people the creeps. Be friendly and confident, but chill the attitude. You'll be surprised how young, lonely hearts will respond to a sociable, affable demeanor.

> *It's much easier to speak to a stranger, male or female, if you're both at the party of a mutual friend—at least you know that you have that person in common. If conversation lags, you can always say: 'So, how do you know so-and-so?' Or even if you get a group of people to go out, and your friend's boyfriend brings a few people he knows, it's easier to talk to them because you already have a small connection.*

Be watchful for people who might share some of your interests. In Barnes and Noble, for example, you might glimpse a good-looking browser engrossed in the Nick Hornby novel you just finished and adored. Approach. Taking a breather from rollerblading in the park, you notice a potential sporty sweetheart taking the same break—and wearing the latest blades that you've been debating whether to buy. Approach. On the train, you spy a fellow music lover listening to your favorite band—a possible rhythmic rendezvous? Approach.

> *When I moved to Los Angeles, I didn't know anyone, so I decided to ask out every person I met who interested me. If I am having a great conversation with someone, I ask for their number—I don't wait for them to ask me—that's too passive. I have enough confidence to risk being rejected. I figure that more people in this world will be wrong for me than right for me anyway. And I've been rejected hundreds of times because someone is gay or already involved or moving to Austria the next day, but I can't be afraid of that.*

## Go Blind

Among cynical singles, the running joke is that a blind date is someone whom you need to be blind to actually date. What a shame. Blind dating is actually about as rational a way to meet new people as one could invent. Most of the time, the people being introduced have mutual friends and perhaps even mutual interests. Both know the purpose of the meeting is a date, a possible relationship. There's none of the awkwardness of a chance meeting, none of the uncertainty about availability.

And even if romance doesn't bloom, a blind date is a way to go to a nice restaurant, see a good band, spend an afternoon in a museum, attend an evening at the theater or cinema, and just meet another person. Build the date around events that you like; that way you'll see whether your date shares your interests. It might be love at first sight or maybe just a new friendship. Even if the entire evening's a bust, at least you have a war story for your next cocktail party.

> *I've had great luck with dates referred to me by my mom. Living in a major city I every so often get a call from her telling me that so-and-so's daughter graduated from University X and is now working for Company Y in my city and that I should take her out to dinner. These are generally not established as dates, but that's effectively what they become once my mother begins talking to this poor girl's mother and both are hoping that they'll share a grandchild some day. On the other hand, I've got to give my mother credit in that she's come closest to the mark.*

Dating friends of friends tends to have a higher rate of success. After all, you both have the same taste in something.

> *I've gained notoriety with my friends as a bit of a blind date expert. If quantity is any measure, I might indeed be a pro. For me, the most successful source for potential blind dates has been coworkers, since there's little personal stake involved on their part—and that's what you're looking for in a referee. The beauty of getting a blind date through coworkers is that they usually know you well but not too well and they can draw from a more diverse pool than your standard weekend*

## Real World Etiquette: Who Pays for What on Dates?

Conventional wisdom and current social mores dictate that the person who asks for the date should pay for it. But what about the second date, or when you and that Certain Someone mutually agree to meet for brunch or for coffee or for a drink? Complications arise.

A good rule here is not to have any. Don't be too rigid with your expectations. "I had all these fixed rules about how as an 'independent woman' I did not want any man ever to pay for me. I used to be so offended when my date would insist on picking up the bill," says Mattie Jones, a Mount Holyoke grad. "But then I realized that I should be more flexible and not too self-righteous about the whole thing. There are plenty of opportunities for both sides to pay for things."

Start with the assumption that a date is split 50–50 and go from there. Ideally, you and your date should talk the money thing out before it becomes a problem; for instance, if there is a big income differential you may wish to set some parameters after the first few dates. Or split the costs of every rendezvous: "I get the movie tickets, you buy the popcorn." But be a good sport and don't play Ebenezer Scrooge to your date's Bob Cratchit. You should insist on picking up a bill every once in a while and vice versa.

*friends, who tend to cluster in tribal groups, which afford few cross-fertilization opportunities. Another great thing I've found about dating friends of coworkers is that you receive instant feedback—they generally give your outing a score and you get informed of your performance the next day in post-game commentary.*

A caveat: Things don't always end happily ever after. Match-makers are ostensibly well intentioned, so don't be upset with them if the date is not perfect. Ditto for all the Dolly Levi's out there: A failed blind date is not a personal affront. Your two friends just don't jive. Leave it at that.

## Online Connections

There was a time when newspaper and magazine personal ads were considered a last resort for the terminally pathetic. But times—and the venue—have changed. As the first generation to come of age in a world with Web surfing and Instant Messaging, we're less intim-idated by the prospect of online dating. Cyberdating is as easy as checking your e-mail. The personal ad has gone electronic and gotten hip.

Many twentysomethings have found Web-based love. Think of the advantages. It's noncommittal: You can spend as much time as you like at it, or as little. It's nonthreatening: The initial infor-mation you learn about your prospective date is similar to that in a newspaper ad—height, weight, hobbies, occupation, and whether the person drinks or smokes. And it's economical: Dating sites charge as little as $20 per month to keep you in the game.

If you are shy, being online makes it much easier to commu-nicate with others and helps you to lose or hide your inhibitions. If you're picky, you can more easily filter out the drones from the dreamboats—without ever having to date them.

*After much cajoling from my friends, I signed up at an online matchmaking site and filled out a profile. Most people put a picture up, so I did, too. Now, I am a nice-looking person, no goddess, but nice-looking. I received*

*120 emails in two days! It was overwhelming but confidence boosting at the same time. Guys write and tell how beautiful and awesome you are. It's funny. The first one who wrote me said something like, 'Hi, my name is Greg, you sound really cool. I would like to get married and have two kids. I was wondering what you are doing this weekend.' Ultimately, I went on six dates with four different guys. No love, but I am still looking.*

Although cyberspace may be a reasonable place to meet potential mates, no amount of scintillating electronic banter can guarantee romantic success. It's a starting point, but electronic dating is no substitute for the real thing. Eventually you'll have to meet *in person*—always in a public place like a coffee shop or diner, maybe with a friend along for support and feedback—to see for yourself if the person's right for you.

*I met a guy online in a political chat room. He suggested we go in a private room and from there we exchanged e-mail addresses. It started out slow—breezy one-liners here and there. And then we were e-mailing three or four times daily. We talked about books, our families, our jobs—all with a flirtatious undercurrent. I really liked him, plus he was a surfer: what a turn-on! He suggested we meet and I agreed. When I first laid eyes on him there was no instant attraction. He said something like, 'Gee, I thought you'd be taller,' which I read as 'I thought you'd be better looking.' We lacked the chemistry that we had online. He was more reserved in person—and not nearly as funny. Online, he*

## Looking for Love in All the Wrong Places? Helpful Web Sites

These are subscription-based dating Web sites where members create profiles, place pictures, and are allowed to search the databases for potential matches. Nerve is the most racy of the three; Date and Match target a slightly older crowd.

**www.Nerve.com**

**www.Date.com**

**www.Match.com**

Or, if you just want a place to kvetch, check out: "Tell Me About It," Carolyn Hax's funny advice column for the under-thirty crowd, which appears in the *Washington Post*. She writes about love, relationships, jobs, money, and family. It's also available online at www.washingtonpost.com.

*seemed like a dreamer with big ideas. In real life, he seemed more like an unambitious slacker. We never e-mailed again.*

Now we've all seen those episodes of *Dateline*—roll scary stills, crescendo ominous background music—about sinister stalkers on the Internet salivating at the chance you might log on. It's understandable that you're leery of online dating sites, so do some homework and find chat rooms and other sites that are trustworthy and reputable. And obviously, don't give away too much personal information over the Internet.

If you're unlucky at love and feeling hopeless, take heart. True love takes time, and you still have plenty of that to find your special someone. But it also takes a little courage and an epic amount of persistence.

Look at it this way: If all else fails, you can always get a dog. They're fun-loving and playful and great babe magnets—believe me.

# Maintaining Relationships

When you finally settle in to your first real job, it can suddenly feel as if you are a slave to routine. The simple acts of going to work each morning, getting exercise, and shopping for and cooking meals seem to consume all your waking hours. Somehow your concept of "being grown up" had more going for it than this.

One of the places you may find yourself making large and unhappy sacrifices is in the maintenance of your relationships with friends and family. What you wouldn't give for the carefree, relaxed environment of college, where meeting up at midnight at the local saloon or coffeehouse was commonplace. Now you've got a work schedule that's more regimented and often more frenzied than college. It's not as easy to squeeze in a visit to Mom and Dad during what used to be your languorous three-week winter break. And those unscheduled, widely roving conversations with friends that lingered into the early morning are mostly just a memory now.

## Friendships Face Time Constraints

How will you ever be able to make time for old friends, let alone new ones? It's a challenge that calls for new strategies and new habits. You never had to think much about how to communicate with the people closest to you before. They were always readily

accessible. But now they're not and you have to be more organized and thoughtful about staying in touch.

> *I liked school because there were so many more*
> *spontaneous meetings, meals with friends, chats on the*
> *steps of the library. You feel so much more connected*
> *with your friends in school. Once you are out, you can*
> *really feel yourself drifting apart.*

Start with e-mail. It's a godsend—a cheap, efficient way to
communicate with friends and family who are geographically
scattered. You'll find that the REPLY function of most e-mail programs makes this very easy. On the other hand, even e-mail can
be a burden. It becomes another, sometimes overwhelming demand on your time.

> *One of the hardest parts of growing up, and*
> *something that has remained difficult despite seeming*
> *trivial, is that my correspondence skills have fallen to*
> *pieces. I used to be very good about writing messages*
> *and keeping on top of my inbox. But work leaves little*
> *time for keeping up with old friends. I'm still six*
> *months behind on responding to letters, and my e-mail*
> *inbox has on average twenty old messages waiting to*
> *be answered. I guess this is one of the inevitable condi-*
> *tions of adult life.*

Phone calls are cheaper than ever, too, especially if you negotiate a calling plan with low long-distance rates or invest wisely
in calling cards.

Staying in touch with everyone you know is a challenge. You get a few days behind and it feels like you'll never catch up. Something has to give, and it's usually the high standard of communication you had hoped to maintain with your friends after college.

*Contact with friends from high school or college that I was no longer living near was a challenge. I was initially living with a friend from college, so we were mutually keeping in touch with most of our friends. As time has passed, however, contact with these people has become less frequent as we have all become more rooted in our current lives. No regrets, it's just the way our lives have progressed.*

Keeping in contact with friends requires planning. You prioritize what and who is really important to you and worth your time. Your friendships go through a process of natural selection. You'll gravitate toward the people you care about and deem worthwhile. We outgrow some old friendships as we grow into new ones.

*It wasn't a conscious decision, more of a winnowing process, survival of the fittest. Certain friends took precedence over others and mere college acquaintances fell out of my social circle altogether. I guess that after college I thought, 'Who are the people that I want to exert energy to be with and stay in contact with? And who are the people that I hung out with during college just because they were there?' It's not coldhearted, just reality. I have a few friends that I've made it a point to stay in touch with. But I've found that you have to constantly renew those relationships and make time for them.*

You may discover that after college you can't manage the harem of friends you once had, and that two or three close friends can be enough. Unfortunately, but logically, this means you lose touch with some people; some friendships will fade. It might help to be philosophical about it: Think of it as a mature thing to do to make the best of a sad but inevitable situation. Then again, different doesn't always have to mean worse.

*After college, my friends spread out across the country and I had to put in a lot of effort to stay close. This transition was particularly sad for me and I really miss having a lot of friends. Instead of coincidentally running into my ten closest friends at the dining hall and all having dinner together, I had to plan a month in advance to have dinner with two friends. We had to accept the new terms of our friendship and go from there. I've planned my week so that I have some evenings allotted to exercise and some for socializing. We've learned that even though we may only see each other every couple of months, our relationship is the same as it always was.*

## Retaining the Romance

If you already have a significant other—either a long-term, committed relationship from college, a summer romance that blossomed into something more, or even a high-school-sweetheart thing that's still going strong—it can be a real challenge to maintain that bond in the Real World. Good relationships are about adapting, and there are few stiffer tests for any relationship than adapting to the transition from school to adult independence and responsibility.

Graduating from college, getting a job, living on your own, and paying your own way will force you to get to know yourself better. You'll come to understand what you want, what you don't want, and what you can tolerate in a partner. You'll grow to appreciate what you need and what you thrive on. And that's when you'll start to identify these qualities in somebody else with whom you may want to spend time or even share your life.

You may even start to see your relationship in a whole new light as your compatibility suddenly revolves around more than your devotion to Steve Martin movies or your proximity to dining halls. You'll have to make a decision about whether the energy consumed in bustling between apartments—or cities, or countries—and the constant scramble to deal with the logistics of who's coming over when and keeping clothes in two places overwhelms the pleasures of the relationship.

*My boyfriend and I did not expect that the transition would be so hard, so we were caught unaware. For me, one of the hardest things was watching him fall in love with something else other than me. He was in love with his work. I saw a level of commitment and discipline and passion in him I had never seen in school. In school there was always a very high level of focus and priority that he could give our*

*relationship. It took me a long time to be genuinely
happy about his newfound love rather than feeling
threatened.*

To top it off, there are other new sources of stress. Like money problems: One of you wants to make gobs of cash and live a lavishly yuppified lifestyle; the other is happy to subsist on peanuts, shop at Goodwill, and enjoy a lot of free time. Or differing views on commitment: One of you wants to cohabitate or—pressure, pressure—get married; the other is content to spend a few more years playing Sally to your Harry. Or job-related anxiety: One of you is a gung-ho career maven; the other is uncommitted about a career and not particularly worried about it. Any of these can be key ingredients in the recipe for relationship problems.

*I got a job before my boyfriend did, but he hadn't
bothered to get a résumé together and apply for anything. I felt like he would just sleep in 'til noon, hang
around his house, play Nintendo, not do much. It
bothered me. I wanted him to move on in some way.
And he seemed stuck. So we were stuck. We broke up
eventually because we realized that we wanted different things.*

Relationships stumble when one or both partners are unhappy. Of course, there's also infidelity, boredom, neglect, and issues between the sheets. It's a wonder any duo survives. Such differences can either be insurmountable roadblocks to your relationship, or you can work through them. The choice is up to you both.

> *In college, my girlfriend and I didn't have to decide how serious we wanted to be, it all seemed to be fun and crazy and carefree, but once we were in the 'real world' it wasn't that simple. We needed to clarify where the relationship was going, whether or not we wanted it to be serious. It was hard to figure out and it involved many fights, but luckily, we made it through and are still together.*

"You're at an age where maybe you're beginning to think more seriously about finding a life partner," says Dr. Pat Pacek, author of *Almost Grown: Launching Your Child from High School to College*. "You're peeling away layers of yourself and deciding how to balance work and play and family. You're deciding how ambitious you are. So ask yourself the tough questions: Am I deeply in love with this person? Do I see a future with him or her? If problems have arisen then it's good to face those issues squarely. Sometimes people realize that there are just too many differences."

## Keep the Home Fires Burning

Suddenly you and your parents are peers in a way you never have been before. You go to work, pay taxes, you're self-sufficient, and you have responsibilities. But in other ways, you're still the child and they're still your parents. It's a different relationship, but not altogether different.

Parents can grow to see you as an individual, with interests and concerns outside their sphere of influence. And yet it's new to them, a little foreign. It can be terrible or terrific.

> *My mother had high hopes. Because I chose a job fairly close to home, a two-hour drive, she expected to see me a lot. But I had a crazy work schedule and I couldn't get there as often as she would have liked. I decided to make an effort to spend time with her—but set limits. And communicate those limits. We compromised on dinner once a month. I think eventually she understood.*

But your parents may be ready to see you in new light—a grown-up, more mature light, with new expectations. Your efforts to be understood, respected, and perhaps even admired are coming to fruition. You may be pleasantly surprised to find that your parents have a sense very much like your own of this new relationship.

> *I have always felt really close to my parents and I try to stay in close contact. But since college my relationship with them is not as stressful. I don't feel pressure to be perfect for them because they no longer feel completely responsible for me. I am independent and what they consider a finished product. All I have to do is enjoy life and stay out of jail and they're pretty happy. We also communicate in a more even, adult manner since I left college.*

But some parents have difficulty basking in the glow of their so-called finished product. You may want independence and freedom while your parents still want to nurture or hold sway over you. You'll always be their child.

"Money is the number-one dependency; it's how parents control their children. As long as they're paying, they call the shots. Cut yourself off and establish financial independence," says Dr. Elizabeth Stirling, a life change coach. "How you're seen by your parents has to do in part with what you're doing and whether they approve of it. If they're not offering support, you need to find it in other places."

But what happens when your parents believe that you are beholden to them and should heed their wishes about a career choice? Or if they hound you about your values, your choices in friends and partners, how you spend money, or your religious beliefs?

Dr. Dori Winchell, who specializes in coping with life changes, recommends straightforward dialogue. "Say, 'I respect your opinion but I wished you'd waited till I'd asked for it.' Or, 'I know that I am going to make mistakes but I really think it's important that I make them on my own right now.' This is really the first time that you're asking to be treated like an adult and it may be hard for some parents."

Or maybe it's the other way around and you're the one who needs to break away.

*When I first got out of school I found I was talking to my mom a lot on the phone, always calling when I was bummed about something or having a problem. But I knew that had to change. These first few years*

*out of school have been all about adjusting my rela-*
*tionship with my family. I had thought that when I*
*went to school I had really branched out on my own,*
*but I think that real independence from your family*
*comes when you finally start to make your own life in*
*a more complete way.*

Experts say that if you have always turned to your family for support or help in problem solving, try not to call them right away. Try to figure out some things for yourself. Experience the real separation and differentiation between you and your parents.

It's up to *you* to make the decision to build and maintain a healthy relationship with your family. Try to accept your family members' frailties and foibles. As long as they're not hurting themselves, perhaps you don't have to approve of your parents' sudden interest in Harley Davidsons or your sister's green-haired boyfriend.

*My relationship with my sister has improved as*
*I've grown older. I've become less demanding of her*
*since I graduated college by reserving judgment. I re-*
*alize she has a life and interests that don't always lie*
*with my own and I respect that. I think I have become*
*more tolerant of her viewpoints and priorities since*
*graduating.*

It's difficult at times to juggle your needs and wants and available time off with your family's expectations, especially around holidays and other important family events. There are bound to be disappointed looks and offhand remarks, but your family is your original and probably most important support group. Don't squander that over petty disagreements.

## Cheap Ways to Entertain Yourself

It's a conundrum that has stumped some of the finest thinkers of our time. When you're young and have the vigor and stamina to do all sorts of things, you have no funds with which to do them. When you're old, all you've got is time, and probably more money, too, but it's harder to have fun when you're wearing orthopedic shoes.

Don't spend your early twenties bemoaning your social life of too few friends and too little fun. There are countless cheap ways to amuse yourself—to socialize while you economize. You're young—be creative. Here are some suggestions to get you started.

### Eat Out

Dining out is great fun but hard to do when your wallet has been on a diet. There are ways, however, to shrink the tab down to about the size of available funds.

Breakfast is usually most affordable meal to eat out, followed by lunch or brunch. Dine out during the week rather than on weekends because prices may be a couple of dollars cheaper and crowds are usually smaller.

*I have found that small ethnic restaurants are relatively inexpensive and have great food. Granted, you are sacrificing glitz and glamour, and they can be*

*cramped, but they provide a very relaxed atmosphere.*
*There are hundreds of these places that are not preten-*
*tious and have excellent food and wine.*

Make every restaurant a tapas bar by ordering an assort-
ment of appetizers instead of an entrée. The markup on alcoholic
drinks is very high—so scout out BYOB restaurants. Check out
the special of the day first, since it normally provides good value
for your dollar. Some especially generous restaurants will offer a
free meal for the birthday person as long as there is an accompa-
nying paying customer.

Investigate a frequent dining card. Restaurant weeks in various American cities make it affordable to see and be seen at all
the hottest, and usually prohibitively expensive, restaurants. And
local food festivals are a great way to sample cuisine.

## Throw a Party

College parties have been your way of life for the past four years.
But somehow, "Kegger in the hallway, dude!" no longer has the
allure it once did. So get creative. Host a movie marathon. Throw
a theme party: retro 1980s nights or, a personal favorite, Tactile
Sensation Time, where everyone must wear an item of clothing
that's interesting to touch. Or a costume party. Holiday gatherings are always a good standby. If you're in the mood for a small,
more subdued, and more adult party, host a wine tasting where
each guest brings a bottle of vino from around the globe.

*Parties are expensive, so I've learned to plan them*
*with a group of friends so that we split the expenses*
*evenly. My friends and I divvy up the cost of the food*
*and alcohol so it ends up being much more manage-*

## Free and Cheap Fun and Games

"I'm in graduate school and always flat broke, so I have to be creative in finding cheap things to do," says Trish Eaton, who went to Williams. "Sometimes I take my books to Denny's and study there over milkshakes and greasy food. I like to go to basketball games—they're free for students—and ogle the undergrads. They're so young now!"

Bring back all the games of yore like mini-golf, ice skating, bowling, billiards, pool, and roller skating—all cost-effective ways to spend an evening. Attend a book reading, usually held at bookstores or local colleges, and almost always free. Visit museums in your area. They're typically free or inexpensive. Look into summer theater productions or movies in the park. Spend an afternoon in a make-your-own pottery shop or tag along at karaoke night.

*able. All our guests bring over a six-pack of beer or a bottle of wine to share so we invariably end up with more liquor than we started with. We throw another party the very next weekend to get rid of it all.*

Before you party on, Wayne, be sure to have plenty of chips, sandwiches, and nonalcoholic drinks on hand to soften the blow of booze. The last thing you want is people getting physically sick from all the alcohol—especially in *your* apartment, on your carpet or your couch.

## Cook Dinner

Dinner parties are making a comeback among the twentysomething set as a less expensive, civilized way to socialize. Choose a

# Real World Etiquette:
# Being a Good Guest

*Visitors, like fish, begin to stink after three days.*
*—Benjamin Franklin*

While you may have hosted countless pizza parties and an
overnight guest or two at school, there are best practices to abide
by when you are on the receiving end of such hospitality.

Upon accepting an invitation to a dinner party, first ask what
you should bring. Dessert? Hors d'oeuvres? A date? And then
follow up. No matter what sort of party you're attending, you are
expected to bring something: a good bottle of wine, a hunk of
exotic cheese, a baguette, a small box of chocolates, or a bouquet
of flowers. (You are also expected to return the invitation at some
future date.) Never, ever arrive as an invited guest at a party or
dinner without a gift in hand.

theme for the dinner—perhaps a type of ethnic cuisine or an era;
barbecues work, too. Or make it potluck—no tuna casseroles
allowed, of course—and invite friends and friends of friends.
Voilà! Instant party, and at half the price of going out to dinner.

> *Lately, I am really getting into dinner parties—*
> *a sure sign that I am getting older and becoming*
> *my parents. It turns out you can actually have fun*
> *in your own home and still keep your clothes on. This*
> *is new to me. And you get to choose the music too, a*
> *bonus.*

If you're spending the night at a friend's place, make your stay as short as possible. A guest is a burden on a host, even when they're best of friends. The burden is heavier still if the host's abode is humble and space is tight. Try to help out a little: make your bed in the morning, wash a dish or two, clean up after yourself. Bring your cell phone or use a calling card to avoid making long-distance calls at the expense of your host. Send a handwritten note soon afterward thanking your host for having you.

Getting together with friends should always be a treat. But overnight stays can test any friendship. Be alert to that fact and take the steps necessary to make your visit a happy, not a harrowing, event.

There are a few basic considerations for putting a menu together for a dinner party. The dishes should be attractive, enticing, and complementary in taste. The dishes should be interesting but not too pretentious; no need to introduce your guests to the beguiling world of foie gras and petit fours, at least not at the same sitting.

*Dinner parties are a great alternative to the tired bar scene, and what I like to call taking ownership of my evening. The key to a good dinner party is making an adventurous dish. Don't make something like pasta*

## One Is Not the Loneliest Number

One sure long-term cure for loneliness is learning to like being alone. Part of growing up is not feeling the need to be surrounded by people all the time to feel good about yourself. Even if you're a social animal, learn to have fun being by yourself. Discover ways to amuse and nurture yourself.

Relish time alone; savor solitude. "I don't like my schedule to be too jam-packed. I like having time to be alone and see a movie or read a book. If that happens to be my Friday night activity, so be it," says Sophie Milford, a Northwestern grad. "Even though I live in Chicago, a cool city with lots of fun places to go, my interest in hanging out with acquaintances has waned. I'm looking for good, real, wonderful conversation—not just the small talk that you'd have with someone you just met at a bar."

*or lasagna. Anyone can do that. Instead, I like to buy fish or a nice cut of steak, then make an interesting sauce and a fresh salad.*

The food should vary in color. Seasonal foods shouldn't be served out of season. And the preparation should not be too time-consuming so that you'll actually have time to entertain your guests. Always, always serve dessert.

## Head for the Hills

Take off on a day trip and discover the joys of weekend getaways. An hour or two away from almost every city in America lies beautiful countryside. So hop in your car or jump on a bus or train and

"At first I felt this great urgency to meet a ton of friends and re-create the community of college. I was a mess," says Hope Myers, who went to Wesleyan. "After a while, I relaxed a bit and just started to do my own thing. I went to lectures and galleries, did some volunteer work. I became more comfortable with myself. And if I met people, it was just a bonus."

Take time out from your go-go-go life and a break from the constant stimulation of other people. Cultivate a new hobby. Or be your own best company and see a movie, go to a play, or take yourself out to dinner.

see the sights and environs not far from home. Go fishing, go for a bicycle ride, throw a Frisbee around the park, take a hike or a swim. All cheap. Ask tourist offices for hiking maps, scenic routes, and traffic peaks. Bring a picnic with some of your own food from home, granola bars, and other snacks so that you don't always have to drop cash when hunger pangs hit.

If you're more interested in an urban jaunt, investigate new and different neighborhoods in your city. Check out weekly news-paper listings and magazine entertainment schedules to find out about upcoming concerts, restaurant openings, shows, or festi-vals. Most towns now have online guides—usually linked from its chamber of commerce site—that showcase points of interest. Or, be your own guide.

> *I thought I was a millionaire when I got my first job, and I didn't really think about money at first. Then I got deeper and deeper into debt. Luckily there were so many parks in the Washington, D.C., area that it was always easy to get outside and experience nature. There were also a lot of cool neighborhoods in the city to explore. That made for a cheap, easy way to share time with friends.*

## Planning Your Vacation

It had been a long first six months on the job, but I had finally accrued a week of vacation. An unadulterated, uninterrupted seven days away from the office. Pure bliss.

Desperate to get away from the bleak Northeast winter, my best friend from college and I started dreaming. We wanted a sunny, tropical getaway, someplace with palm trees, white sand, and little paper umbrellas in the drinks. We wanted a place that was not too near and not too far, as we didn't want to spend the whole time traveling but we wanted to feel as though we'd truly gotten *away*. Remote, but not too isolated. Good food, but not gourmet. The Bahamas would do nicely.

We were determined to do it all ourselves, thank you very much. We researched fares on the Internet, called travel agents for the best hotel deals, and shopped around for rental cars. We were women on a mission of fun. On a budget, of course.

Things don't always work out as you plan. Our plane was late and we missed our connecting flight in Charlotte. The cost of the cab from Nassau International Airport was about equal to the

## Rely On a Travel Agent

If you're a first-time trip planner or anticipating a complicated itinerary, consider using a travel agent. Travel agents are experienced professionals who plan trips for a living. They book everything from plane tickets to Amtrak to hotels to specialized tours. They have up-to-date information, plus they're privy to all kinds of travel deals and promotions. While some may charge a nominal fee for their services, it's a safe bet that you'll save money using a travel agent.

"My three roommates from college and I wanted to go on a two-week Brazilian getaway. But none of us was willing to organize it," says Alicia Tyler, a fun-loving Duke grad. "Luckily, I found a travel agency near my apartment that specializes in packages to Rio. I befriended the owner, Carlos, a São Paulo native, and entrusted him with organizing the trip. He did it all: booked our hotels and also our air passes and even set us up on our rafting trip. He saved us a lot of hassle in Brazil."

GDP of the Bahamas, and the hotel had misplaced our reservation. But we eventually made it to the beach.

There we sat in our bikinis, oiled up, basking in the hot Caribbean sun, sipping our Bahama Mamas, and congratulating each other on a vacation well done. We're so grown-up, so smart and savvy, we thought. Is there anything we can't do?

A few minutes passed. The self-congratulation continued. Sergio, the tanned activities director of the resort, approached us, looking like he'd just come off the set of *Baywatch*. There was a party later on the beach and he wanted to know if we were available. We smiled coyly at the prospect—he handed us each a bright pink invitation. "I hope to see you both there," he winked. "Just be sure to ask your parents if it's okay because the hotel has rules on minors and that sort of thing." He nodded purposefully and walked away.

The nerve.

## Making the Most of Your Days Off

The worst part about vacationing in the Real World is that there's so little time in which to do it. Most entry-level professionals are allowed a paltry two- to three-week vacation, if that, so it's up to you to make the most of your time away.

> *The lack of vacation days is really horrifying to me. It is very important to me to have decent vacations because time away from work makes me a more sane person. I love Europe and save all my money so that I can make it over for one week every year. Another week goes to various family gatherings. After that, it's a desperate three- or four-day weekend trip here and there. As a New Yorker, places like Atlantic City and Philadelphia got my business just because of convenience and cost.*

Vacations may come in various incarnations that might even surprise you. A holiday weekend spent alone in your apartment can be heavenly. A day trip to a local beach, state park, sports event, or historical site might release a month's worth of pent-up stress. Going back home to visit Mom and Dad, for example, becomes a welcome break.

## Before You Go, Remember To ...

Before you leave for your big trip, make sure that your professional life is in order. Tell your boss about your plans at least one month prior to the trip. Complete all projects (good for your peace of mind, too), set up your voice and e-mail to let callers know that you're out of the office, and give the office manager your contact information while you're away in case coworkers need to get hold of you in a pinch.

And don't forget to make arrangements in your personal life, too. Put a hold on your newspaper subscriptions and mail if you're going to be away for more than a few days—a stack of papers and an overflowing mailbox call attention to an empty apartment. Bring your plants into the office and ask a coworker to water them while you're away; also, let a trusted neighbor know that you will be gone and ask her to check on your place every few days.

For your own security and convenience, make two photocopies of important documents—passports, visa, credit cards—and keep one copy in a separate location from the originals, which you should carry with you; leave the other copy with a friend or the folks back home, in case you hit any snags in your travels abroad. And make sure you have your cell phone, chargers, adapters, and a list of emergency numbers for all of your destinations with you when you go. Check ahead to make sure that your service plan covers the areas that you're traveling in—otherwise it's just a useless gadget.

*Unfortunately, I can't afford a luxurious trip right now, so vacationing has somehow turned into visiting my family. Going back to my home state of Oregon is now a real treat, since I am starved for fresh air, a home-cooked meal, and a slower pace of life for a few weeks. Also, family vacations are a lot cooler now than when I was in college—especially when they're subsidized by my parents.*

For the first time ever in your life you're not on an academic schedule, and vacation is really precious. The quicker you learn how to be creative with your vacation time, like molding a miraculous five days off around a simple holiday weekend, and competent in your planning, the better.

## The Destination

The first step to planning the perfect getaway is also the most fun: deciding where to go. What kind of vacation experience do you wish to have: relaxing and sunny? Sporty and snowy? Adventurous and wildernessy? Cultural and urban? Then decide how much time you wish to devote—or, more accurately, how much time your company is willing to allow you to devote—to your vacation and how much money you have to spend.

Now is a good time to visit your local travel agent to get an idea of the current hot—and cheap—spots. Also, don't overlook the many travel consultants all around you. As when you're looking for a job or an apartment, tap into your network of friends and family to help you come up with a target destination. Ask around for recommendations of affordable getaways. Maybe some friends or family members living in different cities will invite you to stay with them—a good way to save on lodging costs.

> *I wanted to get away but I didn't have a lot of money. So I decided to take advantage of my friends who were sprinkled around the country. I chose the most appealing place: Aspen. All I had to take care of was the airfare. I crashed with my friends and they were even able to hook me up with ski passes. I was able to vacation in a very ritzy town on a tight budget. With friends in the right places, vacationing can be very affordable.*

Be aware of your timing, too. Know when the high season occurs. Your goal is to pinpoint the best off-season weather so that you avoid the tourists *and* the jacked-up prices. For example, Costa Rica in November is just as lovely as in December through February, which is the country's so-called season. Paris in the spring is *parfait*, but if you're going there to soak in the museums and cafés, go in January when it's cheaper.

If you're traveling abroad, pay attention to currency rates so that you'll know where in the world the dollar is strong compared to the local currency. A robust dollar signifies a good time to travel abroad.

If you're eager to vacate your city and your workaday rut but lack the necessary funds, take heart. There are plenty of ways to plan an affordable escape. Volunteer for an environmental project through the Sierra Club or Earthwatch, which typically is situated in exotic locales and often includes free or discounted room and board. Or build homes for another good cause, Habitat for Humanity, and get to see a new part of the country.

If you really need some serious R&R, get a room at a B&B, which can be cheaper than your average hotel. Better yet, pitch a tent for the weekend and explore small towns, hike up mountains, swim in a river, or just lay in the sun all day—with sunscreen of course. Again, be creative: You could luck out with a free night's lodging for you and a friend by sitting through a no-strings-attached time-share presentation at some beachfront condo. Hey, you have a job and are on your own now—you might as well use that to your advantage.

## The Accommodations

Vacationing today can be a do-it-yourself enterprise if you keep your travel plans simple. If you're going by plane, use the Internet to find the best deals on airlines. Never accept the first price an airline ticket agent gives. Always ask if there are cheaper rates. Check for specially priced days or times. Sometimes if you travel at night or adjust your plans by one day, you may get a better fare. Book your flight in advance or during airline sales. If timing is immaterial, you can try last-minute deals. Cut costs by flying to an alternative airport, the city next door for example. Sign up for every frequent flier program available, particularly if you travel a lot for work and can accumulate miles quickly.

Travel plans include organizing accommodations, too. Always ask for the least-expensive room when booking at a hotel. Weekend deals? Corporate coupons? Discounts for AAA members? They'll always quote you a high price—what hotels call the "rack rate"—and usually will have something cheaper. Say something simple but leading, like "I'm sure you could do a little better than that."

You might also consider staying in a suburb of your destination. Stay in a hotel suite, usually only marginally more expensive, where there's a kitchen. That way you won't have to eat out every night. Or consider renting a house with a group of friends and sharing the costs—in the end, much cheaper than piling into a hotel where you'd have to go out for all your meals.

Hostelling is another viable option, and it's a very inexpensive way to travel.

> *I'm pretty low-maintenance so I always stay in backpacker motels or youth hostels when I travel. They're basic dormitory rooms. But the other guests are usually eager to talk about their travels in the area and they can give you the scoop on which beaches were great, which temples were a waste of time, and how much a moped rental should really cost.*

## Do Your Homework

Once you know where you're going and where you're staying, pick up tour guides with maps of your destination. *The Lonely Planet* and *The Rough Guide* are two bibles of budget travelers. Read about the cuisine, history, and the culture of your destination. You don't have to have your trip mapped out entirely, but if you're going someplace new it's wise to know how you'll be getting around and some sights you're interested in seeing, otherwise you'll spend your vacation planning your vacation.

> *Before I take a trip anywhere, I ask around to my coworkers and friends who've been there for recommendations of interesting places to go, cool restaurants*

*and bars, and other fun things to do in a particular city. Of course, I'd rather operate in terms of happy accidents, but when I only have a couple of days to spend someplace new, I'd rather not eat mediocre food.*

If you're traveling abroad, try to find out about social norms of the places you'll be visiting. What are the accepted forms of dress? You don't want to have packed tank tops for a country where it's considered taboo for a woman to reveal her shoulders. Is it safe for a woman to be out after dark? Is it acceptable for a woman to drive a car? Upon arrival, don't say yes to the first person who offers to be your guide—there are some untrustworthy people out there. Give yourself a chance to acclimate to your surroundings.

## Be Mindful of Your Budget

Perhaps the biggest pitfall of vacationing is spending much more money than you'd planned. Or maybe you didn't plan. Maybe that's the problem. Try to find places in your guidebook that correlate to your budget. Then, while traveling, watch your money closely.

Before you go, draw up a basic forecast of your expenditures: hotels, rental cars, meals, gifts, and miscellaneous expenses. "Be realistic about the actual dollar amount and total cost of your vacation," recommends Kathy Sudeikis, vice president of the American Society of Travel Agents. "There's always a few sneaky costs. Car rental agencies charge more for registering two drivers, for instance. And be sure that you're comparing apples to apples. If you see a great deal on airfare and hotel in Hawaii, be sure that you're actually staying on the beach."

Bring a credit card for large purchases, or use travelers' checks. Only bring a small amount of cash with you each day, especially if you're traveling abroad, which only accentuates the Monopoly money syndrome—you know, where you spend more than you'd planned since it's only play money. You can get cash from an ATM in most countries these days, but banks and many exchange bureaus are closed on weekends, so plan ahead. Hotels or retail outlets may change your money but usually at a poor exchange rate.

Remember to save enough foreign currency to pay for any exit fees or taxes you are obligated to pay before leaving the country. And be sure to use up foreign currency before you leave; otherwise you end up paying two exchange fees—one to buy it and one to change it back to U.S. dollars. Even if it means that everyone in your family gets a Mexican sombrero for Christmas, use up those pesos in the airport duty-free shop.

# afterword:
# WHAT NEXT?

OKAY, SO NEGOTIATING THE REAL WORLD after leaving the comforting confines of school isn't easy. Situations that later in life you'll take in stride are bound to seem scary and complicated the first time you face them. And chances are in your first year out of college you are doing lots of grown-up things for the first time: looking for a "permanent" job, confronting stingy landlords, maintaining a car, working full-time, paying your own bills, trying to stay healthy while living it up a little (or a lot), and maybe even whittling away at that mountainous student loan. Someday you'll react instinctively to these chores and choices, but for now you are treading new ground, and that's intimidating.

Just remember that much of your post-college ordeal is just the stuff of growing up. Everyone struggles with writing her first, albeit meager, résumé. Everyone spends too much money moving to and furnishing his first apartment. Almost everyone eventually starts a retirement fund—or should. And, like a rite of passage, nearly everyone deals with a penny-pinching insurance company or at least a flinty landlord some time along the way.

Yes, big decisions loom, but your first year or so out of school is a thrilling time of liberation and independence, too. You're learning what it means to have your own place and make your own money. How to battle bureaucracy and get what you want. You might even experience a defining moment when you recognize that you've truly arrived. Said one grad, "I knew I had 'arrived' when my parents came to visit me in my new city and I took them out for dinner." You're learning that despite all the uncertainty and misgivings—your own and everybody else's—you definitely do have a future, and—like it or not—the future is now.

Luckily, you don't have to come to any hard and fast conclusions about the future right away. And you can always change your mind. You've got plenty of years to get the hang of the Real World: the adult responsibility, the career, the bills, and tax returns. Resourcefulness comes with life experience, and the further you get from the ivory tower or the ivy-covered walls, the more practical knowledge you will gain. Some people call it wisdom.

A few years have passed since my own graduation, and my life has settled down a bit. I've endured apartment searches in a couple of different cities. I've lived with good roommates and bad. I've paid off my car loan. I've quit one job and found another. I made a little money my first year out, a little more in my second, and learned to live on it.

Every once in a while I am struck by the fact that I'm getting older. A pimply-faced high school kid working at my neighborhood Stop 'N' Shop refers to me as "Ma'am." I now prefer *Behind the Music* on VH1 to the MTV *Spring Break* specials. And I've come to some painful realizations. My father was right: The shower curtain does indeed grow more mildew when it's pushed to one side. My mother was right: Electricity *is* expensive, and it's more economical to just put on a sweater.

All in all, I'm really enjoying adulthood. I've started reading for pleasure again. I regularly attend movies by myself. I finally have enough money to go on nice vacations and occasionally buy a fabulous pair of shoes on a whim. I've discovered that I love to cook. My friendships have gotten deeper. I have a knack for investing. And I never, *ever* have to study for tests anymore. After getting over that first-year-out hump, life is getting easier.

As you adjust to your new life, you'll have your own experiences and your own advice to pass on; you will have earned the right with the scars that you will pick up along the way. Until then, here are some final tips from grads just like you who've survived the transition.

- Take risks—don't let your anxieties about what might go wrong or how you might fail stop you from doing what you think you want to do.
- Try not to worry too much about money in your first year out. Money is probably going to be an issue for your entire life, so learn to breathe without lots of it for a while, and you'll appreciate that salary, large or small, even more.
- Stop comparing yourself to what your friends are doing with their lives or jobs or internships. Don't take a job to satisfy anyone else's expectations of you. Let yourself do what you want to do instead of what you feel you have to do, or what others feel is successful.
- It's so easy to get stressed about jobs, apartments, and friends, but remember that none of it is forever. Think of it as a series of learning experiences and try to maintain a sense of humor about all of it.
- Don't forget about the values you learned in college: a respect for ideas, the environment, and political issues.

Keep up with intellectual debate. Maybe even take a few classes when it's convenient or affordable. You just might come to the realization that you want another degree someday, and it would be nice to have a few credits under your belt to put toward that.

A year from now you'll be in a position to discern for yourself whether these are words to live by, or about as informative as a David Letterman Top Ten List. You'll have your own tales to tell by then.

In my first year out of college, I relied on strengths I didn't even know I had. I got to know myself better: what I love, what I hate, and what I can tolerate. I found out, and am still finding out, how to make the best of difficult situations. It's a good feeling, and you will get to experience it too, as you graduate into your second year out—and beyond.

# index

Boldface page references indicate illustrations. Underscored references indicate boxed text.

## A

Abuse, by bosses, 153–54
Accident, car
  checklist, post-accident, 128–29
  claims, filing, 127
  information, exchanging, 126, 128
  insurance, 116–18
  medical treatment, 127
  police, calling, 126, 128–29
  repair, car, 128–29
  reporting to insurance company, 126–27, 129
Accountant, hiring, 210
Action Without Borders, 278
Acupuncture, 240
Ads, classified, 18
Aerobics and Fitness Association, 263
AIDS, 233
Airlines, 312
Alcohol
  health effects of drinking, 231–33
  at parties, 300, 301
  at restaurants, 300
Allowances, tax withholding, 180–81
Alumni, networking with, 21
American Council on Education, 203
American Dietetic Association, 250, 251

American Management Association, 150–51, 160
American Society of Travel Agents, 314
Annual percentage rate (APR)
  auto loan, 110
  credit card, 197
Answering machine, 17, 23
Apartment
  break-ins, 268–70
  brokers, 62–65
  discrimination, 62
  eviction, 67, 90
  finding, 47–49, 50–53
  furnishing, 83, 85–88
  information resources, 52, 88
  insurance, renter's, 71–72
  jargon, 48
  landlords, dealing with, 57–62, 69–71, 89–90
  lease, 57, 65–67, 66–67
  location, 53–55
  moving into, 68
  moving out of, 89–90
  negotiations, 57
  neighbors, 72–74
  planning, importance of, 49
  problems with, 69–71
  renovating, 57, 59, 82–83
  rent, 55–57
  repairs, 69–71